BUILDING CULTURAL
INTELLIGENCE

NINE MEGASKILLS

RICHARD D. BUCHER

Baltimore City Community College

with contributions from

PATRICIA L. BUCHER

PEARSON

Prentice
Hall

UPPER SADDLE RIVER, NEW JERSEY
COLUMBUS, OHIO

Library of Congress Cataloging-in-Publication Data

Bucher, Richard D.
    Building cultural intelligence (CQ) : nine megaskills / Richard D. Bucher.
        p. cm.
    Includes bibliographical references and index.
    ISBN-13: 978-0-13-173895-9 (pbk.)
    ISBN-10: 0-13-173895-X (pbk.)
    1. Diversity in the workplace.   2. Cultural awareness.   I. Bucher, Patricia L.   II. Title.
    HF5549.5.M5B827 2008
    650.1'3—dc22

                                                            2007020920

Vice President and Executive Publisher: Jeffery W. Johnston
Senior Acquisitions Editor: Sande Johnson
Editorial Assistant: Lynda Cramer
Production Editor: Alexandrina Benedicto Wolf
Production Coordination and Text Design: Thistle Hill Publishing Services, LLC
Design Coordinator: Diane C. Lorenzo
Cover Designer: Jeff Vanik
Cover Image: SuperStock
Production Manager: Susan Hannahs
Director of Marketing: David Gesell
Marketing Manager: Amy Judd
Marketing Coordinator: Brian Mounts

This book was set in Janson Text by Integra Software Services. It was printed by R.R. Donnelley & Sons Company. The cover was printed by Phoenix Color Corp.

Pearson Education Ltd.
Pearson Education Singapore Pte. Ltd.
Pearson Education Canada, Ltd.
Pearson Education—Japan

Pearson Education Australia Pty. Limited
Pearson Education North Asia Ltd.
Pearson Educación de Mexico, S.A. de C.V.
Pearson Education Malaysia Pte. Ltd.

10 9 8 7 6 5 4 3 2
ISBN-13: 978-0-13-173895-9
ISBN-10:   0-13-173895-X

PREFACE

• • • • • • • ━━━━━━━━━━━━━━━━━━━

One common request from students, employees, and other participants in courses, workshops, and training is "Give me something I can use tomorrow." I hope that this book provides you with an array of tools that you can take with you and use, reflect on, share, improve, and evaluate.

As you read *Building Cultural Intelligence (CQ): Nine Megaskills*, you will be an active participant in acquiring and using knowledge. Specifically, you will be able to recognize, evaluate, and adjust to a dynamic work environment.

Learning and performance aids such as "Your Turn," "Reflect Before Reading," "To Learn More," "Individual Action Plan," and "Where Am I Now?" illustrate the conversational, interactive nature of this book. You will assess your own skills and develop new skills. By addressing "bottom-line implications" throughout the book, the rationale for developing specific CQ megaskills becomes clearer and more relevant to you.

I encourage you to e-mail me with your thoughts and suggestions. As a teacher, trainer, and fellow learner, I highly value your feedback. You may reach me at **rdbucher@aol.com**.

ACKNOWLEDGMENTS

I am deeply indebted to the many people who have made significant contributions to this book. *Building Cultural Intelligence (CQ)* is truly a team effort. My family, colleagues, students, and a group of caring, talented, and supportive individuals at Prentice Hall have made this undertaking possible. In addition to their constant and unwavering encouragement, I have relied heavily on their diverse talents, perspectives, and experiences.

First and foremost, I would like to thank my wife, Patricia. In addition to being a wonderful mother and wife, she is an accomplished educator and writer. Her ability to help me organize and expand my thinking is invaluable. Furthermore, as *Building Cultural Intelligence (CQ)* took shape, she was always there to help in any way possible. With her computer skills, cultural intelligence, and commitment to excellence, we make a great team.

My writing reflects the love and support I receive from my children, Jimmy, Katie, and Suzy. I am blessed to have children who support, stretch, and stimulate me emotionally, intellectually, and spiritually. Being a family man has always been a priority in my life. The "lessons" my children teach me every day keep me grounded and provide me with much needed perspective. I have learned so much from their ability to understand, value, and bridge cultural differences.

Throughout my life, my family exposed me to the value of cultural diversity, long before I became a social scientist and developed my passionate interest in this field. In particular, my parents modeled unconditional respect for each individual, regardless of race, ethnicity, religion, gender, social class, sexual orientation, disability, or any other socially constructed difference. My upbringing helped prepare me for my eventual immersion in diversity as the father of a son with autism, a graduate of a historically black college, and a professor in a college population comprised of students from more than 80 countries.

Even though I have been teaching for more than 30 years, my students and colleagues continue to amaze me. Their diverse life experiences and perspectives, and their willingness to share and learn from each other, deepen and broaden my cultural intelligence.

My team at Prentice Hall, and Sande Johnson in particular, gave me the latitude I needed to be creative and explore on my own, all the while providing me with guidance and help whenever necessary. Sande's assistant, Lynda Cramer, has made my job much easier. Lynda's communication skills and promptness, along with her expertise, have made it possible for me to meet deadlines and get answers to my many questions.

The input and fresh and insightful comments of the following reviewers were absolutely critical: Monica Gravino, St. Xavier University; Neisha McNeal-Pellegrino, North Park University; and Juan Meraz, Missouri State University. They allowed me to critique my work from a variety of perspectives.

Finally, I would like to thank Alice Barr, my Prentice Hall book representative, who started me thinking about writing many years ago. Because of her encouragement, and her interest in me and my family, writing became more than just a dream.

Richard D. Bucher

CONTENTS

CHAPTER 3

CQ Megaskill: Checking Cultural Lenses 51

CHAPTER 4

CQ Megaskill: Global Consciousness 77

CHAPTER 5

CQ Megaskill: Shifting Perspectives 103

CHAPTER 6

CQ Megaskill: Intercultural Communication 127

CHAPTER 7

CQ Megaskill: Managing Cross-Cultural Conflict 151

CHAPTER 8

CQ Megaskill: Multicultural Teaming 177

CHAPTER 9

CQ Megaskill: Dealing with Bias 201

CHAPTER 10

CQ Megaskill: Understanding the Dynamics of Power 229

Note: Every effort has been made to provide accurate and current Internet information in this book. However, the Internet and information on it are constantly changing, so it is inevitable that some of the Internet addresses listed in this textbook will change.

CHAPTER 1

CULTURAL INTELLIGENCE (CQ): AN OVERVIEW

Performance Skills

- *Understanding cultural intelligence*
- *Understanding the importance of cultural intelligence*
- *Identifying nine essential megaskills*
- *Understanding the bottom-line importance of cultural intelligence*
- *Identifying three key strategies for developing cultural intelligence*

REFLECT BEFORE READING

How is cultural diversity changing the skills we need in the workplace?

_____

_____

_____

_____

"As a Muslim, I choose to wear a head scarf. While this is an external symbol of my deep faith, I choose not to discuss my religion with others unless they ask me. When I walk into interviews wearing my head scarf, I tend to notice the surprise in people's faces. They seem to lose interest in me, and I wonder if it has anything to do with my appearance. This is very different from the treatment I get over the phone."

"I am a female technician. I work for a phone company. On the job one day, I was climbing up a telephone pole. The homeowner and four of his friends were watching from below. One of the men yelled up, 'Fix it right or we'll spank you.' A short while later, I told the men I needed a tool from my truck. I came down the ladder, locked the doors, and took off."

"I am not comfortable being singled out for praise from my supervisor. What does this say about my coworkers? It implies that they are not doing a job as well as I am. In my native country of Indonesia, this is frowned upon."

"In a meeting where I'm the only woman, I quietly suggest an idea but nobody acts like they are interested. A few minutes later, a man firmly says something very similar and all of a sudden people are acknowledging his input and running with it."

"I teach math in a suburban high school to the north of Washington, DC. I come from Puerto Rico and have a noticeable accent. The first year I taught calculus, I spent endless hours defending my ability to teach this class. Parent after parent called to try to get me removed from my position. I persevered. At the end of the year, our high school got the highest number of passing scores on the AP Calculus test in the history of our school."

"As a childless worker, I find I have to put in more hours at work than my coworkers with kids. They are the ones who are allowed to leave early or come to work late."

"I was an intern with a nonprofit agency that serves homeless families. On my first day of work, I was assigned to my client, Marie, and her two-year-old son. Marie had been in the U.S. for 2 weeks. Marie spoke Spanish only. I spoke English only. I was supposed to work with Marie once a day helping her with all aspects of daily living."

"To me, the Bible dictates how I should think and act. When I come to work, I bring my religion with me. I got into an argument with a coworker. I told him how uncomfortable I felt when he talked about what he did after hours—the partying, the relationships he has, even his values. Ever since, I have noticed considerable friction between us."

"I no longer wear a tool belt. Instead, I keep my tools in a carrying case. When I first wore the belt, I found that male customers were coming up to me and touching the tools on my belt."

"I work at a hospital. The diversity of the staff has given rise to a number of problems. Recently, patients complained about a group of Filipino nurses who were talking in their own language within earshot of them."

"The candidate I was interviewing kept looking down and did not establish eye contact. This made me question his qualifications. I was aware of his cultural background and thought maybe this was his way of being respectful. But then I started to think. He was applying for a position for which interpersonal skills are extremely important. What does this say about his ability to handle this job?"

"How many times has a customer entered my department and walked right past me to the closest nonblack face? Too many. But now I take pleasure in the fact that the person they choose to talk to sends them right back to me. They have to talk to me whether they want to or not."

Ll of these real-life personal experiences involve ordinary interactions in today's workplace. It is a world of potential misunderstandings, bias, conflict, and missed opportunities. It is also an exciting, vibrant, and emerging world where cultural differences give rise to all kinds of possibilities.

How well prepared are we to excel in an environment in which these multicultural scenarios continue to increase in frequency and importance? Do we have the necessary knowledge? And, if so, do we have the wisdom to know when, where, and how to apply this knowledge? What do we do when we find ourselves stymied or taken aback by how much we do not know? Perhaps most importantly, do we have the motivation to make a long-term commitment to learn, change, and adapt?

Each day, we are reminded of the skills we need as we increasingly cross borders, encounter ambiguous behaviors and gestures, and seek to make sense of a seemingly endless variety of values. At home and abroad, many of us struggle to relate to cultural strangers. Whether we have the ability and drive to thrive in this global, changing environment will be pivotal in determining our success.

CHANGING REALITIES

Data from the most recent U.S. Census illustrate how demographic and cultural change is transforming the world in which we live. People are living and working longer. Since 1980, the number of people in the United States 65 and older working or looking for work has grown by more than 50%. Religious diversity is increasing. Gay, lesbian, bisexual, and transgender people are becoming more open about their identity. Increasingly, people with disabilities are gaining access to the workforce. Racial and ethnic minorities now constitute roughly one-third of the U.S. population, and by the year 2050, the Census estimates this figure will grow to one-half. In particular, the number of Hispanics and Asians is expected to continue to experience dramatic growth in the future.

> *Nearly one in five people in the United States are potential customers for businesses accessible to people with disabilities.*
>
> *(U.S. Census Bureau)*
>
> **DID YOU KNOW?**

These demographic changes impact every facet of business, including customers and clients. **Buying power** refers to the total personal income that is available, after taxes, for purchases of goods and services. Data from a recent report by the University of Georgia's Selig Center for Economic Growth shows the buying power of racial minorities increasing much faster than that of Whites. The figure for Hispanics, who can be of any race, is projected to jump 357% during this same time span (see Figure 1.1).

As the multiethnic and multiracial consumer markets expand dramatically, women, seniors, and people with disabilities are changing the face of consumers as well. The growth of the senior market (age 60 and older) will far

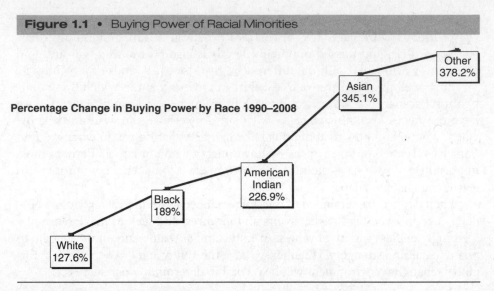

Figure 1.1 • Buying Power of Racial Minorities

Percentage Change in Buying Power by Race 1990–2008

Other 378.2%

Asian 345.1%

American Indian 226.9%

Black 189%

White 127.6%

SOURCE: Selig Center for Economic Growth, Terry College of Business, The University of Georgia, May 2003.

outpace the growth of the rest of the adult market (see Figure 1.2). At present, women represent slightly more than half of the U.S. population but account for 85% of all consumer purchases.[1] According to the U.S. Department of Justice, the percentage of people with disabilities (about 20%) is greater than any single racial or ethnic group in the United States today. Their buying power is almost two times the buying power of teens (U.S. Department of Labor).

As customers and markets become more diverse, so does the U.S. labor force (see Figure 1.3). The labor force participation rate for women has increased significantly during the last few decades, from 43% in 1970 to a projected figure of 62% by 2010 (U.S. Census Bureau, 2004). As Figure 1.3 shows, the labor force growth rate of minorities is outpacing Whites, and this trend will continue. This trend is a reflection of the recent upsurge in minority populations. The influx of immigrants contributes to much of this growth.

While these changes are significant, they do not reflect the impact of global business and cross-cultural relationships in which boundaries and time zones are increasingly irrelevant. The global economy is diversifying the world's workforce and changing how we think, team, communicate, and do business.

As these trends contribute to new social and economic realities, more attention is being directed at **inclusion**, the feeling of belonging and acceptance. Inclusion means moving beyond tolerating or just putting up with diversity. People feel validation and genuine appreciation.

Diversity does not guarantee inclusion. In some cases, diversity is accompanied by barriers, including bias, cultural misunderstandings, and a

Figure 1.2 • Market Growth: Seniors vs. Remainder of Adult Market

Age 18–59

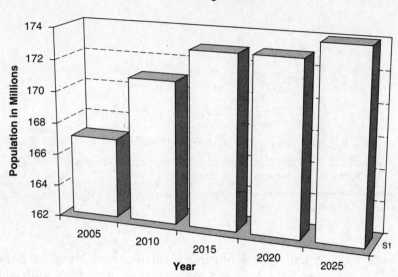

Age 60 and over

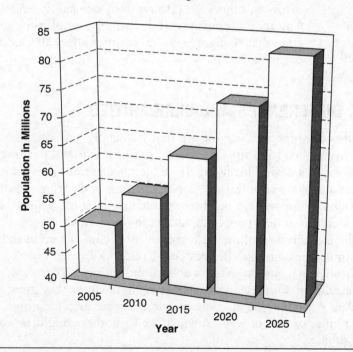

SOURCE: U.S. Census Bureau, *Statistical Abstract of the United States (2004)*.

Figure 1.3 • Labor Force Growth Rates of Minorities Will Outpace Whites

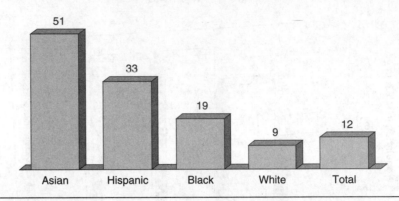

Projected percent change, 2002–2012

| Asian | Hispanic | Black | White | Total |
| 51 | 33 | 19 | 9 | 12 |

SOURCE: Bureau of Labor Statistics.

general lack of cultural intelligence. These barriers contribute to a lack of inclusion in today's multicultural workplace.

While some organizations fail to capitalize on cultural diversity, others are cashing in by constantly adjusting the way they do business. Increasingly, employers acknowledge that changing cultural realities affect all aspects of an organization.

CULTURE: DIFFERENCES AND SIMILARITIES

Culture refers to a people's way of life that is socially learned, shared, and transmitted from generation to generation. Perhaps it is useful to think of culture as a tool kit or a design for living. If we look inside our kit, we might find tangible creations such as our favorite books, clothing, and perhaps a computer. Other creations are intangible or abstract, such as personal values, religious beliefs, and ideas about how people should act in different situations.

Given the inclusiveness of the term *culture*, it becomes apparent that differences and similarities among cultures could refer to any number of things. People might share a common ancestry and history, family background, political viewpoint, or religion. Or they might differ in terms of where they grew up, their age, social class, education, or exposure to cultures other than their own. Hence, there is an infinite variety of ways in which we and others might be culturally alike and dissimilar.

It is important to familiarize ourselves with two dominant views of cultural differences and similarities. One view overemphasizes how much we are alike and pays scant attention to our differences. Because we are all one big "melting pot," our cultural differences are insignificant or irrelevant. The other view trains our eye on the different ingredients in the "pot." When we take this to the extreme, we focus so much on the differences that we forget how much we are alike.

Both of these viewpoints can be problematic. Viewing culture one way *or* the other narrows our perspective, restricts our understanding, and impairs our ability to relate. What is needed is the ability to integrate and modify both viewpoints by recognizing and respecting both our similarities and differences.

UNDERSTANDING CULTURAL INTELLIGENCE

Today's employees need **cultural intelligence (CQ)**; that is, those key competencies that allow us to effectively interact with people from diverse cultural backgrounds in all kinds of settings.

 ## Where Am I Now?

DIRECTIONS: For each statement, mark M (most of the time), O (often), S (sometimes), R (rarely), or N (never).

1. _____ When I meet someone from another culture, I am aware of the physical space between us.

2. _____ When I communicate with someone from another culture, I am aware of my tone of voice.

3. _____ When I participate on multicultural teams, I am aware that my experiences may be very different from the experiences of my teammates.

4. _____ I realize that I have a difficult time listening to certain people because of my biases.

5. _____ I am aware of the different ways in which I might express bias.

6. _____ I am aware of my cultural values when I interact with people from very diverse countries and cultures.

7. _____ I understand that gender roles may vary significantly among people from various cultural backgrounds.

8. _____ I understand the difference between prejudice and discrimination.

9. _____ I understand how cultural intelligence (CQ) promotes an organization's ability to achieve its goals.

10. _____ I understand why it may be necessary for me to change my nonverbal behaviors in a new cultural setting.

11. _____ I understand why CQ requires more than just good intentions on my part.

12. _____ I understand why it is important to be aware of differences in power and privileges.

13. _____ In a new cultural setting, I vary my verbal and nonverbal language when necessary.

14. _____ When I communicate with people from culturally diverse backgrounds, I ask questions to make sure I have heard and understood all of the relevant details.

15. _____ When I observe people showing cultural insensitivity or bias, I intervene in some way.

16. _____ I seek feedback from others regarding my biases.

17. _____ I seek feedback from others regarding my ability to manage cross-cultural conflict effectively.

18. _____ When I interact on multicultural teams, I check the accuracy of my knowledge about other cultures.

The preceding self-assessment provides insight into your current CQ. Questions 1 to 6 relate to your awareness, questions 7 to 12 measure your understanding, and questions 13 to 18 deal with your behaviors or skills. What do your answers reveal about your CQ, and specifically your awareness, understanding, and skills? When you examine these three competencies, are there any differences or similarities that stand out?

If you marked "M" for most or all of the statements, you see yourself as culturally intelligent, at least as far as these indicators are concerned. If you responded "N," "S," and/or "R" to many statements, you do not rate yourself as high on CQ. What this means varies from individual to individual. For example, individuals may have similar competencies but rate themselves differently because their expectations and self-awareness vary. Regardless of how we evaluate ourselves on these and other indicators of CQ, we must view building CQ as a never-ending process for continual improvement.

The competencies that make up CQ are constant awareness, cultural understanding, and CQ skills:

Constant Awareness. This competency refers to our ability to always be mindful or cognizant of oneself, others, and the cultural context. For example, this awareness allows us to tune into our biases at any given moment and how those biases reflect our cultural upbringing.

Figure 1.4 • CQ Components

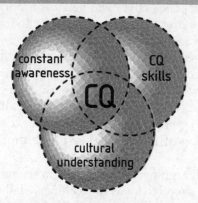

Cultural Understanding. This involves exposing oneself to information about cultural differences and similarities *and* grasping what this information means as well as its significance.

CQ Skills. This refers to our ability to do something and do it well as a result of training, experience, and practice. Clearly, there is a difference between knowing what to do and actually doing it. As we practice and refine these skills, they become more automatic.

As Figure 1.4 shows, these three competencies are interdependent. Each competency impacts the others. To illustrate, our *skill* level in communicating effectively with others who are culturally different is dependent on our awareness of them and ourselves as well as our understanding of this process.

UNDERSTANDING THE IMPORTANCE OF CULTURAL INTELLIGENCE

We often do not respond well to cultural diversity. CQ changes that. It allows us to view people, and what they "bring to the table," differently. Through CQ, differences become possibilities for learning, personal growth, and relationships. Our world becomes bigger and more complex as we develop CQ. We move from assuming that cultural diversity is a deficit to understanding that cultural differences embody potential. What we do with that potential is up to us.

More specifically, CQ opens us up to new experiences. In addition to being more informed about what we might encounter in cross-cultural relationships, we are better prepared to deal with **culture shock**, or the disorientation we experience when encountering new, radically different situations. Because we can appreciate multiple perspectives and make appropriate adjustments in our behavior, we are much better able to quickly adjust and relate effectively to others whose backgrounds are not at all like ours.

As realities change in today's multicultural, global environment, CQ becomes a critical component of everybody's résumé. Unfortunately, research shows that while employers desperately need workers with CQ to adjust to changing workplace and workforce realities, many employees do not measure up. To complicate matters further, CQ cannot be manufactured in a short period of time. It takes work, motivation, and constant practice.

It is not unusual for employees with excellent technical skills to possess low CQ. Often, there is a singular focus on technical skills: the ability to use the "tools" and procedures unique to a specific field. According to a new study by Leadership IQ, a leadership and training company, nearly half of newly hired employees fail within 18 months. What these new hires lack are interpersonal skills rather than technical skills, such as the inability to manage their own emotions and accept feedback from others.[2]

YOUR TURN   • • • • •

Which of your competencies would you rank higher—your "technical" expertise in a specific area or your CQ? Why?

_____

_____

_____

_____

IDENTIFYING NINE MEGASKILLS

Different situations require a variety of skills. With regard to CQ, there are certain skills that are of paramount importance. This book refers to these as the nine megaskills (see Figure 1.5). A **megaskill** is a powerful, fundamental skill that is absolutely necessary for excelling on the job and in other areas of life.

Building CQ is no easy task. We need to nurture and practice those cognitive and behavioral skills that allow us to adapt and excel in any and all environments. Further, retooling and reeducating ourselves is an ongoing process that can be humbling and uncomfortable at times. With the proper mindset and motivation,

Figure 1.5 • Nine CQ Megaskills

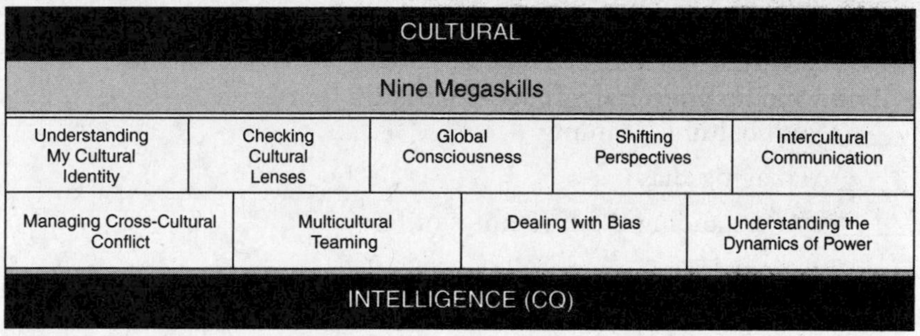

CULTURAL				
Nine Megaskills				
Understanding My Cultural Identity	Checking Cultural Lenses	Global Consciousness	Shifting Perspectives	Intercultural Communication
Managing Cross-Cultural Conflict	Multicultural Teaming		Dealing with Bias	Understanding the Dynamics of Power
INTELLIGENCE (CQ)				

we can develop the following nine megaskills that are absolutely critical in any workplace:

1. *Understanding My Cultural Identity*—Understanding how we think about ourselves as well as the people and ways of life with which we identify.

2. *Checking Cultural Lenses*—Recognizing the ways in which cultural backgrounds differ and how they influence thinking, behavior, and assumptions.

3. *Global Consciousness*—Moving across boundaries and seeing the world from multiple perspectives.

4. *Shifting Perspectives*—Putting ourselves in others' shoes and cultures.

5. *Intercultural Communication*—Exchanging ideas and feelings and creating meanings with people from diverse cultural backgrounds.

6. *Managing Cross-Cultural Conflict*—Dealing with conflict among people from differing cultural backgrounds in an effective and constructive manner.

7. *Multicultural Teaming*—Working with others from diverse cultural backgrounds to accomplish certain tasks.

8. *Dealing with Bias*—Recognizing bias in ourselves and others and responding to it effectively.

9. *Understanding the Dynamics of Power*—Grasping how power and culture interrelate and the effect of power on how we see the world and relate to others.

⍰ Where Am I Now?

DIRECTIONS: Rank yourself on the following megaskills. For each, mark M (need much improvement), S (need some improvement), or L (need little improvement)

1. _____ Understanding My Cultural Identity

2. _____ Checking Cultural Lenses

3. _____ Global Consciousness

4. _____ Shifting Perspectives

5. _____ Intercultural Communication

6. _____ Managing Cross-Cultural Conflict

7. _____ Multicultural Teaming

8. _____ Managing Bias

9. _____ Understanding the Dynamics of Power

UNDERSTANDING THE BOTTOM-LINE IMPORTANCE OF CQ

 REFLECT BEFORE READING

In what ways might promoting CQ improve an organization's success?

In the past, cultural intelligence was seen as an extra; that is, something that *might* be useful to some people in the workforce. Cultural diversity issues were ghettoized, meaning they were only dealt with within a particular department such as human resources or community relations. "One-size-fits-all" products and services were marketed to the average consumer. When interacting, cultural differences were ignored or seen as irrelevant.

Because monocultural organizations were the norm, issues dealing with diversity were often seen as divisive and counterproductive. In short, cultural diversity was something to control, curtail, and avoid if possible.

A major challenge in all types of organizations is the ability to understand the bottom-line importance of cultural intelligence. In one study, one of the most significant findings had to do with the fact that many respondents did not understand what impact diversity had on them personally; nor did they understand why diversity is important.[3]

Now, leaders in areas such as business, education, health care, government, military and law enforcement, and human services are much more apt to approach cultural intelligence as a **bottom-line issue**. In other words, employees with CQ megaskills impact the overall success and survival of an organization (see Figure 1.6). CQ changes the way employees interact with their customers and clients. As employees develop their CQ megaskills, their ability to assess and understand the cultural context of any social interaction increases. This, in turn, allows them to increase customer/client satisfaction by building relationships and adapting to the diverse needs of individuals. Even small changes in the range and magnitude of one's skills can have a profound influence on productivity, profitability, and other bottom-line issues.

Figure 1.6 • CQ and the Bottom Line

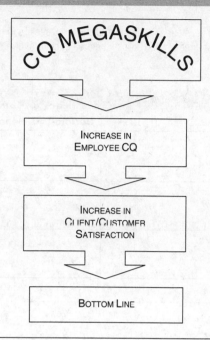

Since the cultural diversity of workers and customers affects everyone within an organization, CQ is now viewed as an essential rather than a "nice-to-have" competency. CQ impacts the bottom line for a variety of reasons (see Table 1.1).

Table 1.1 • Rationale for CQ

Bottom-Line Issue	Rationale for Developing CQ
Avoiding lawsuits and other forms of intolerance that devalue diversity and threaten productivity	Bias, including discrimination, is expensive. Even if it does not result in a lawsuit, bias wastes human potential and alienates customers.
Being flexible and innovative	Being able to shift perspectives makes it possible to continually reexamine basic, traditional assumptions. In turn, this can foster development of new and better products and services and recognition of new opportunities.
Maximizing utilization of human capital	Respecting and valuing differences breaks down walls, increases trust, and improves performance.
Solving problems	Seeking, understanding, and evaluating multiple perspectives allows for better solutions.
Reaching out to a changing, global marketplace and new populations	Designing and developing products and services are much easier when we understand markets.

YOUR TURN • • • • • •

As our CQ increases, so does our ability to appreciate our own skills in this area and their bottom-line benefits. List three of your skills in the area of cultural diversity and the benefits of each.

Table 1.2 • My Skills and Benefits

My Skills	Bottom-Line Benefit(s)
1.	
2.	
3.	

 Applied • • • • • •

One way of maximizing the potential benefits of diversity is by training workers to develop CQ. As an example, a national department store (Saks Fifth Avenue) uses a customized video-based program to train its employees to provide quality service to a culturally diverse customer base. Vignettes show customers interacting with actual Saks employees in a variety of situations. Jay Redman, vice president of service and selling, is clear about the rationale for the training. "We estimate that every customer interaction for us is about $250 dollars, so if you only treat 1,000 customers inappropriately, that's a lot of money."[4]

CULTURAL INTELLIGENCE MYTHS

I spend a good deal of time discussing the importance of being able to deal with cultural diversity effectively. When I do, myths invariably surface. These myths are usually some variation of the following:

CQ is only important for some jobs and some people. No one group has a monopoly on cultural ignorance or bias. People of all colors, cultures, and backgrounds, regardless of position or line of work, need to continually examine, develop, and refine their CQ.

Developing CQ is all about changing people's awareness. Most of the training in this area is aimed at promoting awareness of self and others.

The assumption being made is that once we become more culturally aware, our behaviors will change. But is this necessarily true? Think back to those times we discriminate or act irrationally even though we know better. Awareness is only a first step.

CQ training aims to change people's values. While this might be true of some diversity training, any CQ training ought to respect all values. Rather than changing or even judging values, CQ is about being aware of our values and those of others, and the relationships among people's values, behaviors, and cultural backgrounds.

There is some simple formula or strategy for developing CQ. This thinking is typical of many training programs, especially those of short duration with little or no follow-through. Most cultural diversity training is one day or less in length. Learning CQ becomes a quick fix: an event rather than a process. While developing skills in making presentations or using the Internet is a fairly straightforward and standardized process, developing CQ is much more complex and variable from person to person and situation to situation. The challenge is not just to learn the skills, but to regularly use the skills effectively.

CQ comes naturally to people with good intentions. In other words, if my heart is in the right place, that's enough. Clearly, understanding and respecting cultural diversity is not just something that happens because you see yourself as a person of character and you mean well.

IDENTIFYING THREE KEY STRATEGIES FOR DEVELOPING CULTURAL INTELLIGENCE

A Chinese proverb states, "I see and I forget. I hear and I remember. I do and I understand." Building CQ involves three key action-oriented strategies—assessing CQ, taking responsibility for learning, and optimizing learning. With sufficient practice, you will learn to employ each of these strategies as you continue to develop CQ.

REFLECT BEFORE READING

What do you think is the most effective way to develop cultural intelligence? Why?

_____

_____

_____

_____

Strategy #1: Assessing My Cultural Intelligence

One of the ways in which we can evaluate our CQ is to be constantly alert to the reactions of others. Another way is to simply ask others who observe our interaction. At work, for example, we might ask our superior, our subordinates, and our peers questions about our CQ. For example, we might inquire about how well we relate to people of different ages or people who do not speak our language.

In seeking feedback, look for your own mentors, especially those people whom you admire. Learn from them, even though you may not identify with them. Compare what others think about you with what you think about yourself, and pay particular attention to those areas where there is a sizable gap.

You can seek input informally, such as when you engage in a casual conversation or send an e-mail to someone. Or you might prefer something more structured, such as asking certain individuals to complete a form such as the following.

My Cultural Intelligence: Please Assess

DIRECTIONS: I am genuinely interested in how you view my interpersonal skills with people of various cultural backgrounds. Please answer honestly, in order that I may identify those areas in which I need improvement. For each statement, write SA (strongly agree), A (agree), D (disagree), or SD (strongly disagree). Thank you.

1. _____ I adjust easily when I sense my behaviors make it difficult for others to approach or talk to me.
2. _____ I spend considerable time with people who are very different from me.
3. _____ I have very good communication skills.
4. _____ People of all different backgrounds enjoy teaming with me.
5. _____ I am able to "shift gears" and adopt multiple perspectives.
6. _____ I am open to suggestions from everyone, regardless of their job or position.

YOUR TURN   · · · · ·

The way we relate to others affects how they relate to us. For example, we might be surprised by a negative reaction we get from people because our perceptions do not align with theirs.

Consider an everyday situation in which a customer pays in cash for a purchase. The cashier reaches out for the money but the customer places it on the counter. What do you think the cashier might read into this?

1. Absolutely nothing.
2. The customer showed a lack of respect by not placing the money in the cashier's hand.
3. The customer did not place money in the cashier's hand for religious or cultural reasons.
4. Any of the above.

Being able to analyze this exchange and understand how different people might interpret what took place is a skill. As part of their diversity training, employees at Denny's restaurant chain analyze this very situation. Depending on their cultural perspective, people may view this interaction between the cashier and the customer in any number of ways. Therefore, the correct answer to the question above is "any of the above."

Another method of self-evaluation involves constant reflection on one's own behaviors. Consider those people with whom you interact on a daily basis. Do you listen more attentively to those people whose communication style is similar to yours? Do you neglect to engage or speak to people who occupy certain positions, such as supervisors, clerical workers, or custodial staff? Whose names don't you know?

Continually assessing and reassessing our cultural intelligence is not an easy task. Sometimes, we are reluctant to evaluate ourselves out of fear of what we might find. Furthermore, it is one thing to become aware of our lack of cultural intelligence; it is quite another to maintain that awareness and commit to change.

TO LEARN MORE

To access a short CQ self-assessment tool, go to **www.culturalq.com/ selfassess.html.** Respond to each of the 20 items. Then, examine how you evaluate yourself in each area of the assessment: CQ Strategy, CQ Knowledge, CQ Motivation, and CQ Behavior.

Strategy #2: Taking Responsibility for My Learning

YOUR TURN   · · · · · ·

What is one specific thing you can do on a regular basis in order to take responsibility for your personal growth in the area of cultural diversity?

_____

_____

_____

_____

Taking responsibility for our own learning means taking advantage of learning opportunities both at work and elsewhere, including experiential, collaborative, and e-learning. In effect, we become the CEO for our own personal development. As CEO, motivation is critical.

Without motivation, we will not persevere or adjust when we encounter obstacles and setbacks. Motivation allows us to keep our focus on our goals during the inevitable failures that arise from cultural misunderstandings. Being aware of why CQ is a bottom-line issue for ourselves and our organizations fuels our motivation.

For example, how do we react when we encounter someone with an accent that makes communication nearly impossible? Do we avoid engaging that person in conversation? If we lack motivation, perhaps we might ask others to listen and interpret for us. If we find ourselves communicating with that person face-to-face, do we go through the motions of listening or do we redouble our efforts? With motivation, we will work harder to ask questions, listen carefully, and acknowledge our own difficulties in understanding.

Developing CQ is a cumulative process. Since culture is fluid and changes from one moment to the next, part of the challenge of developing and applying CQ is adapting, reevaluating, and tailoring how we respond to specific situations.

Learning leads to change, although it may be difficult for us to see. Small, incremental steps lead to major breakthroughs. This is the idea behind the Japanese word *kaizen*, the relentless quest to improve a little each and every day.

We will not maximize our learning unless we become self-directed learners. Even though this requires us to be proactive, it does not necessarily mean participating in formal training. Some of the most valuable lessons occur when we engage in activities that may appear totally unrelated to cultural diversity. This is called **incidental learning**; unintentional learning that results from everyday activities. Opportunities for this type of learning abound. For example, incidental learning may occur during the process of teaming. When working with other individuals on a group project, we might learn valuable lessons about cultural diversity, human interaction, and bias.

Self-directed learners listen actively, ask questions, and then reflect back on what took place. Imagine you are eating lunch with a group of coworkers. One of them comments, "I don't understand why Americans call a sunny day a good day." You can ignore the comment, or probe more deeply. A colleague of mine found herself in this very situation. She wanted to find out more, so she asked her coworker to elaborate. Whereupon the person who made this comment explained that he grew up in India. He went on, "In India, it is not uncommon for temperatures to be in excess of 100 degrees. Where I lived, there is little or no air-conditioning." He added, "A day with lots of clouds is a good day."

By being proactive and asking questions, my colleague learned something about cultural diversity. Although this was not something she planned when she sat down for lunch, she turned a simple comment into a valuable learning experience. And this experience has become a catalyst for more learning, since her coworker is now more inclined to share other parts of his cultural background.

YOUR TURN   · · · · · ·

When it comes to developing your CQ, do you see yourself as a volunteer, a vacationer, or an unwilling recruit? Why?

_____

_____

_____

Steven Covey talks about **modeling,** by which he means taking responsibility for finding one's own mentors and developing a relationship with each of them. Our relationships with others provide feedback on our strengths and limitations. Personal development is a collaborative process. Self-improvement cannot be done in isolation from others.

Strategy #3: Optimizing My Learning

For us to benefit from learning opportunities, planned or incidental, we need to be mindful of a number of things. Learning is optimized when we

- Understand the value of what we learn. What are the bottom-line benefits of those competencies you have been developing and practicing? Many people question the relevance of training that focuses on some aspect of interpersonal skills. To them, mastery of technical skills is what really matters. Research does not support this; rather, both CQ *and* technical skills are essential.

- Actively participate in the learning process. Active learning refers to a continuous cycle of action and reflection. We build on our knowledge by trying it out in a variety of settings and constantly monitoring how successful we are at listening.

- Apply what we learn. Workers at one large restaurant chain take 10 to 15 minutes each morning to learn a new skill aimed at improving customer service. Then they practice that skill for the rest of the day and seek further help or feedback when necessary. Learning is incomplete unless we take it with us, put it to work, and practice it again and again.

- Develop an individual action plan. For instance, target certain megaskills over a period of time. Think through what you can do to develop, measure, and reevaluate them. Reassess your plan continually in light of your priorities and needs. One possible template for an action plan might include the following:

1. Specific skill you plan to work on.
2. Your strategy for developing skill.
3. What you will do and when.
4. Possible obstacles.
5. Necessary resources.
6. Means of assessing your progress.

YOUR TURN   • • • • • ——

Learning Opportunities

DIRECTIONS: For each of the following learning opportunities, describe one specific thing you can do to expand your understanding of cultural differences.

Table 1.3 • What I Can Do to Learn

Learning Opportunities	What I Can Do
Experiential learning—learning by doing rather than simply talking about it	
Collaborative learning—learning by working with others on some project	
Academic learning—learning by taking advantage of a variety of opportunities, including courses and training that are offered in the classroom and online	
E-learning—learning via computer technology, such as surfing the Web	
Incidental learning—learning by taking advantage of every opportunity that presents itself, including those that are unexpected and unplanned	

A Look Back: I Have Learned

✓ _____ How cultural diversity is changing realities.

✓ _____ The meaning of culture.

✓ _____ The meaning of cultural intelligence.

✓ _____ Why cultural intelligence is important.

✓ _____ To identify the nine megaskills of cultural intelligence.

✓ _____ Three key strategies for developing cultural intelligence.

Notes

1. "M2W." Online 6/2/06. Available: **www.m2w.biz/fastfacts.html**.

2. "Interpersonal Failure," *Inside Training Newsletter* (September 28, 2005), 1.

3. National Center for Research in Vocational Education. Online 9/18/03. Available: **http://ncrve.berkeley.edu/Abstracts/MDS-936/MDS-936-Barriers.html**.

4. Jeff Barbian, "Diversity Training." Online 8/29/03. Available: **www.trainingmag.com/training/search/search_display.jsp?vnu_content_id=1809715**.

CHAPTER 2

CQ MEGASKILL: UNDERSTANDING MY CULTURAL IDENTITY

Performance Skills

- *Understanding the complexity of cultural identity*
- *Appreciating the varying importance of cultural identities*
- *Understanding cultural identity development*
- *Understanding why cultural identity matters*
- *Being aware of my cultural silo*
- *Having knowledge of key cultural identity issues*

When others ask us about our **identity**, meaning how we define ourselves, our answers vary tremendously. The concept of *ubuntu*, which comes from Africa, helps explain why. This word from the Nguni language defies simple translation. In English, *ubuntu* roughly translates as "the quality of being human." The *ubuntu* ideal is captured by an African proverb, "A person is a person through other people." In effect, we form our identity as we relate to others.

No two people have the exact same identity. How we think about ourselves is an interactive process that unfolds throughout our lives. As soon as we enter this world, we begin to feel the cultural imprint of individuals, groups, and communities. All leave their mark on us in an infinite variety of ways. As we get older, this process continues and becomes more complex. Each of us is exposed to different individuals and groups who teach us something about ourselves and our cultures. Every lesson we learn contributes toward our uniqueness. The people who impart these lessons include family, peers, coworkers, community members, and many others. Throughout our lives, our identity continues to be shaped and reshaped through our interaction with others.

Examining the numerous and varied cultural lessons we have internalized and their impact on our identity is an eye-opening, challenging, and rewarding process. Who am I? How do I define myself? How do others define me? And why is my answer to these questions so important to me and my cultural intelligence?

◐ REFLECT BEFORE READING

Who are you?

"I am a woman with many types of ethnic groups running through my bloodlines. All of them play a part in who I am. It doesn't make me more or less of a person; it makes me a worldly person. What I mean by this is that since I have different types of ethnic groups in my life I am not just experiencing myself with one group but with different ones."

"I do not see myself as anything. Generally speaking, I do not appreciate being classified in any way. I feel that the color of my skin does not represent anything about me. In no way does it reveal who I am, where I am from, or where I am going."

"I did not want to identify with my ethnic background during my teen years out of fear that I would be labeled as one of those 'banana boat' people, a pejorative term applied primarily to Haitians living in America, regardless of their citizenship status. Consequently, I deliberately concealed any traces of my cultural identity during my social interactions at school and in public. Now I am not ashamed to reveal my ethnicity, especially when I know I may literally be the only Haitian 'living on the block.'"

"I am African American. Although my skin is dark, and I was born in America, sometimes it is difficult for me to relate to either category. I can't trace my ancestors back to Africa so how can I be African? And when I am presented with an image of Americans, what I see does not look, taste, or act like me."

How does your cultural background affect you?

"My cultural background has affected me in many ways. It has given me a sense of pride about who I am and where I am from. Knowing my culture and its history gives me a better perspective of what I have and how much I should appreciate it."

"English is my second language; therefore, I feel uncertainty everywhere because I do not clearly express my questions and my ideas. People feel this uncertainty, lose interest in me, and do not respect me."

"Part of the Jewish laws of modesty is that men and women do not touch each other unless they are related or married. In this day and age, when a man or woman is introduced to a person of the opposite sex, the common custom is to shake hands. However, this is not allowed by my religion. To many people, when I do not shake their hands, it is seen as rude and non-businesslike. However, this is not the case at all."

"Often people judge me based on my age. I have had older clients tell me that I cannot understand what they are going through because I do not have children of my own and I have not had any life experience. I have had younger clients immediately warm up to me because I was young, pretty, and well dressed. They assumed that because of my appearance they could trust me more easily and open up to me."

• • • • • • • ▬▬▬▬▬▬▬▬▬▬▬▬▬▬▬▬▬

INTRODUCTION

For each of us, thinking about our own identity and how it ties in with our cultural background requires effort, knowledge, and awareness. It is much easier to keep the focus on "them" rather than "us," particularly when others seem exotic or just "weird." If we always look beyond ourselves, we fail to see how *our* culture constantly filters what we see and how we make sense of the world around us. We fail to understand how *we* might come across as strange or incomprehensible in another social setting. When we see someone acting in a way that is strange to us, our tendency is to focus on their behavior rather than on our perception of their behavior.

By becoming more aware of our cultural identity as well as the cultural identity of others, we increase our cultural intelligence. We become better communicators and team players because we can relate our own cultural identities to our interactions with others. We find it easier to adjust and change as we recognize our own uniqueness, broaden our perceptions, and respect the cultural identities of other individuals.

Furthermore, understanding our cultural identity enhances our sense of well-being. We are more apt to feel comfortable with our own cultural background in addition to the cultural differences that exist between ourselves and others. By the same token, we are less apt to rely on others to define who we are.

TO LEARN MORE

Go to the Smithsonian Website titled "Cultural Identity and Interaction" at **www.si. edu/history_and_culture/cultural_identity_and_interaction/**. Click on a number of links to find out more about how people from diverse backgrounds express their identities through art and artifacts, bibliographies, music, photography, and more.

WHAT IS CULTURAL IDENTITY?

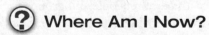 ### Where Am I Now?

DIRECTIONS: For each statement, mark M (most of the time), O (often), S (sometimes), R (rarely), or N (never).

1. _____ I understand how my culture influences the way I think about myself.
2. _____ I understand how my own cultural identity influences my interaction with others.
3. _____ I am aware of the different groups and cultures with which I identify.

Figure 2.1 • Personal, Cultural, and Universal Identities[1]

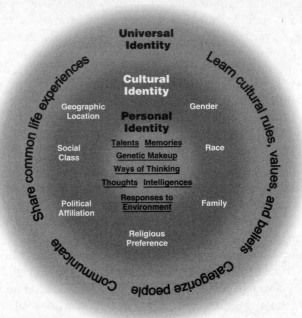

___

4. _____ I often think about how my cultural experiences and background restrict my thinking and influence my behavior.

5. _____ I am aware of what is important to me.

___

In addition to those variables that distinguish us as individuals (personal identity), each of us has a **cultural identity**; the people and ways of life with which we identify. While identity and cultural identity are not synonymous, they interrelate with each other (see Figure 2.1). Components of our identity include our personal, cultural, and universal identities.

Although each of us is unique, we identify with certain people and groups in many ways. This is our cultural identity (note the inner ring of Figure 2.1). Our culture shapes our perception and, specifically, the way we categorize people. Consequently, we identify with some people but not others. In deciding who is similar to us, we may focus on some traits, values, and behaviors and not others. We may consider our affiliation with some groups (age, gender, religion, political affiliation) more than others (occupation, social class).

The outer ring represents our universal identity. At this level of our identity, we realize that in some ways "we are all alike." As an example, we all have common life experiences, such as the life course—birth, growing older, and death. No matter what culture we identify with, we all categorize other people and communicate in some way. Also, we are all born into a culture with values, beliefs, rules, and symbols.

In Figure 2.1, there are no clear-cut boundaries between personal, cultural, and universal identities. Each identity is fluid and ever-changing, as are the relationships among the three identities. Identities change as experiences transform one's knowledge and awareness from one moment to the next. For example, a person living in the United States may see herself as female, middle-class, heterosexual, racially mixed, and single. But when she travels abroad, she also sees herself as American and wealthy. These latter traits are likely to become more visible as she interacts with others whose nationality and standard of living are markedly different.

Lastly, it is important to understand that cultural identities are **socially constructed**; meaning they are based on how we view and define what reality is to us. If we think something is real, it becomes real to us and has very real consequences for our lives. Our racial identity, which is part of our cultural identity, is a good example. If we have been carefully taught that the color of one's skin is important, skin color is apt to be something we see and use to define ourselves.

Gregory Williams's history, as described in his book *Life on the Color Line*, illustrates the fluid, socially constructed nature of cultural identity. Williams grew up in a middle-class family in Virginia thinking he was White. He attended "Whites only" schools and went to "Whites only" movie theatres. At 10 years of age, his parents divorced. While traveling with his father and brother to his new hometown in the Midwest, Williams was made aware of his poor, Black relatives. His father prepared him for his new life as a "colored boy" in Muncie, Indiana. However, he wanted Gregory to keep in mind that he was no different than the boy who thought he was White in Virginia. While other people's perceptions might change, that did not mean he had to change.

We do not define ourselves in isolation from other people. Rather, we only become aware of who we are and what we stand for by comparing ourselves to others. Cultural identity, therefore, is **relational**. It is created out of relationships between and among individuals, groups, and societies.

INDIVIDUALISTIC AND COLLECTIVISTIC VIEWS

YOUR TURN · · · · · ·

If you were asked to describe who you are, would most of your description focus on you the individual or on other people in your life? Explain.

_____

_____

_____

_____

Definitions of identity vary from culture to culture. In **individualistic cultures**, a person is seen as an individual, with a unique personality and a distinctive set of qualities or characteristics that set him or her apart from other individuals. These cultures situate one's identity within the person himself or herself. Moreover, a person's behavior points to his or her identity. Developing a distinctive identity that allows one to function independently is viewed as a necessary part of human development. For instance, part of growing up is learning to be on one's own apart from one's family. Individualistic cultures are found in countries such as the United States, Australia, and the Netherlands.

Collectivistic cultures see people as interdependent. In other words, the person is viewed as an entity that cannot be separated from others or the surrounding culture. Behavior stems from relationships with others. Rather than asserting one's uniqueness, people in collectivistic cultures will be more apt to evaluate themselves in terms of their abilities to interact with others in a harmonious fashion. Collectivistic cultures view growing up differently than individualistic cultures. The emphasis is on "we" rather than "me." In collectivistic cultures, the self is defined through a web of relationships with one's family members and others. This kind of perspective is typical of many cultures in South and Central America, Asia, and Africa.

How might the difference between these two types of cultures, for example, affect how we approach retirement in the United States? Those with an individualistic orientation are more likely to make the arrangements necessary, financial and otherwise, to prepare for their new lifestyle once they retire. Even in old age, self-reliance is valued. Collectivistic-oriented individuals living in the United States are more apt to rely on their children to take care of them as they get older.

THE IMPORTANCE OF ETHNICITY

DID YOU KNOW?

How do Latinos or Hispanics in the U.S. identify themselves? In a national survey, approximately:

- *54% identify themselves by their country of origin, such as Guatemalan or Nicaraguan.*
- *24% prefer to be identified as "Latino" or "Hispanic."*
- *21% use the term "American."[2]*

One significant component of cultural identity is our **ethnic identity**, meaning an awareness of belonging to a social group that shares a common culture. A common culture may embrace a variety of traits, including religion, history, nationality, language, and geography. Given that ethnic identity is such a broad term, there is apt to be considerable cultural diversity within an ethnic group. For example, people in the United States who identify themselves as "American" share many distinctive ethnic identities. Also, people who see themselves belonging to a broader, more inclusive Latin culture may further identify with different Caribbean, Central American, and South American cultures.

In Figure 2.2, data from the Zogby Culture Polls illustrate how six groups in the United States feel about the importance of their ethnic heritage.

Figure 2.2 • How Important Is Your Ethnic Heritage?

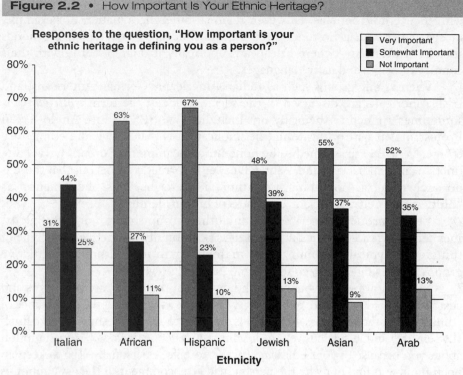

Responses to the question, "How important is your ethnic heritage in defining you as a person?"

- Very Important
- Somewhat Important
- Not Important

Ethnicity

SOURCE: James Zogby, *What Ethnic Americans Really Think.* Zogby International, 2001.

YOUR TURN • • • • • •

What conclusions can you draw from Figure 2.2?

When responses for each of the six groups in Figure 2.2 are broken down into "U.S. Born" and "Immigrants," individuals born in the United States were significantly less likely to see their ethnic heritage as important. For example, 41% of U.S. born Arabs versus 73% of Arab immigrants view their ethnic heritage as important. **Assimilation,** the process by which people lose their cultural differences and blend into the larger society, increases with time. More recent immigrants to the United States may think their ethnicity is more important because they have only begun to experience the effects of assimilation.

Relatively speaking, Italian Americans in this survey do not strongly identify with their ethnic heritage. However, regional differences matter. For example, in large cities such as Boston, New York, and Chicago, there are neighborhoods such as "Little Italy" where European Americans strongly identify with their country of origin and native languages.

When ethnic groups such as Italian Americans, German Americans, and Irish Americans are discussed in the social sciences, the term *white ethnic* is sometimes applied to them. By not including WASPS (White Anglo-Saxon Protestants) as part of this term, the implication is that only white ethnics are ethnic. WASPS are assumed to be nonethnic, meaning they do not have a distinctive cultural background. Ashley Doane Jr. correctly points out that there is no such thing as nonethnicity. Rather, he describes this phenomenon as "**hidden ethnicity**," a lack of awareness of ethnic identity.[3]

When European Americans or any other group shows hidden ethnicity, they tend to view everyone but themselves as culturally distinctive. This type of thinking is typical of dominant or **majority groups**, culturally distinctive groups possessing social, economic, and political power.

One thing we will encounter, both now and in the future, are coworkers and customers who do not share our ethnicity or our views regarding the importance of ethnicity. By preparing ourselves for this eventuality, we can become more culturally sensitive and less defensive. For instance, if someone makes a false assumption about you because of your ethnicity, try not to take it personally. Try to keep an open mind and find out why the person made the comment. If the assumption is stereotypical, explain why it does not apply to everyone who shares your ethnicity.

YOUR TURN · · · · · · ────────────────

What is your ethnic identity?

_____

_____

_____

Is your ethnic heritage very important, somewhat important, or not important in defining who you are? Why?

_____

_____

_____

_____

We cannot assume that all people will view their ethnic identity as important or even relevant. In some cases, their job, family, social class, or disability may be as or more important. Similarly, we cannot assume that ethnic identity impacts all areas of interaction. For example, we might see a person's shyness as a reflection of his or her cultural upbringing. However, shyness in many cases is an individual personality trait that can be found in diverse cultures.

To summarize, people who identify with an ethnic group share a common identity based on cultural characteristics such as nationality, history, language, and religion. However, all people do not see themselves as belonging to an ethnic group, nor does everyone view their ethnic heritage as an important part of their cultural identity.

UNDERSTANDING THE COMPLEXITY OF CULTURAL IDENTITY

Understanding our cultural identity requires us to think about the cultural context of our behaviors. This means understanding that our actions are no more "natural" than anyone else's actions. Like everyone else, our actions can only be understood if we look at all of the cultural influences that surround and impact what we do.

Furthermore, it is important to understand that each individual is affected by his or her cultural environment differently. For example, a number of female workers who are recent immigrants from Nigeria may each feel very differently about their priorities regarding working and fulfilling family responsibilities despite sharing a common cultural heritage.

Likewise, those of us born and raised in the United States may or may not share certain values. Dr. Robert Kohls, a well-known researcher on cultural values in the United States, has identified a number of "basic American values." These include

- Personal control over environment.
- Change is seen as positive and natural.
- All people are created equal.
- Individuals take credit for their achievements.[4]

YOUR TURN • • • • •

Do you agree with Kohls? In other words, do you consider these "basic American values"? Why or why not?

_____

_____

_____

_____

_____

_____

Many people who work in the United States today and consider themselves "American" may not embrace one or more of the four American values studied by Kohls. They believe in the power of fate, see change as disruptive and destructive, see differences in status and authority as desirable, and believe that taking credit for what one accomplishes is boastful and inappropriate.

Even though we may live in the same region and share the same general lifestyle, we do not necessarily embrace the exact same values, beliefs, and ideas. Our individual life experiences and personalities are unique. Therefore, each of us will internalize different things from our culture. Some parts of our culture we will embrace; other parts we will reject, ignore, or modify.

Multiple, Changing Identities

As discussed previously, cultural identity is not one single characteristic of an individual. All of us have multiple identities, meaning we identify with numerous groups and cultures. An individual may "wear many hats," including being a worker, student, atheist, employee, friend, and middle-aged female. Throughout life, our identities change as well. For instance, as we become more experienced in our career and develop a passion for our work, we may increasingly identify with people in our profession.

Some identities we choose for ourselves while others are chosen for us. We have no choice when it comes to our place of birth, age, or **family of orientation**, meaning the family into which we are born. On the other hand, our geographic location, social class, and religion *may* change out of choice.

Being aware of our multiple and changing identities provides us with greater insight into how others define themselves. For example, my ability to understand why I now identify myself as an "American" can help me appreciate why others who have lived in the United States all their lives but whose life experiences are different from mine might not think of themselves the same way. They might prefer the term *African American* or *Asian American*. Having this understanding sensitizes us to the power of words and the importance individuals and groups attach to labeling themselves.

Visible and More Hidden Identities

A popular advertising slogan in the United States proclaims "Image is everything." The slogan points to the importance of visible differentiating characteristics, such as appearance, skin color, gender, and dress. The public may define who we are and assume certain things about us based on one or a number of these observable identities. The visible and concrete nature of these characteristics makes the process of categorization that much easier.

Your hidden identities encompass those differences that people probably do not notice when they first meet you. One's ethnicity, disability, sexual orientation, learning style, and even one's socioeconomic status may be hidden from view. In one exercise I often use when conducting workshops, employees share what parts of their cultural identity make them distinctive. While they typically share a wide range of answers, most focus on more hidden aspects of their diversity such as their concern for others, religious beliefs, family backgrounds, and values.

Mary, who works as a magazine editor, talks about the challenges of having a hidden identity. "Sometimes I'm not sure myself what I am. I blend in easily with normal people." She continues, "To look at me, you'd never guess I once ran naked through my yard or shuffled down the hallways of a psychiatric ward. To hear me, you'd never guess God channeled messages to me through my computer. After my breakdown at 36, I was diagnosed as bipolar, a condition marked by moods that swing between elation and despair."

Mary works at being a functional member of society. She talks about how she feels lucky to blend in with the crowd. At other times, she feels fortunate to be her true self with her closest friends.[5]

YOUR TURN   · · · · · · ———————————

What is one hidden identity most people would be surprised to learn about you?

_____

_____

_____

Appreciating the Varying Importance of Cultural Identities

 Where Am I Now?

DIRECTIONS: For each statement, write SA (strongly agree), A (agree), D (disagree), or SD (strongly disagree).

1. _____ My race is very important to the way I identify myself.
2. _____ My ethnicity is very important to the way I identify myself.
3. _____ My gender is very important to the way I identify myself.
4. _____ My social class is very important to the way I identify myself.
5. _____ My sexual orientation is very important to the way I identify myself.
6. _____ My ability/disability is very important to the way I identify myself.

Reflect on your responses to each of the preceding statements. The statements deal with six dimensions of diversity—race, ethnicity, gender, social class, sexual orientation, and ability/disability. Our culture influences how we define these dimensions, the importance we attach to each of them, and in some cases whether we see them as matters of choice. All, some, or none of these characteristics may be important in how we see ourselves.

As stated earlier, individuals simultaneously carry numerous cultural identities of varying importance. At any given moment, some of our identities may become more important than others. Research shows this is more likely to happen when one of our identities is threatened. For instance, if we work in an environment where people form cliques on the basis of religious differences, then one's religion takes on added importance.

When Dalton Conley, a professor of sociology at Yale University, asks students in all of his introductory courses to list five traits that best describe them, he finds an interesting pattern. With very few exceptions, minorities place race on the top of their list while White students rarely if ever list "Caucasian" or White. Research shows that when we belong to a group that is underrepresented in a particular setting, we become more aware of the characteristic that sets us apart. The underrepresentation of students of color at Yale University may therefore "color" how they describe themselves.

In comparison to Whites, racial minorities in the United States have a history of being threatened or put at a disadvantage because of their race. In contrast, Whites are deracialized, meaning that race is seen as a less important or unimportant part of their identity. Some social critics cite this as an example of what they term "White privilege," those hidden unearned advantages that come with being in the racial majority in the United States.

YOUR TURN   • • • • •

What is one aspect of your cultural identity? Describe a situation in which it becomes more important and a situation in which it becomes less important.

_____

_____

_____

_____

_____

_____

UNDERSTANDING CULTURAL IDENTITY DEVELOPMENT

Cultural identity development refers to the process of learning to identify with larger groups and their ways of life. Identities evolve throughout our lifetime. A wide variety of socializing agents shape our cultural identity, including family, peers, schools, religion, and the media. This process begins in infancy.

Look at your socialization. Think about how you saw yourself and others differently once you started school, and how your identity continued to change as you became an older and more experienced student. Consider the groups you identified with earlier in your life versus the groups that are most important to you now. Depending on your age and your life experiences, you will notice changes in your identity as you move through childhood, adolescence, adulthood, and old age.

The process by which changes of this nature occur varies from group to group, and from individual to individual. Certain theories describe a linear process in which individuals move through different stages toward developing a healthy sense of cultural identity. However, this process is not necessarily straightforward. We may take three steps forward and adopt what we think is a genuine pride in our culture. Only later might we step back and realize that our pride is contrived and our knowledge of our culture is just beginning to develop. At that point, we may realize that there is a significant difference between following certain traditions and developing an understanding and appreciation of these traditions.

The increasing mobility of people throughout the world will continue to affect the development of cultural identities. More people are likely to view themselves as **culturally marginal**, meaning they exist on the fringes of more than one culture. As such, they may have their own set of challenges dealing with diverse and possibly conflicting cultural loyalties and behaviors.

Migration, study abroad, global communication networks, international job placements, military assignments, and culturally mixed marriages are just a few of the social developments that will blur cultural boundaries. Perhaps this is why multiple cultural identities are not necessarily described as all fitting neatly together. Instead, they may be fractured, fragmented, and conflicting.

Consider the case of migrants who return to their native country after living abroad. In one case, a Japanese worker recounts what it felt like to be a stranger in one's home. Back home in Japan, they called her *gaikoku-gaeri* (returned from a foreign country). After a while, she noticed that she was "criticizing the ways of Japan, its people, and its society: the infamous entrance examination system, group orientedness, conformism, etc." She never got used to doing things all together, in harmony, and with no one standing out. She continues to reflect on her cultural marginality, saying, "Sometimes it seemed easier to get along with the foreigners. But I'm not a foreigner, am I?"[6]

As we get older, we are more apt to struggle with questions about ourselves and our people. And as we become culturally conscious, we may have an array of positive and negative feelings about our cultural identity. Events in our lives may change our values and priorities, how we see ourselves, and how others see us. Not only do we discover new friends and new aspects of ourselves, we blend the new with the old. Examples of major events in our lives that bring about changes in cultural identity are becoming a parent, changing professions, contracting cancer, "coming out" as a lesbian at work, adjusting to a disability as a result of a car accident, and returning home as a war veteran.

When stay-at-home moms enter or reenter the workforce, their cultural identity may undergo a significant transformation. Many times, they deal with the psychological issue of what it means to be a good wife, employee, and mother. Employers may view family responsibilities as something that detracts from one's work. Similarly, family members may complain that work is interfering with responsibilities at home.

After staying home with her children for 14 years, one woman writes about what it is like being back at work:

> For years, I have been asked, "What do you do?" and for years I have responded "homemaker." Every time I did I got a look as if to say, "Is that all?" Now, whenever someone asks me, "What do you do?" I get to tell them I teach math and computer science at a nearby high school. The difference in the response I get is appalling. You'd think I was a whole different person. While I was a full-time mom, I already had a college degree from a prestigious women's college but that was hidden. At home, I was surrounded by love, but not a whole lot of respect. The skills of motherhood are notoriously taken-for-granted.
>
> At work, I am treated with respect by my students, peers and supervisors. Moreover, I have privacy that people respect. How can I help but feel better about myself with all of this positive feedback? My job is not as important to me as my home life, not even close. But the difference in my identity is amazing since returning to work. My self-confidence has risen unbelievably and I feel much more appreciated and respected.

YOUR TURN   · · · · ·

During cultural identity development, key questions emerge. Your answers to the following shed light on your identity formation at this point in your life.

Who am I?

_____

_____

_____

_____

With whom do I identify?

_____

_____

_____

_____

What are my values?

_____

_____

_____

_____

How do others see me?

_____

_____

_____

_____

What do others want me to be?

_____

_____

_____

_____

With whom do I want to spend my time?

_____

_____

_____

_____

What do the media say I am?

_____

_____

_____

_____

Where and when do I feel like I belong?

_____

_____

_____

_____

UNDERSTANDING WHY CULTURAL IDENTITY MATTERS

CQ   Applied · · · · · ·

Knowing who we are can give us the power and confidence we need to fight to be seen and acknowledged for who we are. A gay male describes how he deals with identity issues at work. "On more than one occasion, I have had people ask me why I feel the need to 'be out of the closet and flaunt my sexuality' at work. To them, my reply is always, 'This is not about sexuality, it is about my entire being. Being a gay male is far more than being attracted to another guy; there is an entire culture of being gay.'" Ask yourself, when straight people walk down the street holding hands, send out wedding announcements, and display pictures of their family on their desk at work, are they flaunting their sexuality?

On a personal level, cultural identity is important for a number of reasons. First, it provides us with a better idea of who we are and how we got there. By immersing ourselves in our heritage and traditions, our goals at work as well as other areas of our lives become clearer. From our cultural identity, we gain a sense of belonging; we realize that our identity connects us with others with whom we share certain things in common. Understanding cultural identity provides us with insight into why we have developed into the person we are. By recognizing how our identity unites us with others both past and present, we become more confident in the face of stereotypes and more resilient when our heritage is devalued.

YOUR TURN · · · · · ·

Observing traditions, no matter how unimportant they may seem, can reinforce our cultural identity and help us to stay focused and grounded. What is one cultural tradition you observe? Why is it important to you?

_____

_____

_____

_____

Our cultural identity enhances our ability to relate to others. By knowing our own cultural preferences, we grow more aware of differences between ourselves and others, and when and where these differences might surface. Also, we develop a better understanding of how our cultural preferences impact our ability to problem-solve, work on teams, and manage projects. This enables us to recognize that others might possess strengths, perspectives, and talents that we do not.

For instance, ask yourself if you are someone who frequently takes risks or who finds comfort in following the rules almost all of the time. Your answer, according to research by Geert Hofstede, may relate to your cultural upbringing. Hofstede found that workers in various countries felt differently about the need for certainty. **Certainty**, as defined by Hofstede, refers to our need for structure and regulations. Based on his research, workers in countries such as Japan and Mexico were more apt to desire strong codes for behavior. Moreover, they were more intolerant of people who deviate from rules. In contrast, workers in the United States and the United Kingdom had a greater tolerance for risky, ambiguous, or unpredictable situations. In other words, they encourage risk-taking and believe that circumstances dictate whether rules should be broken.[7]

Knowing our own cultural preferences regarding certainty will help us recognize, understand and adapt to people who prefer more or less structure than we do. For instance, if we have a manager who prefers more structure than we do, we are more ready to shift gears and adapt to his or her rules and guidelines. In addition, it is easier to adapt when we depersonalize differences and understand the role played by culture. Having the knowledge and the vocabulary to discuss these kinds of differences with others empowers us and promotes effective cross-cultural communication.

TO LEARN MORE

Go to "The Culture in the Workplace Questionnaire Overview" at **www.itapintl. com/ITAPCWQuestionnaire.htm.** This website is maintained by ITAP International, an organization that focuses on the development of human capability, locally and globally. Read the overview to acquaint yourself with the questionnaire and its uses. Scroll down to the "Preference for Certainty Questionnaire." Answer the questions on this brief questionnaire, complete the contact information, and then click "Submit." You will receive a personal cultural profile based on your responses to the questionnaire.

BEING AWARE OF MY "CULTURAL SILO"

A senior manager at a large IT firm was recently asked what he looks for in prospective employees. One of the biggest considerations, he said, was whether individuals can think about the "silos" in which they have been socialized. **Cultural silos** refer to limited social experiences that restrict our thinking and insulate us from the rest of the world.

Understanding our cultural identity requires us to identify and dissect our cultural silos. In doing this, it is helpful to examine the groups to which we belong. Perhaps you are a member of a synagogue or temple. Maybe you belong to one or more community groups. Think about how you spend your leisure time. What groups do you associate with during the course of a day? How do these groups influence your values and beliefs? And how do these groups restrict and expand your thinking about yourself and others?

YOUR TURN · · · · · ·

DIRECTIONS: Figure 2.3 is an **eco-map**, a drawing that represents relationships connecting you and some of the groups that make up your cultural silo. Within each numbered circle, identify a group to which you belong. Then next to each circle, write the most important value you have learned from that group.

Figure 2.3 • My Eco-Map

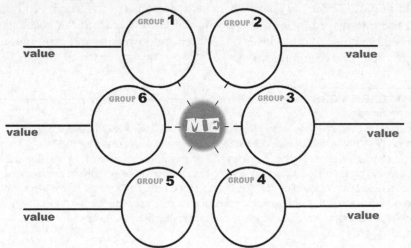

Analysis of Your Eco-Map

DIRECTIONS: Next, examine the groups you identified in your eco-map. Place an "X" beside the answer that best describes each group's cultural diversity.

Group #1 _____
Very Diverse _____   Somewhat Diverse _____   Very Little Diversity _____

Group #2 _____
Very Diverse _____   Somewhat Diverse _____   Very Little Diversity _____

Group #3 _____

Very Diverse _____   Somewhat Diverse _____   Very Little Diversity _____

Group #4 _____

Very Diverse _____   Somewhat Diverse _____   Very Little Diversity _____

Group #5 _____

Very Diverse _____   Somewhat Diverse _____   Very Little Diversity _____

Group #6 _____

Very Diverse _____   Somewhat Diverse _____   Very Little Diversity _____

In general, are the groups in your eco-map culturally diverse? Explain. What groups are most and least diverse?

_____

_____

_____

_____

_____

_____

By increasing the cultural diversity within our cultural silo, we become better able to adjust when we encounter situations that are new to us. For instance, someone's experiences with a close friend who has a speech impairment may make it easier to adjust to other situations where communication might be a challenge.

Within our cultural silo are groups which have a profound influence on our values and priorities. This is especially true of **primary groups**, meaning groups that are relatively small and involve more intimate and informal relationships. Family and close friends are two common examples of primary groups. When you look at the groups in your eco-map, particularly your primary groups, what are the major values or "lessons" you have learned from them?

_____

_____

_____

_____

_____

_____

As we become more aware of our cultural silo, we develop a greater awareness of our own and other cultures. We become more aware of our **ethnocentrism**, the assumption that our way of doing things is superior to any other. Equally important, we realize how ethnocentrism restricts our thinking and intercultural sensitivity. Instead of our cultural identity being the dominant or best, it is simply one of many.

HAVING KNOWLEDGE OF KEY CULTURAL IDENTITY ISSUES
Reconciling Multiple Racial and Cultural Identities

YOUR TURN • • • • •

Do you define yourself as multiracial? Why or why not?

_____

_____

_____

_____

At present, the term multiracial includes various types of mixed heritage, including race and ethnicity. The United States's multiracial population is gaining prominence, as racially and ethnically mixed marriages have increased in recent years and people of all ages have been encouraged to explore their roots. For the first time, the 2000 U.S. Census allowed respondents to check as many racial designations as appropriate. However, the census rejected adding a "multiracial" category.

YOUR TURN • • • • •

Do you define yourself as multicultural? Why or why not?

_____

_____

_____

_____

In _Borderlands_, Gloria Anzaldúa uses the term **mestiza consciousness** to refer to the ability to reconcile conflicting and meshing identities. By doing this, people see reality and themselves differently. She makes it clear this is not an easy thing to do. As a Chicana native of south Texas, Anzaldúa grew up in the midst of many races and cultures. She discusses the challenge of juggling and integrating her multiple identities, including being a Chicana in Anglo culture, a woman in Hispanic culture, and a lesbian in the straight world. In doing so, she developed a tolerance for ambiguity and contradictions. For example, she had to reconcile a white cultural background that historically had attacked the beliefs of her Mexican ancestors. Likewise, she had to juggle a Mexican culture which strongly discouraged her from being selfish and thinking of herself with a white culture that did just the opposite.

Multiracial identities can be difficult to reconcile. It can be a complex struggle that is spiritual, psychological, and social, as Anzaldúa's writings attest. Identities may relate to differences within as well as between groups. Individuals are confronted with a number of options, including identifying with one or more than one racial or ethnic group, or identifying with a new group.

Earlier, I asked whether you consider yourself multiracial. In this country, we view belonging to a single race as the norm. Historically, people in the United States have been socialized to view themselves this way in spite of research that shows we cannot be put into a single racial box on the basis of biological or genetic traits. In other words, individuals who are put in a box labeled as "White" or "Black" are no more alike or different from people who are defined as multiracial or "Others."

In 1997, world-reknowned golfer Tiger Woods acknowledged his multiracial lineage by describing himself as "Cablinasian," a mixture of Caucasian, Black, Indian, and Asian. Because he identified with a group outside of the box, many people reacted with surprise and even hostility.

As discussed earlier, the way in which we define ourselves has implications for how we negotiate the demands of the workplace. By acknowledging his multiracial identity, Woods can take the best from a number of cultures. He can rely on a larger knowledge base, a greater ability to identify multiple perspectives, and a more well-rounded view of the world.

As with other cultural identities, multiracial identities are created, adopted, negotiated, and shared. We can facilitate this process by developing our knowledge and awareness. "What parts of my history are unknown to me?" "What do I believe, and why do I believe it?" "How does what I believe impact on my sense of well-being?" These types of questions, coupled with a commitment to learn more about ourselves, can provide us with direction and promote personal growth.

A theory of cultural self-identity, created by E. R. Oetting and F. Beauvais, acknowledges that greater identification with one culture does not have to decrease our identification with other cultures. In other words, we can feel strongly connected to many different ethnic groups and races at the same time.[8]

One of the greatest challenges of reconciling multiple racial identities comes from trying to fit into a workplace that is still racially segregated. Often, the multiracial population talks about their encounters with exclusion. Many face uncomfortable and inappropriate questions from coworkers and customers, such as "What are you?" or "Where are you from?"

Questions such as these provide learning opportunities, as well as insight into people's cultural silos. When asked, "What are you?" Angela Nissel, author of

Myths: My Life in Black and White, sometimes uses sarcasm to defuse her anger. "When a businessman with argyle socks asked what I was I replied I was 'Argylian.' I ended up having a long conversation about how unspoiled the island of 'Argyle' was and how there was even undiscovered gold in the rain forest." [9]

The Implications of Internalizing Negative Stereotypes

YOUR TURN   • • • • •

Describe one stereotype of a cultural group with which you identify. If you internalize this stereotype, how might it affect your behavior?

_____

_____

_____

_____

_____

The way others see us interrelates with the way we see ourselves. To illustrate, we may reject or embrace or ignore how society thinks we should behave on account of our ethnicity or religion. Research shows that workers from collectivist cultures may find it particularly difficult to discount other people's appraisals of them. Unlike workers in individualist cultures, their self-esteem is more apt to hinge on what people think about them and their group.

As individuals, the various ways we express our culture may clash with other people's stereotypical expectations. The way we look and talk, our clothing, our interests, and our choice of friends can lead to questions in the minds of those with whom we come into contact. "You say you're an American; you don't look American." "You say you're Mexican; why don't you speak Spanish?" "You speak English extremely well. Are you really Korean?" At times, society wants to label us and put us into socially constructed boxes that do not embrace who we feel we are.

Frank Wu, author of *Yellow: Race in America Beyond Black and White*, discusses how easily people can be transfixed by a racial stereotype.

In a casual aside, a business colleague, who I thought knew me well enough to know better, may make an earnest remark revealing that his attempt to connect with me can only come through race. Although they rarely mention their personal lives, people always will make it a point to tell me about the hit movie they saw last night or the museum they toured over the weekend if it had a vaguely Asian theme, whether Chinese, Japanese, Korean, Vietnamese, or whatever, because, "It reminded me of you."[10]

Wu explores how stereotypes can result in a loss of self-control. Some of us may find ourselves internalizing negative stereotypes about our cultural groups. We become who others stereotype us to be rather than who we perceive ourselves to be. This may cause us to withdraw socially. Furthermore, it may have a profound effect on our self-esteem and our confidence. The result may be **stereotype vulnerability**, not performing up to one's potential for fear of perpetuating a stereotype.

Research by Claude Steele amplifies the theory of stereotype vulnerability. Steele found that people's blood pressure tends to elevate when they sense others might judge them on the basis of a negative cultural stereotype. This may be due to the fact that people who encounter the threat of a stereotype may be trying too hard to prove themselves.[11]

In his book *The Rage of a Privileged Class*, Ellis Cose interviewed business executives, law partners, college professors, and other so-called successful African Americans. Many of them discussed how fellow workers and managers assumed they would fail because of their race. Not only did this stereotypical presumption of failure make some of them more anxiety-ridden and fatigued, it also interfered with their ability to excel.

Stereotypes often make us out to be one-dimensional. For instance, research shows that overweight people in the United States are often viewed in negative terms simply because of their appearance. These stereotypical attitudes may be grounded in traditional cultural values such as personal responsibility and self-discipline. Based on weight alone, people may be seen as undisciplined and lazy. Even though these evaluations may be inaccurate and unfair, they may become part of the identities of some overweight people. All too often, these stereotypes impact overweight people's feelings of personal value, worthiness, and professional competence. Moreover, their mental and physical health may suffer.

For many U.S. high school students, many of the stereotypes they encounter revolve around race and ethnicity. According to one study, the way peers define race or ethnicity influences how high school students see themselves. Students as a whole saw White students as studious and hardworking. In contrast, those surveyed viewed African Americans as less studious and less academically successful, because they were thought to lack intelligence or not apply themselves. Asian Americans were seen as studious, smarter, and hardworking. Hispanics were seen as likely candidates for manual occupations such as laborers and gardeners. According to the study's findings, students generally believed that the stereotypes about their own and other groups were true. For example, African Americans were inclined to view themselves as less studious and less capable. Similarly, students as a whole believed the positive stereotypes made about Asian Americans.[12]

Adapting to the Situation

Choosing cultural identities depends on a number of situational factors. For instance, you are apt to make different choices depending on the feedback you get from your employer. Employers run the gamut from those who repeatedly ignore or devalue racial, gender, and cultural differences to those who embrace diversity as part of their overall business strategy.

As we learn more about ourselves and our employers, we may have to make certain identity choices. With each of the following choices, there are assets as well as liabilities.

Assimilation Model. When assimilation manifests itself, we shed or cover some part of our distinctiveness and try to blend into another culture. As an example, an individual from a collectivist culture may work at a job site that emphasizes individual achievement and recognition. After a period of time, this individual's "organizational identity" becomes her identity both at work and at home.

Pluralistic Model. With this identity choice, we retain as much of our cultural distinctiveness as possible, such as language, values, diet, and dress. For example, we might wear accessories, jewelry, or a certain hairstyle at work as a way of identifying with our native culture. Or we might join a minority networking organization at work. With the growing trend toward cultural self-awareness and pride in the United States, this model has become more common in recent years.

Integrative Model. When we adopt this model, we bring some aspects of our cultural distinctiveness to work but we also blend into the new culture when the opportunity presents itself. For instance, a religiously observant conservative Jew might wear a yarmulke on most days but take it off in those situations when he thinks it might make some people reluctant to approach him.

Separate Identity Model. This model entails compartmentalizing our cultural identities; such as bringing one identity to the workplace and another to life outside of work. For example, an employee who is a lesbian may engage in "straight acting." In the workplace, she may constantly monitor her speech to avoid giving off cues that might raise suspicion about her sexual orientation.

The perception that minorities have to assimilate to succeed puts the individual in a difficult dilemma. By hiding their cultural identities, minorities do not bring all of their assets to work. These assets might include unique language skills, a keen understanding of global markets, or simply the ability to look at challenges from different perspectives.

In summary, developing a knowledge base can help us understand who we are. As an example, do we have more than one racial identity? If so, how do we reconcile these identities? How and why might negative stereotypes influence the way we view ourselves? Additionally, how might we adapt our cultural identity depending on situational factors? Building CQ depends on our ability to understand these issues and their implications.

THE BOTTOM LINE

Before organizations identify areas of human relations that require their attention, they generally conduct something called a "cultural audit." This allows organizations to take stock of their values and mission, how they are doing, and how they can improve. Before we improve our cultural skills on an individual level, we need to do the same. The questions and issues raised in this chapter will help us do that. If we are not aware of our cultural identity and our personal development in this area, we will not be able to manage ourselves.

By understanding our cultural identity, we make it possible to identify strategies to improve our cultural intelligence and understand why this is important. We expand our learning, adapt and change our behaviors when necessary, become better team players and communicators, and become more valued employees.

• • • • • • • •

A Look Back: I Have Learned

✓ _____ Why understanding my cultural identity is a critical component of cultural intelligence.

✓ _____ What is meant by cultural identity.

✓ _____ How individualistic and collectivistic cultures view identity.

✓ _____ To acknowledge differences in the way people view their ethnic identity.

✓ _____ People view the importance of ethnicity differently.

✓ _____ Why identities are multiple, changing, hidden, and visible.

✓ _____ What is meant by cultural identity development.

✓ _____ Why cultural identity matters.

✓ _____ How to become aware of my cultural silo.

✓ _____ Key cultural identity issues.

✓ _____ How we adapt our cultural identity to different situations.

✓ _____ Why understanding cultural identity impacts the bottom line.

Individual Action Plan

Think about one specific thing you can do to improve your skills in the area of understanding your cultural identity. Then complete the following plan during the next _____ (state time period).

Specific skill I want to improve first (refer to list of Performance Skills at the beginning of the chapter):

_____

My strategy:

_____

_____

_____

_____

_____

In order to develop this skill, I will:

_____

_____

_____

_____

Possible obstacles include:

_____

_____

_____

_____

Resources I need:

_____

_____

_____

_____

I will measure my progress by:

_____

_____

_____

_____

Notes

1. Model adapted from D. W. Sue, "Multicultural Facets of Cultural Competence," *Counseling Psychologist*, 29, 2001, 790–821.

2. Pew Hispanic Center/Kaiser Family Foundation, National Survey of Latinos, 2002.

3. Ashley Doane Jr., "Dominant Group Ethnic Identity in the United States: The Role of 'Hidden' Ethnicity in Intergroup Relations," *Sociological Quarterly 38* (3), 1997, 375–397.

4. R. Kohls, *The Values Americans Live By* (Washington, DC: Meridian House International, 1984).

5. Mary Seymour, "Call Me Crazy, But I Have to Be Myself," *Newsweek*, July 29, 2002, 16.

6. Atsushi Furuiye, "I Am Plural, and I Am Singular." Online, 7/9/2006. Available: **www.digitrends.com/crossingcultures/fury.htm**.

7. Geert Hofstede, *Culture's Consequences: International Differences in Work-Related Values* (Beverly Hills, CA: Sage Publications, 1980).

8. E. R. Oetting and F. Beauvais, "Cultural Identification Theory: The Cultural Identification of Minority Adolescents," *International Journal of Addiction*, 25, 1991, 655–685.

9. Angela Nissel, "What Are You? Life as a Bi-Racial," NPR's Morning Edition. Online May 10, 2006. Available: **www.npr.org/templates/story/story.php?storyId = 5395390**.

10. Frank Wu, *Yellow: Race in America Beyond Black and White* (New York: Basic Books, 2003).

11. Tori DeAngelis, "Thwarting Modern Prejudice," *Monitor on Psychology*. Online 10/30/2006. Available: **www.apa.org/monitor/apr01/prejudicc.html**.

12. Grace Kao, "Group Images and Possible Selves among Adolescents: Linking Stereotypes to Expectations by Race and Ethnicity," *Sociological Forum 15*(3), September 2000, 407–430.

CHAPTER 3

· · · · · · · · · ·

CQ MEGASKILL: CHECKING CULTURAL LENSES

Performance Skills

- *Adjusting my cultural lenses at work*
- *Understanding the impact of cultural lenses*
- *Becoming aware of our own culture*
- *Recognizing the consequences of cultural encapsulation*
- *Identifying different cultural truths*

- *Making cultural adjustments*
- *Seeing and appreciating commonalities*
- *Respecting a variety of cultural lenses*
- *Critically evaluating assumptions*
- *Understanding the limitations of the Golden Rule*

 REFLECT BEFORE READING

Common sense tells us that "seeing is believing," meaning that we assume something is true because we saw it with our own eyes. However, is it also true that believing is seeing? How do our cultural beliefs influence what we see?

· · · · · · ·

INTRODUCTION

In prior chapters, we have discussed the meaning and significance of culture. Culture is our way of life; it provides us with rules, recipes, and instructions for living. Furthermore, culture shapes the way we perceive and understand the world around us.

Cultural lenses refer to those social influences that shape our vision and evaluation of the world around us. For instance, our cultural lenses filter our perceptions of others. We view people through aspects of our culture, such as religion, nationality, gender, family, and community. Additionally, culture helps us make sense of what we see and shapes how we communicate and interact with others. Our cultural lens, like the world in which we live, can change from one moment to the next.

In building cultural intelligence, adjusting our cultural lenses is a key megaskill for today's dynamic, multicultural environment. It permits us to understand better, for example, divergent needs, values, behaviors, communication styles, and teaming styles. But it is not easy. In the process of donning and adjusting multiple lenses, we need to appreciate a wide array of cultural possibilities and options without stereotyping. If we master this megaskill, we will become better communicators and team players, more aware of who we are, and more appreciative of our cultural commonalities and differences.

YOUR TURN   · · · · · ————————————

In all likelihood, you have had any number of opportunities to check your cultural lens during the past month. Can you think of one? Explain.

_____

_____

_____

THE NATURE OF CULTURE

We belong to many different cultures. Culture embraces all of the groups with which we identify, starting with those into which we are born. Examples include family, race, and national origin. It also includes the groups that we become part of as we get older, such as friends, coworkers, and community groups. Furthermore, we might join groups as we move to another region, move into another social class, or make new friends.

Although people tend to think of culture as nonmaterial, it can be material as well. **Material culture** refers to the tangible things that you can see, touch, or feel, such as jewelry, clothes, books, and art. **Nonmaterial culture** takes the form of abstract ideas, including language, beliefs, and values. As part of our cultural upbringing, we learn, share, and pass on both material and nonmaterial culture from one generation to the next.

Furthermore, our individual and collective histories are an integral part of our culture. Knowing our history and the history of other people and cultures expands our personal and social awareness and understanding. It is not uncommon to hear people talk about the importance of knowing where they came from. This knowledge empowers us, providing a clearer picture of our past, present, and future.

SUBCULTURES

Subcultures are distinctive ways of life within the larger, mainstream culture. Subcultures may revolve around ethnicity, social class, region, religion, language, occupation, and any number of other differences that affect our everyday life.

One such difference is disability. For example, people who are hearing-impaired share certain experiences, but at the same time, their individual lives are tremendously different from each other. Even their means of communication vary significantly. Some hearing-impaired individuals rely more on sign language, others rely more on reading lips, and still others have undergone surgery for cochlear implants to gain hearing.

Terms such as Latino, Muslim, and Asian American tend to hide ethnic subcultures, or cultures within a culture. We may talk about Asian Americans, for example, as if they are all alike. When we talk about Asian American values and Asian American families, there is a tendency to stereotype Asians as a whole and ignore the tremendous diversity that exists within and among the nearly 50 countries found in Asia. People who share a common cultural background are unique individuals with their own identities. Moreover, individuals may identify strongly or weakly with their ethnic or cultural groups.

For example, a recent national survey by the Pew Hispanic Center and Kaiser Family Foundation found significant differences among Latinos on a number of attitudes. Attitudinal differences toward family issues and migration were found among Latinos from various places of origin, including Cubans, Dominicans, Salvadorans, Colombians, Mexicans, and Puerto Ricans. Other variables related to attitudes included sex, educational attainment, whether Latinos were born in the United States or abroad, and whether they are primarily Spanish or English speaking.[1]

Think for a moment about the individuals who make up those cultural groups with which you identify. If you examine the values, behaviors, lifestyles, and interests of these individuals, the differences from person to person are significant. Because we are not as likely to be familiar with individuals in cultures other than our own, individual differences are less visible.

ORGANIZATIONAL CULTURE

Within organizational settings, culture manifests itself in a variety of ways. **Organizational culture** is the underlying values and beliefs of an organization. An organization's culture can profoundly affect people's comfort level and success.

Culture may vary from department to department within an organization. For example, employees in one department may feel very much at ease using flexible hours in an effort to juggle responsibilities at home and work. Within the same organization, in another department or location with the same policy, employees may be hesitant to use flexible hours.

Recently, I was talking to Rosemarie, a teacher who had recently given birth to her first child. After staying home with the child for the first few months, she was having second thoughts about going back to work because of the school's organizational culture. Rosemarie's principal is a career woman. She has no children and, in Rosemarie's words, her work is her life. The principal expects everyone to put in long hours and is not terribly flexible when it comes to giving teachers time off for family matters. Because of Rosemarie's familiarity with the values and expectations of her job, she decided to take a two-year leave of absence.

Traditionally, culture in the workplace reflects the values of those in power. Historically, organizational cultures have been monocultural rather than multicultural. For instance, a traditional monocultural workplace may reflect the values of white males in leadership positions; that is, it caters to the needs and expectations of white men. In such a setting, females and people of color may feel as if they need to adapt their dress, speech, or body language to fit in or at least avoid negative attention.

Earl Graves, founder and publisher of *Black Enterprise* magazine, authored the book, *How to Succeed in Business Without Being White*. In his book, Graves argues that people of color have less latitude than Whites to be themselves. Consequently, people of color may believe they need be more aware of themselves—their speech, their choice of music, or even their hairstyle. Over time, they may learn to seamlessly shift gears between home and work.

As organizations become less monocultural and more inclusive, their complexity increases. They allow for the expression of cultural diversity, including diverse opinions and behaviors. Everyone shares responsibility for adjusting to an inclusive organizational culture. Finally, cultural diversity is not treated as a separate entity; rather, it is integrated into the organizational structure.

ADJUSTING MY CULTURAL LENSES AT WORK

 Where Am I Now?

DIRECTIONS: For each statement, write SA (strongly agree), A (agree), D (disagree), or SD (strongly disagree).

1. _____ As I interact with people in multicultural settings, I seek to expand my knowledge about other cultures.
2. _____ As I interact with people in multicultural settings, I seek to check the accuracy of my knowledge about other cultures.
3. _____ I am ready to shift my perspectives and behaviors according to the cultural environment.

4. _____ My actions demonstrate respect for cultural diversity.

5. _____ When I encounter a new cultural environment, I feel confident I can deal effectively with practically any situation that might arise.

6. _____ When I learn something unexpectedly in a new cultural environment, I try to retain and use this knowledge to adjust more effectively in the future.

7. _____ Whenever I meet someone new, I keep in mind that people from the same culture may have very different values, beliefs, and customs.

> **DID YOU KNOW?**
>
> The Model Minority Myth (MMM) highlights the economic successes of Asian Americans. However, the MMM also hides the high poverty rates and low educational attainment of diverse groups within the Asian American community. As an example, roughly 40% of Laotians and Cambodians live below the poverty line. More than 94% of Tongans, Cambodians, Laotians, and Hmongs do not graduate from college.
>
> (2000 U.S. Census)

Responding positively to cultural diversity in the workplace is anything but easy. Competencies, such as those in the assessment you just completed, are made possible by constantly adjusting your cultural lens.

Organizational expectations vary considerably, including:

- Blend in, and leave your differences behind.
- Celebrate diversity, but keep it separate from our day-to-day operations.
- Treat everybody the same—diversity is not an issue.
- Tolerate diversity—but only some forms, and keep it superficial.
- Draw on and respect the diverse perspectives of others.

Depending on the organizational expectations and our cultural lens, we might suppress, accept, deny, tolerate, or respect diversity. Each of these responses is likely to change the way we act; and each has both positive and negative consequences for us as individuals (see Table 3.1).

Table 3.1 • Five Adjustments to Organizational Expectations

SUPPRESS:

I must change, blend in, and adapt for my own good and for the good of the organization.

Behavioral Changes	*At work, I might change the way I look, speak, dress, and act in order to conform.*
Positive Consequences	*I know what to expect because everybody plays by the same rules, meets the same expectations, and puts organizational loyalty above all else.*
Negative Consequences	*Sometimes, I feel I cannot be myself. Attempting to hide who I really am can be physically and psychologically stressful.*

(Continued)

Table 3.1 • Continued

ACCEPT

My coworkers and I have very different values. But I can live with that.

Behavioral Changes	*I acknowledge people's differences and accommodate them as part of my job.*
Positive Consequences	*I do not have to hide my heritage or identities. Consequently, I can focus on my job rather than fitting in.*
Negative Consequences	*When I embrace people's differences, I may lose sight of what we share in common. This may lead to misunderstandings and threaten unity.*

DENY

Except for our outward appearance, I feel we are all really the same.

Behavioral Changes	*It is not necessary for me to change.*
Positive Consequences	*Not acknowledging differences allows me to focus on myself rather than others. This is less time consuming and requires less commitment on my part.*
Negative Consequences	*Assuming that differences do not exist or do not matter allows me to avoid responsibility for changing my own lens. This heightens the likelihood of misunderstanding and bias on my part.*

TOLERATE

I guess I'll just have to deal with this diversity.

Behavioral Changes	*Broadening my knowledge base helps me put up with other people's differences, but it does not necessarily allow others to enter my world.*
Positive Consequences	*Tolerance can be a major achievement, especially when I move beyond my intolerance.*
Negative Consequences	*I endure differences but do not necessarily embrace them. When I tolerate others, they may feel demeaned.*

RESPECT

While I might not embrace everybody's values and lifestyles, I acknowledge and learn from cultural differences.

Behavioral Changes	*Developing my knowledge base is critical, as is putting that knowledge to use.*
Positive Consequences	*Rather than keeping diversity at a distance, I reflect on it, confront it, and change myself in the process.*
Negative Consequences	*Understanding the impact of diversity is intellectually and emotionally challenging. Conflict is an inevitable part of the learning process.*

UNDERSTANDING THE IMPACT OF CULTURAL LENSES

YOUR TURN   · · · · · · ▬▬▬▬▬▬

According to research studies, when health-care providers interact with poor patients, especially Blacks and Hispanics, there is a greater likelihood that patients will be treated in a childlike manner and receive inadequate counseling. Do you think this treatment has anything to do with the cultural lenses of these providers? Why?

_____

_____

_____

_____

_____

Our cultural lens filters our perceptions of others. Imagine if you grew up in a culture wearing yellow lenses. Everywhere you go, things appear yellow. You then take a trip to a distant country where everybody wears red lenses. Ideally, it might be nice to put those red lenses on and experience the world as they do. But that is not what typically occurs. As hard as you try, your yellow lens remains. The best you might be able to do is see this new culture in varying shades of orange.

More often than not, we perceive what we expect to see, or what we have been conditioned to see (see Figure 3.1). Similarly, we do *not* see what we have *not* been conditioned to see. In other words, we are blind to certain things because they do not mesh with our experiences. We might assume that honoring someone as "employee of the month" is an honor that anyone would enjoy. Perhaps we don't think twice about this because our experiences have taught us that individuals like to be recognized for a job well done. Because of our cultural lens, it does not occur to some of us that employees from Latin American and Asian countries may not like to be singled out in this manner. Receiving an award of this nature is seen as boastful.

We view each other through the filters of our upbringing, nationality, religion, community, gender, and ethnicity. For example, our cultural lens influences our views of who is a "real" American and who is a foreigner. Many Asian Americans, for example, can cite numerous occasions when they have been asked where they are from. If they say they are from New York, this may lead to another question: "No, where are you really from?" To many people in the United States, Asian Americans are seen as perpetual foreigners. When judged this way, differential treatment is more likely.

Figure 3.1 • When you look at this photograph, what assumptions do you make about the two individuals?

_____

_____

_____

_____

_____

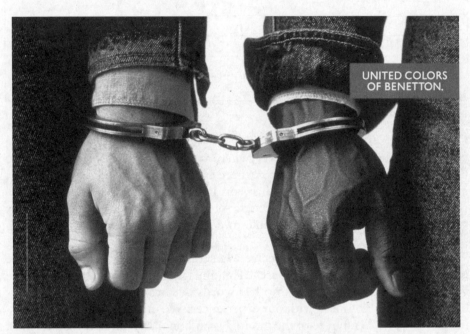

UNITED COLORS OF BENETTON.

This photograph, produced by the United Colors of Benetton, was part of an advertising campaign to show that all of us are linked together regardless of skin color. However, many people's interpretation of this image points to the influence of their cultural biases. In their eyes, this picture shows a White police officer escorting a Black criminal.

© Copyright 1989 Benetton Group S.p.A.—Photo: Oliviero Toscani

According to researchers, our cultural lens explains how we make sense of why people do the things they do. For example, someone who sees individuals as ultimately in control of themselves and their own fate will be more apt to blame unethical or wrongful behavior on a particular person. Another person with more of a collectivistic or group-oriented perspective might be more inclined to find fault with organizational controls or even the norms of the larger community.

Cultural lenses may also account for definitions of what is "normal." Dr. Kathy Morsea's heritage is Native American (Navajo on her mother's side and Ojibwa, Sioux, and White on her father's side). During her medical education, she recalls how there was a standard of "normal" against which everybody was measured. Dr. Morsea remembers a resident in her program asking a physician, who had worked on the Navajo reservation, the question, "How does drinking among Native Americans compare to normal people?" To which Dr. Morsea replied, "Excuse me, normal?"[2]

BECOMING AWARE OF OUR OWN CULTURE

When you talk with someone in a public setting:

- How close do you stand to that person?
- Do you maintain or avoid eye contact?
- How long do you wait for him or her to respond to a question?
- How do you express feelings such as anger, appreciation, or approval?

How we answer these questions reflects our culture.

Often, it is easier to see the presence of culture in the behavior of others. The cultural context of *our* thinking and behavior is more difficult to see. Subconsciously, we may assume that we form our viewpoints independent of social influences such as media, friends, schools, workplaces, and places of worship. This assumption reinforces the notion that *our* language, *our* values, and *our* ways of doing things have no cultural context. We take these things for granted, assuming that it is natural for everyone to do things our way. What I have just described is called **enculturation**, immersion in a culture to such an extent that our way of life seems only natural. The culture of "others," particularly those whose way of life is markedly different from ours, is much more noticeable.

Why are we oblivious to our own culture? Because we have been enveloped in culture since birth, we do not think about it. Anthropologist Ralph Linton offers an interesting analogy. He compares our enculturation to a fish swimming in water. Since the fish is completely surrounded by water, the last thing a fish would see is the water itself.[3]

What Is My Race?

When you identify your race, which of the following characteristics apply?

✓ _____ Skin color
✓ _____ Hair texture
✓ _____ Eye color

✓ _____ Thickness of lips

✓ _____ Curvature of spine

✓ _____ Other (please specify _____)

Seeing our own culture allows us to examine the effect our cultural lens has on us. A good example is how we view our race. Race is a **cultural construct**, meaning that we have some idea of what race means because of what others have taught us. If we grew up in a different culture, the idea of race, or what it means to be Black and White, might make no sense at all.

When we hear the term *race*, many of us think of people who share certain biological traits, such as skin color and hair texture. However, in recent years, scientists have come to the conclusion that race is a biological myth. According to the Human Genome Project, human beings are 99% alike. Furthermore, there are no physical traits that clearly differentiate one racial group from another. Even skin color is unreliable. There are Whites, for example, who are more dark-skinned than some Blacks.

TO LEARN MORE

Visit the website, "What Is Race," at **www.pbs.org/race/001_WhatIsRace/ 001_00-home.htm.** Examine the idea of race in more detail by clicking on the following links: "What Is Race," "Sorting People," "Race Timeline," "Human Diversity," "Me, My Race, and I," and "Where Race Lives."

What Is My Ethnicity?

Ethnicity, or one's cultural heritage, is also a cultural construct. Members of an ethnic group constitute a cultural community. They may share common ancestors, language, religion, and other cultural traits. Like race, ethnicity is complex and not easy to define. At various times, people may play up or play down their ethnicity. Life experiences may change how we view our ethnicity. Furthermore, we may identify with one or numerous ethnic groups.

YOUR TURN   • • • • •

Is your ethnicity a matter of choice? Explain why.

_____

_____

_____

_____

Many of us become more aware of our ethnicity at college or at work. Why do you think this is the case? One's ethnic identity does not evolve in a social vacuum. In college, for the first time in your life, you might find yourself surrounded by people who do not share your ethnic identity. Consequently, you are likely to become more aware of your ethnicity and its relevance in a setting such as this.

For example, when you begin a new job or attend college for the first time, how do your ethnic roots fit into how you see yourself? What choices do you have when you feel out of place because of your ethnicity? Do you "hang" only with those people who share your ethnic background? Do you find yourself being more "ethnic" in certain situations? Are you a cultural chameleon, meaning your ethnicity changes according to the setting?

YOUR TURN   · · · · · ───────

Do you view your ethnicity differently than you did five years ago? Why or why not?

_____

_____

_____

_____

RECOGNIZING THE CONSEQUENCES OF CULTURAL ENCAPSULATION

Cultural encapsulation refers to a lack of contact with various cultures outside of our own. All of us experience cultural encapsulation to some degree. Because social segregation is still pervasive in the United States today, many of us live in communities where most of our neighbors share our social class, race, and cultural heritage. When this occurs, much of the information we receive about "others" with whom we have little or no contact comes from the media and other secondhand information. This information is often incomplete and inaccurate. Yet, we have no way of knowing that.

Because of cultural encapsulation, we are more prone to tunnel vision. Yet, we may not realize this. Consider the following problem. You see four squirrels perched on the branch of a tree. You shoot one of the squirrels. How many are left?

a. three

b. none

c. other (specify # _____)

When I ask this question in workshops, most participants say three (four squirrels minus one). Their focus is on the individual squirrels rather than the group.

But some participants look at the larger situation and choose none. From their point of view, no squirrels are left because they all scatter when they hear the shot. Since they are looking at the squirrels as a whole, they come to a different conclusion. Look at how you answered this question. Might your cultural background have something to do with whether you focused on the individual or group?

Do you think most of the people with whom you regularly interact were raised in environments that exposed them to a wide variety of cultures and lifestyles? What about you? Cultural encapsulation leads many of us to believe that there is a single, morally acceptable way to look and act. We make universal, stereotypical assumptions that reflect our limited life experiences.

The following questions ask you to think about your exposure to other cultures, both now and in the past:

 ## Where Am I Now?

DIRECTIONS: Circle the letter of the correct answer.

1. Growing up, I frequently interacted with people of different races. (a) yes (b) no
2. Growing up, I frequently interacted with people of different social classes. (a) yes (b) no
3. Growing up, I interacted with people from a wide variety of religious backgrounds. (a) yes (b) no
4. At present, my *close* friends include people of different races. (a) yes (b) no
5. At present, my *close* friends include people of different social classes (a) yes (b) no
6. At present, my *close* friends include people from a wide variety of religious backgrounds. (a) yes (b) no

---

YOUR TURN   • • • • • ━━━

Do you think your answers to questions 1 through 6 above are a valid measure of your cultural encapsulation? Why or why not?

_____

_____

_____

_____

Cultural encapsulation takes many forms. In the preceding assessment, the focus is on race, religion, and social class. Additionally, the questions ask us to examine not only with whom we interact but also the frequency and closeness of these interactions. When we examine our life experiences over time, we may uncover certain patterns. As we get older, have our friends become more diverse? Do we continue to keep certain ethnic groups at a distance? Have we grown more aware of cultural differences?

YOUR TURN · · · · · ——————————

Think back to one of the "lessons" you learned about cultural diversity as a child. Describe what it taught you and how it shaped your cultural lens.

_____

_____

_____

_____

CQ Applied · · · · · ——————————

As part of a television documentary entitled Hopkins 24/7, *a female doctor discusses the challenges of dealing with her cultural encapsulation on the job.*

"I kinda came into this job completely naïve. I've lived in my own little White world all my life and I have no experience with what our patients deal with. A lot of them have no money, no health insurance, no job, horrible health problems; and when I first came here I had no way to relate to those kinds of patients. But you learn and you ask them questions. They're very open with us and you try to learn from their experiences; and assimilate that into your practice so that you can be more accepting. You don't want to be judgmental of the patients. They're doing the best they can with the life they have."[4]

IDENTIFYING DIFFERENT CULTURAL TRUTHS

Each of us perceives things differently. For some of us, our age, race, religion, or gender is a major factor in shaping our opinions on various issues. For others, it might be wealth, disability, or sexual orientation. On certain issues, perhaps our marital status or education is a contributing or overriding factor. Consequently, we cannot assume that our lens is identical or even similar to others. This is even true when others share our cultural heritage.

Ask yourself whether you agree or disagree with each of the following statements:

_____ The group is more important than the individual.

_____ We control our own future.

_____ People should avoid being too dependent on others; rather, they should be as independent as possible.

_____ The past is more important than the future.

_____ Being direct, open, and honest are virtues.

_____ In the workplace, your primary concern should be focusing on your task and completing it.

_____ If you do something positive, it is a good idea to let others know about it.

These statements reflect various **cultural truths**, beliefs so embedded in one's culture that they are rarely stated or questioned. Consequently, we assume anyone, anywhere would accept them. Reality proves otherwise. People worldwide believe many different cultural truths, and many of them run counter to what you or I may believe. A number of examples follow:

Time

European Americans are more apt to adhere to strict time schedules. Individuals from many other cultural groups place less emphasis on when an event is held and more emphasis on who participates and the quality of time spent together.

Space

In comparison to European Americans, individuals from Latino or Arab cultures tend to be more comfortable with physical touching as well as sitting and standing relatively closer to each other.

YOUR TURN · · · · ·

When you describe yourself, are you more apt to emphasize your individual traits and accomplishments or your relationships with other people? Do you think your response to this question has anything to do with your cultural upbringing?

Explain. _____

_____

_____

_____

_____

Individualism and Collectivism

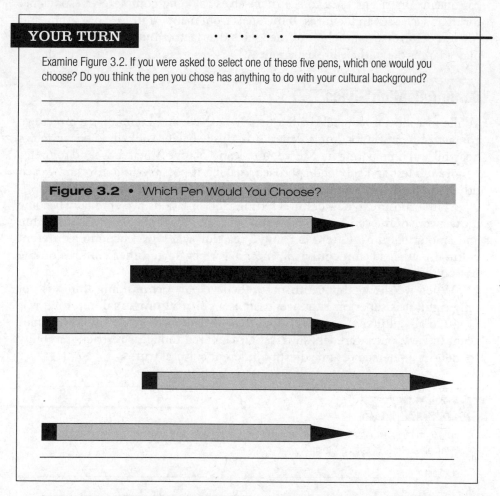

YOUR TURN · · · · · ·

Examine Figure 3.2. If you were asked to select one of these five pens, which one would you choose? Do you think the pen you chose has anything to do with your cultural background?

_____

_____

_____

_____

Figure 3.2 • Which Pen Would You Choose?

When Kim and Markus asked both Americans and Asians to select one of the pens shown in Figure 3.2, they found significant differences.[5] Seventy-seven percent of the Americans selected the different color pen, while only 31% of the Asians made this choice. According to researchers, the findings point to Americans' cultural preference for uniqueness while Asians place more emphasis on conformity.

In individualistic cultures, the needs, values, and goals of the individual are a priority. In collectivistic cultures, individuals are more apt to focus on others and their relationships with others. The needs, values, and goals of the group are of paramount importance. As an example, European Americans tend to value independence and bringing attention to themselves, while individuals from African, Asian, or Latino backgrounds tend to prioritize the group as a whole.

Ability to Control Our Fate

European Americans tend to see themselves as being completely responsible for their successes and failures. Individuals from many Arab, Asian, Latino, and African cultures are more apt to recognize that factors outside of their control play a large role in their life experiences.

Communication Styles

While introducing yourself with a firm handshake and maintaining direct eye contact is the norm for Anglo Americans, this behavior is likely to be viewed as boastful and dominating by Native Americans. Native Americans tend to prefer a more modest and subdued approach, making it possible to get to know each other and their backgrounds. Building a sense of relatedness is important.

With exposure to new cultural settings and situations, we gradually become more aware of the variety of beliefs and behaviors that are possible, both within and among cultures. Often, our initial reaction when we encounter different cultural truths is **ethnocentrism**, meaning we evaluate other cultures on the basis of our own cultural standards.

When we show ethnocentrism, we believe our way of doing things is not only right, it is superior. Ethnocentrism is a **cultural universal**, meaning it is found in all cultures. When we adopt this "be like me" or "do things like me" point of view, our awareness suffers. Self-centered thoughts restrict our ability to identify, understand, and adjust to different cultural truths.

YOUR TURN   · · · · · · ▬▬▬▬

The term *culturally disadvantaged* is still used today. What does this term mean to you? Is this term an example of ethnocentrism?

Explain. _____

_____

_____

_____

MAKING CULTURAL ADJUSTMENTS

Some individuals may find adjustment more difficult and challenging because of who they are and where they work. In certain cultural settings, we may feel uncomfortable or even afraid sharing parts of our culture. And sometimes, people refuse to adjust to their surroundings. For any number of reasons, the process of cultural adjustment may not be smooth.

YOUR TURN · · · · ·

When you left home this morning, what parts of your culture did you leave behind? Check all that apply.

_____ Your first language?

_____ Your religious beliefs?

_____ Your real views about cultural diversity?

_____ Your taste in music?

_____ Your real hairstyle?

_____ Your political opinions?

_____ Your gender?

_____ Your sexual orientation?

_____ Your hidden disability?

When individuals from different cultures interact, the result is often some degree of assimilation. **Assimilation** refers to an adaptive process in which people blend in to the mainstream culture.

Assimilation is not the universally good thing it is sometimes made out to be. As a learning process, it involves learning the negative as well as the positive. For example, some research studies indicate that immigrant students in the United States who are the hardest working and most respectful tend to be those who recently arrived in this country. Conversely, those who have undergone more assimilation may have picked up negative values and bad habits since coming to this country.

One of the most comprehensive national surveys ever conducted of Latinos asked students about their desire to assimilate *and* their desire to maintain traditions. The results, shown in Figure 3.3, indicate that assimilating and maintaining traditions are not mutually exclusive. The vast majority of Latinos in this study believe it is important to change so they can blend in. But nearly 9 out of 10 also say it is important to hold on to their native culture.

The experiences of immigrants in the United States show that they are likely to assimilate, but only to a certain degree. Rather than stripping themselves of their history and traditions, many add on to these aspects of their culture. For example, while learning the mainstream culture, including the language of the

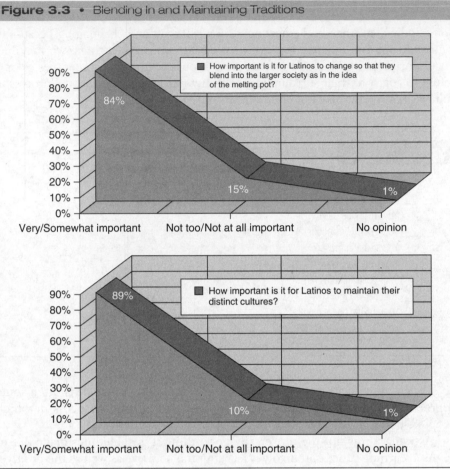

Figure 3.3 • Blending in and Maintaining Traditions

How important is it for Latinos to change so that they blend into the larger society as in the idea of the melting pot?

84% Very/Somewhat important
15% Not too/Not at all important
1% No opinion

How important is it for Latinos to maintain their distinct cultures?

89% Very/Somewhat important
10% Not too/Not at all important
1% No opinion

SOURCE: Amy Goldstein and Robert Suro, "A Journey in Stages," *The Washington Post,* January 16, 2000.

United States, many Latino immigrants preserve their culture in a variety of ways, including speaking Spanish themselves and teaching their children to speak Spanish, holding on to family values, and watching Latino channels on TV.

The ability to balance "fitting in" and "blending in" is a skill that allows us to adjust and adapt. When we go to work, we are expected to buy into certain rules and adjust to certain values. At the same time, there are some things that we cannot relinquish because they are just too meaningful to us. How we decide when to put our values aside and when to conform, even momentarily, depends on the situation, our cultural background, and our own individual priorities. While there are consequences for whatever cultural adjustment we make, no one can make that choice for us.

SEEING AND APPRECIATING COMMONALITIES

YOUR TURN   • • • • • ─────────

When you meet people for the first time, are you more apt to notice how different they are from you, or how much you share in common? Why?

_____

_____

_____

_____

Given our inclination to focus on what makes people different from us, it is easy to ignore our similarities when we look through our cultural lenses. While we see, celebrate, and reward uniqueness, it is immensely important that we acknowledge, celebrate, and understand our human commonalities as well. We can be proud of our differences but at the same time recognize and share our common humanity.

Often, issues of race, gender, ethnicity, and physical appearance restrict our ability to see similarities. In his autobiography _Days of Grace_, Arthur Ashe talks about how we can be proud of our culture and ancestors and proud of ourselves. But at the same time, we can see our identities as extending far beyond our racial and ethnic identities, colors, and creeds. Recognizing our common humanness, according to Ashe, requires us to see beyond what he calls "the barbed-wire fences" of looks and labels.

Seeing and appreciating commonalities is just as much a part of CQ as valuing diversity. When we understand that we are all capable of showing ignorance, stupidity, insensitivity, and cultural incompetence, we can relate to each other more effectively. By the same token, when we share and see that we are just as capable of displaying insight, genuine concern for others, love, and cultural sensitivity, we affirm our individual and collective strengths as well as our unity.

Cultural commonalities tie us together. For instance, all of us share things in common such as

- Using symbols to express feelings and ideas.
- Being able to accumulate culture and pass it on to our offspring.
- Sharing the experience of the life cycle, from birth to death.
- Sharing certain so-called universal languages, such as dance, art, and music.
- Having some concept of time, and the ability to recall the past and look into the future.

- Categorizing people and showing bias.
- Living in groups.
- Recognizing kinship and some form of family.
- Experiencing some type of inequality.
- Having the capacity to love and hate.

YOUR TURN   · · · · · ·

Add two more things that all people or all cultures share in common.

1. _____

_____

2. _____

_____

Staying humble and being aware of our own cultural lens allows us to build on what we share in common. When we are tempted to think too highly of ourselves and our culture, it is important to remember that no individual or way of life is perfect. Whenever we become blinded by our differences, it helps to explore and uncover those similarities which often remain hidden. Only then will we be able to think and act more inclusively.

RESPECTING A VARIETY OF CULTURAL LENSES

When we respect how different people perceive the world, we acknowledge, try to understand, and value their uniqueness as individuals. Respecting and agreeing are two different things. When I team with other individuals, I might not agree with everyone, but I try to respect their individuality and diverse points of view. Similarly, I can respect people who practice different religious beliefs without endorsing those beliefs.

Respecting a variety of lenses does *not* mean identifying people with certain behaviors because of their culture. Rather, it means learning to be skeptical of cultural do's and don'ts that do not apply to all people in all situations. Some diversity programs, for example, teach us to view Whites as more materialistic, analytical, and individualistic than Blacks. Latinos are portrayed as less competitive, more family-oriented, and affectionate; Asians as religious and passive, while Native Americans are described as spiritual and living in harmony with the earth. Cultural stereotypes such as these ignore individual and group differences within cultures. Furthermore, they promote a lack of respect by restricting and distorting our views of each other.

By adjusting our cultural lenses we can recognize cultural differences without stereotyping. Employees at one large insurance company found that marketing and relationship techniques need to take generational differences into consideration. When relating to older people, salespeople generally found it helpful to cultivate a relationship with the individual beforehand. Moreover, many older customers preferred to have people come to their homes and provide ample time for any transaction. On the other hand, younger people were more interested in quick interactions, using technology such as cell phones, faxes, and e-mail. By adopting an approach that considers the different relational styles among generations, these salespeople are respecting diversity. In the process, they are becoming more adept at communicating, building trust, and relating to people of all ages.

CRITICALLY EVALUATING ASSUMPTIONS

YOUR TURN • • • • • ────────────────

When a manager comments to an Asian American employee that she speaks excellent English, what assumptions are being made? Why might the employee interpret this comment negatively?

_____

_____

_____

_____

When you see a Muslim woman wearing a burqa, what assumptions do you make? The burqa, an outer garment covering almost the entire body, has a mesh screen to see through (see Figure. 3.4). Do you assume women wear it to obey their husbands? Do you assume it is oppressive to have to wear a burqa all the time? Whatever your assumptions, they may be false. Wearing a burqa may be a woman's choice, a way of expressing herself and her faith. From a Muslim woman's perspective, wearing a burqa might be a form of liberation. Why? It liberates them from having to worry about the shape of their bodies or their appearance.

Figure 3.4 • What does a burqa symbolize to you?

YOUR TURN • • • • • •

Read Situation 1 and Situation 2 and answer the questions for each.

SITUATION 1. Recently, a very religious Southern African American woman with breast cancer visited a hospital in a suburb of Charlotte, North Carolina. The woman refused to undergo chemotherapy. Instead, she and other family members participated in prolonged and intense prayer. The staff on hand, including the attending physician, assumed that the woman had given up all hope of getting better. Can you think of another reason for the woman's behavior?

_____

_____

_____

_____

_____

SITUATION 2: A police officer, talking to a small group of Central American immigrants in a suburb of Washington, DC, warns them of robberies in the area. He describes a number of incidents in which immigrants have been targeted because they keep large amounts of cash in their pockets. The officer tells them to protect themselves and put their money in a bank. As the officer sees it, these people do not understand the risks they are taking. Can you think of a different reason for the immigrants' behavior?

_____

_____

_____

_____

_____

Note: See the end of the chapter for other possible explanations (pp. 74–75).

UNDERSTANDING THE LIMITATIONS OF THE GOLDEN RULE

According to the Golden Rule, we should treat others as we would like to be treated. On one level, the Golden Rule, "do unto others as you would have them do unto you," makes sense. After all, don't we all want to be treated with respect, fairness, and courteousness? The answer is clearly yes.

But if we deal with more specific expectations, we may find that others do not necessarily share our views regarding how they wish to be treated. Even though I might want people to wish me Merry Christmas, I cannot assume that others practice my religion and feel this way. Treating others as *they* wish to be treated allows us to respect differences, including different cultural traditions and holidays.

The Golden Rule assumes that if I treat you the way I want to be treated, you should like it. In other words, it assumes we all think and act alike. It is quick and easy, because we do not have to take the time to get to know another person.

The Golden Rule is a good start, but we need to modify it. While we should never hesitate to show respect, *how* we show it varies depending on the cultural setting and the individual with whom we are interacting. To not offend other worshipers in a mosque, I would show respect by taking my shoes off. However, this same behavior is not necessary nor does it mean the same thing where I may worship. Cultural intelligence requires us to check our lenses, be sensitive to differences and other lenses, and then make the effort to treat others as they wish to be treated.

THE BOTTOM LINE

Why is the ability to check our cultural lenses a bottom-line issue for organizations? Given the changing demographics across the United States and beyond, it is irresponsible, ignorant, and just plain bad business to ignore the subtle and not-so-subtle cultural differences of consumers and clients. Our cultural lens can act as a revenue driver or it can have just the opposite effect. By continually checking and adjusting our cultural lens, we are less apt to stereotype, make false assumptions, and ignore emerging markets.

With the proper adjustments, our cultural lenses can empower us in a variety of ways. It provides us with the rationale and motivation to develop a broader, more inclusive view of people and their cultures. Once we develop our knowledge base, we are better able to determine how to manage, team, communicate, and problem-solve. Our CQ increases as we learn to recognize a variety of cultural scripts and react accordingly.

A Look Back: I Have Learned

✓ _____ What is meant by the terms *culture* and *cultural lens*.

✓ _____ How culture manifests itself in organizations.

✓ _____ How cultural lenses filter what we see.

✓ _____ Why we cannot assume our cultural lens is similar to others.

✓ _____ How we adjust our cultural lens at work, and the implications of these adjustments.

✓ _____ How cultural lenses impact our perceptions of others and our views of the world.

✓ _____ How cultural lenses shape our views of race and ethnicity.

✓ _____ What it means to respect a variety of lenses.

✓ _____ How cultural encapsulation influences what we see.

✓ _____ How cultural lenses may lead to false assumptions.

✓ _____ Why the Golden Rule has certain limitations.

✓ _____ Why checking cultural lenses is a bottom-line issue.

Individual Action Plan

Think about one specific thing you can do to improve your skills in the area of checking cultural lenses. Then complete the following plan during the next _____ (state time period).

Specific skill I want to improve first (refer to list of Performance Skills at the beginning of the chapter):

_____

My strategy:

_____
_____
_____
_____

In order to develop this skill, I will:

_____
_____
_____
_____

Possible obstacles include:

_____
_____
_____
_____

Resources I need:

_____
_____
_____
_____

I will measure my progress by:

_____
_____
_____
_____

Answers

Your Turn *(see p.73) Possible explanations for Situations 1 and 2:*

SITUATION 1. Among some cultures, health is viewed as a blessing from God. By the same token, illness is seen as a consequens of sin. Therefore, prayer takes precedence over medical intervention, at least initially.

SITUATION 2. Immigrants may be distrustful of financial institutions because of their experiences in their home countries. Some immigrants remember a lot of corruption back home and therefore, do not trust banks in the United States. Also, undocumented immigrants hesitate to open checking or savings accounts, fearful that they will be turned over to authorities, even though financial institutions may assure potential customers they do not engage in this practice.

Notes

1. Arturo Vega, "Americanizing? Attitudes and Perceptions of U.S. Latinos," *Harvard Journal of Hispanic Policy*. Online 11/23/2006. Available: **www.ksg.harvard.edu/hjhp/vol/2006/vega/pdf**.

2. "Interview of Dr. Kathy Morsea," in Lois Crozier-Hogle and Darryl Babe Wilson, *Surviving in Two Worlds* (Austin, TX: University of Texas Press, 1997).

3. Ralph Linton, *The Study of Man* (New York: Appleton-Century-Crofts, 1936).

4. ABC News, "Hopkins 24/7," September, 2000.

5. H. Kim and H.R. Markus, "Deviance of Uniqueness, Harmony, or Conformity? A Cultural Analysis," *Journal of Personality and Social Psychology*, 77, 1999, 785–800.

CHAPTER 4

CQ MEGASKILL: GLOBAL CONSCIOUSNESS

Performance Skills

- *Understanding globalization*
- *Increasing awareness of cultural differences*
- *Questioning assumptions*
- *Becoming a global communicator*
- *Recognizing ethnocentrism*
- *Practicing critical cultural relativism*

- *Showing respect for diverse world views*
- *Optimizing global teamwork*
- *Creating global Websites*
- *Avoiding culture shock*
- *Doing your homework*

 REFLECT BEFORE READING

Experiences in other countries and with other cultures provide us with valuable insight into our own culture. Similarly, experiences at "home" can promote international understanding. Can you think of experiences in your life that promoted this kind of insight and understanding?

YOUR TURN

DIRECTIONS: Answer true or false.

_____ 1. Many perceptions of the United States throughout the world come from movies and television shows shown abroad.

_____ 2. Outside of the United States, describing yourself or another person as a "foreigner" is a good idea since people generally view this term favorably.

_____ 3. Business cards are used more frequently in the United States than in other parts of the world.

_____ 4. Good business is good business; if a business practice is successful in New York City or Los Angeles, it will be successful elsewhere.

(Note: See answers on pp. 99–100.)

INTRODUCTION

Tom, an employee of an educational tutoring firm in the United States is meeting a group of employees in India. His objective is to outsource tutoring. At their first meeting together, Tom tries to come across in a friendly and informal manner. He begins by telling the group he does not consider titles all that important, so people should feel free to just call him Tom. He then applies the training he received back in the States. Instead of telling them what to do, he asks them for feedback regarding how to make this business venture successful. "What are your ideas?" he says.

At this point, there is a long period of silence. When no one responds, he calls on an individual named Kanwar and asks him what he thinks. The other Indian employees give Tom a bewildered look. They cannot understand why Tom is asking these questions. If he needs to ask these questions, then he must not know. Their confidence in him is shaken.

Tom needs to rethink his approach. In India, it is usually expected that someone like Tom will present his ideas first. Then, brainstorming and decision making by the group follows. When they eventually issue their report, they will do so as a group.

The global marketplace is not some futuristic concept. It is here and now. Given the changing nature of the marketplace and workforce, our ability to be good, knowledgeable, and sensitive citizens of the world will go a long way toward enhancing our chances for success.

Global competition affords consumers the opportunity to choose the best available products and services from around the world. If we think of the world as a pool of potential customers, the numbers are mind boggling. Furthermore, U.S. employers are increasingly expanding their reach for talent. Workers throughout the world are competing with each other for more jobs and particularly for the best jobs.

Ask yourself if you have the skills to compete in this type of environment. More specifically, what skills do you have that will be an asset in the global marketplace? What skills do you need to develop in order to be competitive? What is the best way for you to acquire these skills? Lastly, why are these questions important to you and your future?

DID YOU KNOW? *David Smith, author of* If the World Were a Village, *posits what the world would look like if it were shrunk to 100 people. The graphic in Figure 4.1 shows the diversity of this global village.*

UNDERSTANDING GLOBALIZATION

Globalization refers to the growing interdependence among people and cultures throughout the world. Instant messaging, e-mail, Web conferencing, and other technologies make it possible to communicate and collaborate across cultures and countries. Travel, economic and government policies, trade, outsourcing

Figure 4.1 • If the World Were a Village of 100 People

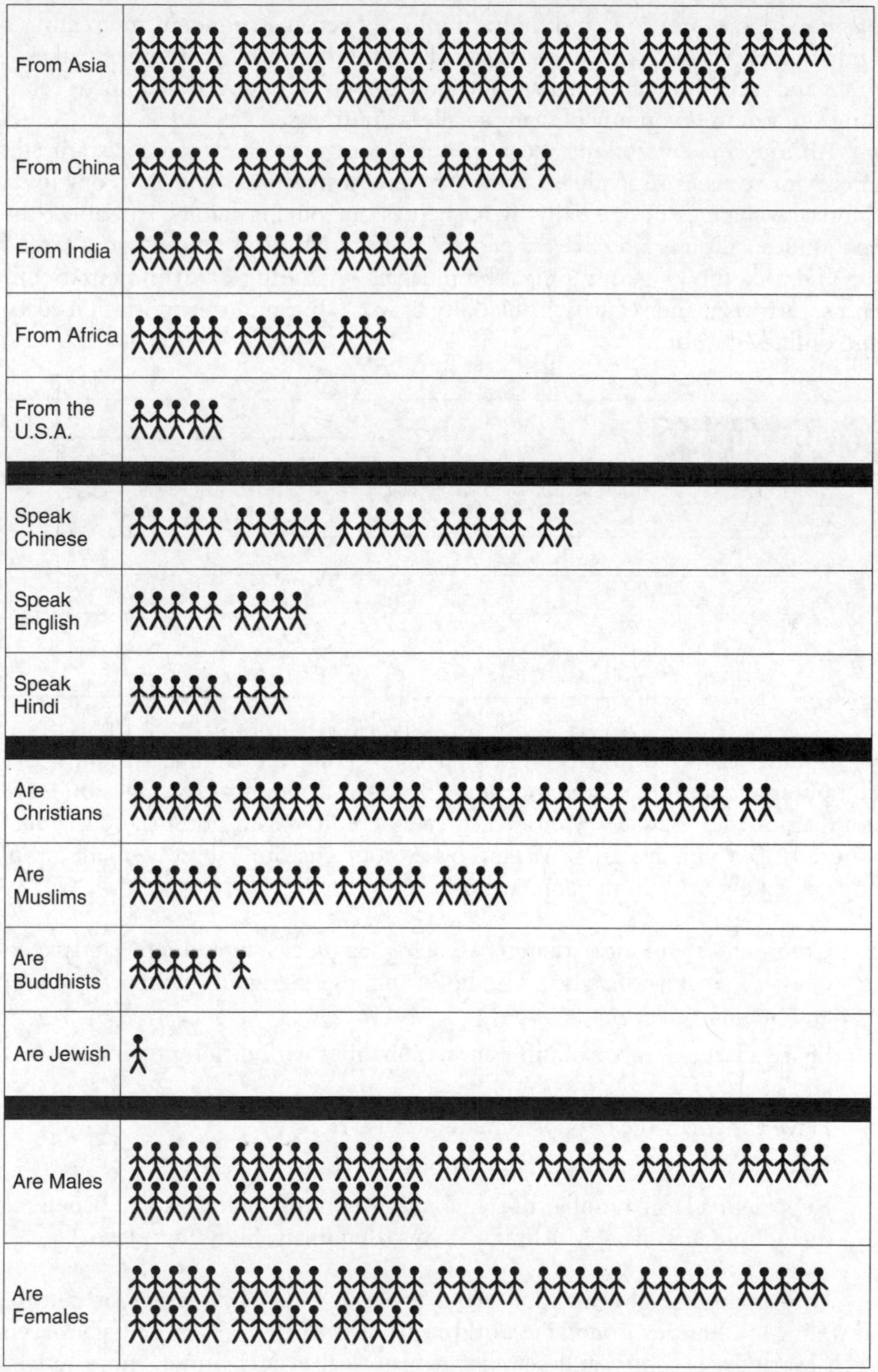

From Asia	𝖎𝖎𝖎𝖎𝖎 𝖎𝖎𝖎𝖎𝖎 𝖎𝖎𝖎𝖎𝖎 𝖎𝖎𝖎𝖎𝖎 𝖎𝖎𝖎𝖎𝖎 𝖎𝖎𝖎𝖎𝖎 𝖎𝖎𝖎𝖎𝖎 𝖎𝖎𝖎𝖎𝖎 𝖎𝖎𝖎𝖎𝖎 𝖎𝖎𝖎𝖎𝖎 𝖎𝖎𝖎𝖎𝖎 𝖎𝖎𝖎𝖎 (57)
From China	𝖎𝖎𝖎𝖎𝖎 𝖎𝖎𝖎𝖎𝖎 𝖎𝖎𝖎𝖎𝖎 𝖎𝖎𝖎𝖎𝖎 𝖎 (21)
From India	𝖎𝖎𝖎𝖎𝖎 𝖎𝖎𝖎𝖎𝖎 𝖎𝖎𝖎𝖎𝖎 𝖎𝖎 (17)
From Africa	𝖎𝖎𝖎𝖎𝖎 𝖎𝖎𝖎𝖎𝖎 𝖎𝖎𝖎 (13)
From the U.S.A.	𝖎𝖎𝖎𝖎𝖎 (5)
Speak Chinese	𝖎𝖎𝖎𝖎𝖎 𝖎𝖎𝖎𝖎𝖎 𝖎𝖎𝖎𝖎𝖎 𝖎𝖎𝖎𝖎𝖎 𝖎𝖎 (22)
Speak English	𝖎𝖎𝖎𝖎𝖎 𝖎𝖎𝖎𝖎 (9)
Speak Hindi	𝖎𝖎𝖎𝖎𝖎 𝖎𝖎𝖎 (8)
Are Christians	𝖎𝖎𝖎𝖎𝖎 𝖎𝖎𝖎𝖎𝖎 𝖎𝖎𝖎𝖎𝖎 𝖎𝖎𝖎𝖎𝖎 𝖎𝖎𝖎𝖎𝖎 𝖎𝖎𝖎𝖎𝖎 𝖎𝖎 (32)
Are Muslims	𝖎𝖎𝖎𝖎𝖎 𝖎𝖎𝖎𝖎𝖎 𝖎𝖎𝖎𝖎𝖎 𝖎𝖎𝖎𝖎 (19)
Are Buddhists	𝖎𝖎𝖎𝖎𝖎 𝖎 (6)
Are Jewish	𝖎 (1)
Are Males	𝖎𝖎𝖎𝖎𝖎 𝖎𝖎𝖎𝖎𝖎 𝖎𝖎𝖎𝖎𝖎 𝖎𝖎𝖎𝖎𝖎 𝖎𝖎𝖎𝖎𝖎 𝖎𝖎𝖎𝖎𝖎 𝖎𝖎𝖎𝖎𝖎 𝖎𝖎𝖎𝖎𝖎 𝖎𝖎𝖎𝖎𝖎 𝖎𝖎𝖎𝖎𝖎 𝖎𝖎𝖎𝖎𝖎 (55)
Are Females	𝖎𝖎𝖎𝖎𝖎 𝖎𝖎𝖎𝖎𝖎 𝖎𝖎𝖎𝖎𝖎 𝖎𝖎𝖎𝖎𝖎 𝖎𝖎𝖎𝖎𝖎 𝖎𝖎𝖎𝖎𝖎 𝖎𝖎𝖎𝖎𝖎 𝖎𝖎𝖎𝖎𝖎 𝖎𝖎𝖎𝖎𝖎 (45)

partnerships, education, and migration have been instrumental in creating a global marketplace. Nowadays, the global integration of economies makes it more and more difficult to talk about the German economy, the Chinese economy, or even the economy of many smaller countries such as Cuba.

Although events taking place in other continents may seem distant and irrelevant to us as individuals, they may have a profound effect on our lives. Similarly, changes in our daily lives, such as our buying habits, can affect the economies, cultures, and lives of people far away. More and more issues extend beyond a country's geographical boundaries, including environmental concerns, terrorism and security, availability of work, fuel and transportation costs, and online education.

YOUR TURN   · · · · · ———————

What two recent international developments are impacting your lifestyle at the present?

1. _____

   _____

2. _____

   _____

Today, organizations large and small can become global in an instant with a computer and an Internet connection. IBM is just one of a growing number of companies that view *every* citizen in *every* country as a potential customer. Therefore, if you are an IBM employee, your customer base is made up of approximately 6.5 billion people who

- Communicate in more than 6,000 living languages, including Mandarin Chinese, Spanish, English, Hindi, Portuguese, Bengali, Russian, Japanese, and Standard German.

- Share a large number of different nationalities with different perspectives and goals.

- Have a median age of approximately 28 years.

- Have an average life expectancy at birth of about 65 years.

- Represent a large number of religions with unique practices and beliefs, including Christians, Muslims, Hindus, Buddhists, Sikhs, and Jews.[1]

Understanding globalization requires us to peel back layers of culture. Traveling to countries around the world acquaints us with outer, more visible layers such as foods, fashions, and significant historical events. Inner, more hidden layers take the form of values, everyday norms and customs, and body language.

By reading novels and other works by authors from other cultures, living and studying abroad, developing friendships with people who are vastly different from us, reflecting on diverse customs and points of view, and immersing ourselves in other cultures wherever we find ourselves, we can deepen our understanding and appreciation of globalization. As we immerse ourselves in other cultures, we expand our knowledge base with regard to the meaning of culture, the interconnectedness of cultures, and cultural similarities and differences throughout the world.

YOUR TURN   · · · · · · ─────────

The International Programs Center of the U.S. Bureau of the Census provides continuous updated projections of the world's population. Access the "World POPClock Projection" on the Internet at **www.census.gov/ipc/www/popclockworld.html** to find the most recent estimate of the world's population.

Total World Population = _____ as of _____ (date).

WHAT IS GLOBAL CONSCIOUSNESS?

 Where Am I Now?

DIRECTIONS: For each statement, mark M (most of the time), O (often), S (sometimes), R (rarely), or N (never).

1. _____ In culturally diverse situations, both at home and abroad, I think and act flexibly.

2. _____ In culturally diverse situations, both at home and abroad, I am very confident in my ability to adjust to any situation.

3. _____ As a global communicator, I am aware of my body language and what it communicates from culture to culture.

4. _____ I understand how being globally conscious opens up all kinds of opportunities for me.

5. _____ When I find myself in a "new" cultural environment, I have an easy time socially interacting and adjusting.

With globalization taking hold, the costs of cultural misunderstandings and biases are increasing. As borders become less important for travel, trade, and the media, expanding our vision becomes imperative. Put another way, employers need workers who exhibit **global consciousness**, meaning the awareness, understanding, and skills necessary to adjust to different cultures. Globally conscious employees understand how globalization affects virtually every aspect of their work.

How might our global consciousness affect the way we do our job? At one U.S. company with ties to Singapore, workers reevaluated the scheduling of routine meetings due to differences in time zones. Websites, such as timeanddate.com, facilitate the process of checking time zones in different countries and cities. Instead of asking their coworkers in Singapore to get up in the middle of the night, meetings are now held at different times in order to periodically accommodate everyone's preferences.

UPS, which operates in more than 200 countries, has created a global trade curricula for all "UPSers." Given the global marketplace in which it operates, UPS seeks new hires who are

- Conversant in multiple languages.
- Sensitive to foreign cultures.
- Able to learn how to learn.
- Capable of managing complexity and uncertainty.

A lack of global consciousness makes it difficult for us to know what constitutes ethical behavior in different cultures. What is **ethical**, or those standards for determining what conduct is right and wrong, varies from one part of the world to another. A few years ago, a U.S. nuclear submarine collided with a Japanese high school training vessel. Eight Japanese died in the collision. Formal statements of regret from top government officials and the submarine commander, Scott Waddle, only fueled Japanese resentment and skepticism. Next, a written statement by Waddle, issued through the Japanese consulate in Hawaii, was viewed as too little, too late, and too formal.

Only after the commander offered a sincere apology in person to families of the victims was an international crisis averted. If this incident had taken place in the United States, counsel would have instructed the parties involved to exercise their constitutional right to remain silent because of legal liability issues. But in Japan, the ethical thing to do is an immediate, heartfelt, personal apology to the victim by the person at fault. Apologies from an official or third party are not sufficient.

TO LEARN MORE

Go to **www.worldcitizensguide.org.** Click on the tab "World Flags." You will see small icons for 120 countries. As you move your mouse over each icon, you are given an interesting fact about each country and the major languages spoken there. For example, if you mouse over Bangladesh, you will learn: "Some people here use their chins to point at things."

INCREASING AWARENESS OF CULTURAL DIFFERENCES

Some trainers who lead workshops on global cultural differences advise people to "assume difference instead of similarity." Why? Because we tend to assume similarity. Perhaps you use a red pen to write a suggestion to a coworker who is a native of China. Later, your supervisor informs you that the coworker was highly insulted by the note. The problem was not the message. Rather, it had to do with the color red. In her culture, using that color to write a note such as this means "I wish you would die."

Assuming difference, as well as assuming similarity, has its downside. If we focus too much on our cultural differences, we run the danger of ignoring the many commonalities that unite us. Among other things, we all send messages and have a need to be understood, all of us live in groups and classify people in categories, and each and every one of us possesses a culture. These are **cultural universals**, meaning those behaviors, values, and beliefs found in all cultures.

Making a habit of assuming difference or assuming similarity locks us into a mode of thinking. Global consciousness requires us to be more flexible. By developing our cultural intelligence, we learn to be sensitive to possible differences and similarities among cultures. Not if but when we fail to show this sensitivity, we need to learn from our mistakes. If we mistakenly suggest a steak dinner to visiting staff from India, neglect to inspect a business card from a Japanese associate before putting it in our pocket, or offend a colleague by using written documentation rather than more personal face-to-face communication, these cultural missteps do not make us bad people. Rather, they simply indicate we need to expand our global consciousness.

CQ Applied · · · · · ·

Companies in the United States frequently use focus groups for market research. Recently, one U.S. drug company considered marketing one of their products in Japan. Before launching this venture, the company wanted to find out more about their new client base. Marketing materials for this drug would be evaluated by assembling a focus group of physicians in Japan. Soon, it became evident that this marketing strategy would not work.

In Japan, hierarchy is very important. People lower in the chain of command are hesitant to question higher-ups. Therefore, if a senior doctor likes the marketing approach, other doctors are quick to agree. After some thought, it was decided that doctors would be questioned individually. By taking into account the norms of Japanese culture, the drug company gathered the feedback it needed.

QUESTIONING ASSUMPTIONS

As we develop our global consciousness, we learn to question our assumptions—and then ask certain questions. As an example, when meeting with foreign clients, do we assume that punctuality is valued? What constitutes inappropriate dress? If we give gifts, do we even think about the color of the gifts and what it might signify (see Table 4.1)?

Stereotypical assumptions about a nation's personality are far from the truth, yet they are pervasive and often unquestioned. A recent survey of almost 4,000 people in 40 countries revealed that people everywhere believe stereotypes about a nation's personality, even their own. The researchers, Robert McCrae and Antonio Terracciano, discovered that we form misconceptions based on a country's leadership, historical events, and personal encounters traveling abroad.

Table 4.1 • Looking Beyond My Assumptions

Assumptions @	Predominant View in U.S.	Examples from Other Countries
Appointments	Punctuality is valued; after all, "time is money."	Punctuality is not valued in many Middle Eastern countries such as Israel and Saudi Arabia. Making a client wait is standard practice.
Dress	Business attire varies from conservative suits and skirts to more informal wear. Accessories, such as leather briefcases and handbags, are common.	Wearing or carrying anything made of leather will be offensive to Hindu clients, who view cows as sacred. In Saudi Arabia, Muslim beliefs dictate very modest attire for women. High dress, especially necklines, long sleeves, and long skirts are appropriate.
Gifts	A wide range of gifts is permissible. Flowers of any color are a common way of showing appreciation. Alcohol is a common gift during the holiday season.	In Japan and China, white flowers are associated with funerals. In China, even the color of the wrapping paper is significant. Alcohol is illegal in Muslim countries.

For instance, we may think of Germans as aggressive, based on Germany's role in World War II. Or we may think of Swedes as being conscientious, but they are no more so than the rest of us according to the researchers' data.[2]

YOUR TURN   · · · · · · ──────────

Briefly explain each of the following sayings and what values it supports. Are these U.S. values? And are they universal values? Explain.

1. "Pick yourself up by your own bootstraps." _____

_____

_____

_____

2. "A rolling stone gathers no moss." _____

_____

_____

_____

3. "The nail that sticks up gets hammered down." _____

_____

_____

_____

4. "I scratch your back, you scratch mine." _____

_____

_____

_____

(*Note:* See answers on p. 100.)

BECOMING A GLOBAL COMMUNICATOR

Global consciousness allows us to reconsider our traditional thinking, interactions, and communication skills. Thinking of ourselves as citizens of the world helps us move beyond nationalistic boundaries. Pearce and Pearce talk about the process of becoming a **cosmopolitan communicator**; that is, understanding and responding to situations as worldly people. Instead of thinking of ourselves solely as Americans, Koreans, or Russians, we need to consider our ties to a larger, interdependent community.[3]

> **DID YOU KNOW?**
>
> *According to the U.S. Department of Education, 24,000 U.S. elementary and secondary students study Chinese. In contrast, more than 200 million Chinese children study English.*

Global communicators consider their audience. What if you speak English much more fluently than your audience? If this is the case, it is a good idea to use gestures and a lot of visual aids. Do not talk fast and avoid the use of slang. If translation is necessary, be careful.

Since some words have multiple meanings and those meanings vary from one context to another, a straight translation using software is apt to create misunderstandings. For example, one international company explained they were terminating employees. In translating statements in English to Chinese, the company issued a statement to the effect that it would execute employees.

With cyber global communications, becoming multilingual is an extremely valuable skill. Although English is the primary language of international business, people still prefer doing business in their native language. For this reason, companies are rapidly globalizing their Websites, in part by making their sites available in a wide variety of languages.

Becoming a global communicator involves becoming more informed about how and why people from different cultures communicate the way they do. Understanding the cultural context of communication is critical. In Japan and many other Asian countries, mail says something about the sender. Therefore, the quality of the printing or other things that might distinguish the mailing assume more importance than in the United States.

 **Applied** · · · · · ·

Roger Axtell, author of Gestures: The Do's and Taboos of Body Language Around the World, *shares a wealth of advice to increase the knowledge base of globally conscious business travelers. Axtell, former vice president of worldwide marketing for Parker Pen Company, focuses on gestures, greetings, and business protocol in general.*

As an example, he explains that the process of exchanging business cards takes on a different meaning in Japan. Upon receiving a business card, Axtell recommends looking at it closely rather than quickly putting it away. Because the card represents one's personal and professional identity, it should be treated with respect. When presenting your own card, Axtell suggests doing so with both hands and bowing slightly. The lettering on the business card should face the recipient.

YOUR TURN · · · · · ·

Global communicators pay attention to body language, and what it communicates from culture to culture.

Look at Figure 4.2. What do each of these gestures mean to you?

- In Iran, Greece, and Turkey, nodding your head up and down means just the opposite of what it means in the United States. It means no. Moreover, in these countries, a yes can be indicated by moving one's head from side to side (no in the United States).

- A two-handed handshake in Saudi Arabia would be highly offensive. The left hand is considered unclean since it is used for certain hygienic functions. Consequently, you should not touch someone with this hand.
- The A-OK in Germany is an obscene reference to one's anatomy; while in some South American countries it can mean "f——— you."
- In Australia, thumbs up is interpreted as "up yours."
- In Argentina, circling your finger around your ear means you have a telephone call.

Figure 4.2 • Body Language, Culture, and Meanings

Nodding head up and down   Two-handed shake

A-OK   Thumbs up   Circling finger
around ear

RECOGNIZING ETHNOCENTRISM

YOUR TURN

Imagine you are participating in a workshop on careers, CQ, and globalization. One of the participants states, "I am studying to be a physical therapy assistant. My job will be to rehabilitate people without regard for who they are. I will bring someone back to their highest functional capacity. It doesn't matter if they are from Honduras, Mexico, or Spain. I don't need this training."

Do you agree with the position taken by this individual? Explain.

_____

_____

_____

_____

Margo Monteith, a psychologist at the University of Kentucky, conducted a test in which she asked people to associate certain words with America and a fictitious country called Marisat. Under time pressure, Monteith found that people were inclined to connect words such as *sunrise*, *paradise*, and *loyal* to

America. On the other hand, Marisat was more easily associated with words such as *death*, *evil*, and *poison*. According to Monteith, our self-esteem is closely related to our group membership. By feeling our group or nationality is better, we feel better about ourselves.[4]

Ethnocentrism is the assumption that our way of doing things is right and therefore superior. Ethnocentrism is found throughout the world. Because of their ethnocentric behavior, travelers from the United States are sometimes viewed as insensitive, ignorant, and "full of themselves." In the 1950s, Lederer and Burdick coined the term *Ugly American* to describe people from the United States who travel the world thinking that their society is the most culturally advanced and civilized. Since U.S. values were considered superior, the Ugly American did not feel it was necessary to understand, much less appreciate other cultures.[5] Even today, this reputation survives. Many people in other parts of the world think of U.S. citizens as loud, boastful, and selfish.

Ethnocentrism is pervasive in the United States and elsewhere. For example, many of us think there is one universal or acceptable way of doing business, and that way is our way. If we encounter people who do not understand or practice our way, then we assume they are misguided, or we try to teach them how to become more like us.

Even the term *American* is ethnocentric. People in the United States use this term to describe only themselves, when in fact Americans populate the entire continents of North and South America. For this reason, I avoid using the term *Americans* to describe the population of the United States.

All humans share the same basic priorities in life: true or false? As we develop our cultural intelligence, it becomes increasingly clear why the answer is false. Culture influences how people judge what is most important. As an example, people in the United States tend to place more importance on individual priorities such as personal fulfillment and autonomy. Japanese, on the other hand, may sacrifice personal concerns for social acceptance. In contrast, Middle Eastern cultures often place a higher priority on reaching out to others and being hospitable.

 ## Where Am I Now?

When interacting with people from a country whose culture is very different from mine, I:

Might judge them by my own cultural standards.

Example:

_____

_____

_____

Might have a condescending attitude toward their lifestyles.

Example:

_____

_____

_____

Might assume they should do things just like I do.

Example:

_____

_____

_____

Might be unaware of my own cultural values.

Example:

_____

_____

_____

PRACTICING CRITICAL CULTURAL RELATIVISM

In contrast to ethnocentrism, cultural relativism does not assume that any one culture is perfect or always right. **Cultural relativism** maintains that any culture's values and beliefs must be understood on the basis of its own standards. In other words, we should not use our own standards to judge another culture.

Cultural relativism promotes understanding and tolerance. However, it has a downside. For example, **absolute cultural relativism** says we should not even question what takes place in another culture. To do so promotes ethnocentrism. However, what if we think the behavior in question harms people or violates their basic rights?

Another form of cultural relativism offers an alternative view. **Critical cultural relativism** poses questions about cultural beliefs and practices in an effort to understand better why they exist, who accepts them, and who they benefit or harm. When we employ critical cultural relativism, we evaluate all cultures, including our own, with the understanding that no culture is perfect. This allows us to respect and understand cultural differences and at the same time maintain a critical perspective.

In Trompenaars and Hampden-Turner's best-selling book, *Riding the Waves of Culture: Understanding Cultural Diversity in Business*, the authors discuss cultural differences that revolve around relationships with people. From their perspective, one of the most important is "universalism" versus "particularism." The universalist approach is founded on the idea that certain rules or contracts should be followed regardless of the circumstances. The particularist approach sees universalism as too rigid. It maintains that special circumstances and personal relationships take precedence over any abstract rule.

According to Trompenaars and Hampden-Turner, much of the research on universalism and particularism has been done in the United States. Perhaps this is why some researchers have concluded that all societies should emulate universalism, since this approach underlies business dealings in the United States.

However, the authors caution against assuming that any one approach is necessarily the best. They argue in favor of critical cultural relativism. By critiquing both approaches, we can see the advantages and pitfalls of each. For example, an employee based in the United States (universalist culture) might be conducting business with a supplier from Japan (particularist culture). For these employees to be successful, cultural self-awareness and flexibility are key skills. The U.S. employee might conclude that while a contract is necessary, putting too much emphasis on a contract might imply a lack of trust and limit flexibility. Similarly, the supplier from Japan might come to realize that contracts and personal relationships are both necessary and can even reinforce each other. In some situations a contract might be necessary, for without it, there might be confusion as to the exact nature of an agreement or what recourse is available if both sides do not uphold their end of the deal. By seeing the benefits and disadvantages of both approaches, it may be possible for these individuals to avoid the extremes of ethnocentrism and absolute cultural relativism by critically evaluating and integrating their cultural differences.

SHOWING RESPECT FOR DIVERSE WORLDVIEWS

Different cultures have different **worldviews**, frameworks for making sense of the world. Each day, we see and hear a smorgasbord of worldviews, relating to things such as religion, the universe, humanity, nature, or other philosophical issues that address who we are or our concept of being. For example, different worldviews exist regarding our relationship to nature. Many Asians and Native Americans emphasize unity with nature and reverence for nature. In other cultures, humanity and nature are seen as separate. To many North Americans, nature is something to overcome or control. However, in some African cultures, people believe that nature is beyond our control.

Whether or not we recognize it, these worldviews affect all aspects of culture, including our priorities, behaviors, and how we express ourselves. In a culture that attaches great importance to personal expressiveness, we are likely to observe people engaging in a wide variety of facial expressions and gestures. To offer another example, we would expect to find a great deal of emphasis on the *process* of communication in a culture that values harmonious group relations. In a culture such as this, the emotional exchange of communicating and the relationships communication gives rise to are apt to be valued as much as the end product of communication.

In spite of globalization, individuals may find themselves working in organizations that do not respect multiple worldviews. Fortunately, this is slowly changing as evidenced by recent corporate developments such as the following:

- Employees of a major airline in the United States are now allowed to wear turbans, yarmulkes, and hijabs as part of their uniform.

- A multinational power equipment maker which operates in 128 countries has rewritten its corporate statement of principles. It now reflects not just its traditional Lutheran values, but Muslim and other values as well.

- A large hotel in a major metropolitan area in the United States has set aside a room for its Muslim employees who need to pray several times during their shifts. This provides those employees with a private room in which to place their prayer rug when they pray towards Mecca.

CQ Applied · · · · · —————————————————————

Cultural beliefs regarding modesty differ. In her research, Dr. Caryn Andrews found people's beliefs about modesty can affect health-care utilization. As an example, certain procedures, such as disrobing or having personal contact with a technician, might be at odds with tzeniut, *the Hebrew belief in modesty. Research on other cultures, such as Muslims, Hispanics, Asians, and the Amish, show modesty can interfere with screenings, check-ups, and overall health care.*

In order to study this issue in more detail, Dr. Andrews created a questionnaire to measure patient modesty. The result is a modesty scale, used by hospitals nationwide to measure degrees of modesty. By taking cultural modesty into account, providers show utmost respect and sensitivity.[6]

What are some ways in which health care providers are adapting? Solutions can be relatively simple, such as putting up a curtain or making it possible for the patient to cover her body while waiting for a provider. In some cases, hospitals now provide gowns that cover the entire body. When discussing private issues, providers can make sure the door is closed and ask the individual if he or she would like to have a family member or someone else present.

Respecting worldviews requires extra thought, knowledge, and sensitivity. If you are setting up a meeting in a multicultural workplace, numerous considerations are important. For example:

1. Does the scheduling of the meeting conflict with holidays, local festivities, or religious observances?
2. What are the attendees' cultural norms?
   - Should you get right down to business or first spend some time building rapport?
   - What are appropriate topics for getting to know each other?
   - What are the hours of a normal workday; and when is it OK to break for lunch?

3. What is the protocol for decision making?
   - Should you make information available before or during meetings?
   - Are decisions made by individuals or group consensus?
4. What is the structure of meetings?
   - Does everyone attend, or just certain people, such as implementers and/or evaluators?
   - Should people be seated randomly, by position, or in some other way?
5. What are the speaking norms?
   - Who opens the meeting? Who speaks first?
   - What gestures are taboo?

OPTIMIZING GLOBAL TEAMWORK

Because of computer technology, work is becoming a thing we do rather than a place we go. As businesses expand throughout the world and as technologies facilitating collaborative work improve, global teams become more commonplace. The idea behind global teamwork is that people from countries and cultures worldwide will be better able to problem-solve and offer a variety of perspectives. While communication technologies such as e-mail, team rooms (members collaborate on a real-time basis), teleconferencing, and videoconferencing make virtual teamwork possible, they cannot eliminate problems caused by distance.

Even when members of teams know each other and can sit down in the same room and talk, efficient and productive teamwork is not necessarily easy. When team members live in different countries, talk different languages, and barely know each other, the challenges are formidable. The geographical and cultural distance separating team members creates a number of challenges besides the obvious ones of sharing information and cultivating team camaraderie and spirit.

Different needs and customs regarding team reward system. Rewards are things that motivate individuals and groups. If not tailored to the culture, rewards meant to motivate can actually alienate. As previously mentioned, some cultures do not want to bring attention to themselves as individuals; and therefore, seek to avoid individual rewards. In a situation such as this, acknowledging the efforts of a group in some manner might be more appropriate.

Cultural clashes. Misunderstandings may result from lack of awareness and respect for cultural expectations of dispersed team members.

Different work cultures may have different beliefs regarding decision making. Teams in some companies and regions of the world are more apt to follow top-down decision making. Elsewhere, there may be more input from people at different levels. If members of the same global team unknowingly employ different decision-making styles, it can seriously impair their ability to work together.

Lack of trust. As social distance increases or as interaction and familiarity decrease, there tends to be less trust. Generally, we are less apt, at least initially, to trust people with whom we do not identify. For example, consider who you would *not* welcome as family, close friends, coworkers, or neighbors. Now ask yourself: Would you trust these same people? Since trust is such a sensitive issue, we tend to ignore it.

Exclusion. Any perceived difference, especially if it is seen as important, can marginalize team members and create disunity. In a team, certain individuals may not feel included. One way of minimizing exclusion is to be responsible with the words and symbols we use to communicate. Anticipating multiple perspectives and reactions goes a long way toward tapping, sharing, and using everyone's input.

Meeting the challenges of global teamwork requires us to

- Seek agreement regarding team goals as well as individual roles and responsibilities.

- Make a concerted effort to stay in touch. For instance, you and other team members might agree to answer e-mails within 24 hours.

- Meet in person as much as possible in order to build trust and if necessary rebuild shattered trust. Kickoff meetings, celebrations of major milestones in a project, and discussions at critical junctures are good times to meet.

CREATING GLOBAL WEBSITES

At any given time, millions of people are using the Internet to shop, read the news, or research some subject. According to the *Computer Industry Almanac*'s recent estimate, more than 1 billion people worldwide use the Internet. Regardless of what people are looking for, they usually have little or no awareness of where the information they access originates. What matters is whether the information is personally and culturally relevant to them.

Given the nature of the Internet, any website is inherently global. Or is it? According to a recent Web Globalization Report Card, most Websites are lacking in terms of their worldwide reach and local usability.[8]

While Web globalization removes geography as a factor, the cultural comfort level of a Website provides a competitive edge. When content is in their native language, Web surfers stay at a site much longer. Additionally, consumers are much more likely to buy a product or service from a Website in their native language because they can research it more thoroughly.

What do the global Websites have in common? With one click, you can access the information you need in a variety of languages including your own. As an example, Google offers more than 100 different language interfaces, and more than half of Google's traffic comes from outside of the United States.

Furthermore, a Website should be culturally relevant. For instance, research on car buying habits shows how the appeal of certain vehicles and even the process of buying those cars varies from culture to culture. A global Website utilizes this information in tailoring its content to different cultures.

TO LEARN MORE

Go to the BBC homepage at **www.bbc.co.uk/languages**, home of the British Broadcasting Company on the Internet. You will be able to read or hear the news in 33 languages. Visit the BBC interactive Website, "Your Voice" at **www.bbc.co.uk/voices/yourvoice.** It was recently named the Best Global Website. BBC's "Your Voice" Website promotes and creates cross-cultural dialogue on topics such as language ecology, language and age, why study language, and when languages collide. You will be asked to share your point of view on these topics and many more, or put your questions to an expert and join the discussion.

YOUR TURN   . . . . . .

Surf the Internet and find a corporate Website that you would rate as excellent in terms of its global reach, and one that you would rate as poor. Compare and contrast the two Websites, as you explain the reasons behind your ratings.

_____

_____

_____

_____

_____

_____

_____

_____

MINIMIZING CULTURE SHOCK

Culture shock, the disorientation we feel when we encounter a significantly different way of life, is a two-way street. We may inflict culture shock on someone else when we do things that offend and alienate others. Additionally, we may be on the receiving end of culture shock when we come face to face with a radically different lifestyle. While we can experience culture shock at home, it tends to be most intense when traveling abroad or returning home after a long absence.

When we find ourselves in an unfamiliar environment, our expectations may not mesh with our actual experiences. This may be due to the influence of the media. As an example, we may experience culture shock upon learning that Australians do not necessarily dress like Crocodile Dundee. Or we may expect all Chinese to know martial arts, all Africans to live in huts in villages, and all Americans to be rich.

Culture shock can take its toll on us. It can make us feel anxious, disoriented, and depressed. We may lose confidence in our ability to socially interact and adapt in new situations. Another consequence is dissatisfaction with the "new" environment and the way people behave. In some cases, culture shock can strain and even ruin relationships.

Minimizing culture shock requires new knowledge and insights as well as a certain degree of flexibility. It is counterproductive to simply think in terms of specific do's and don'ts when visiting a country or region. No one source of information can cover all possibilities. Within a culture, everyone and every group has specific habits, expectations, and norms. Consequently, you will encounter situations that have no script; situations that go beyond previously learned routines. When in doubt, it is wise to follow a saying that comes from Columbia. It says, "When visiting, try to behave the way others behave."

To minimize the likelihood of culture shock, keep in mind the following:

- *Learn what questions to ask and listen actively.* Are there certain conversational topics to avoid? How do people behave at social gatherings? What kinds of gestures are considered offensive?

- *Try to expand and diversify your network.* If possible, develop relationships with males and females of various cultural backgrounds and mentors with international business experience.

- *Conduct environmental scans.* Pay careful attention to the behavior of others as well as the cultural context, status of people, and formality of the situation. For instance, closely observe introductions, eye contact, behaviors toward men and women, and deference toward people in authority.

- *Remember the possible pitfalls of humor.* What is funny to you might be rude or offensive to someone from another culture. If in doubt, do not take a chance.
- *Recognize the importance of humility.* Don't assume that you are better or more able because of your background, education, or credentials. By staying humble, you show that you do not know it all. Rather, you leave room for communication and show that you want to learn and grow.

Minimizing cultural shock is a process. Developing our global consciousness allows us to move beyond confusion and paralysis of action to acceptance and adjustment.

DOING YOUR HOMEWORK

Usually, failures in international business are not due to technical or professional incompetence. According to research, most failures stem from an inability to adapt to diverse ways of thinking and acting. Think about it. Employees living in the United States equip themselves with a vast array of knowledge before they attempt to conduct business. Market research provides them with the latest data on the needs, values, and buying habits of consumers in the United States. Yet, when businesspeople venture into the international arena, they are often woefully unprepared. Whether they deal with managers, fellow workers, or customers, they display a lack of knowledge that would be totally unacceptable at home. Almost unconsciously, we tend to take our own cultural habits and norms with us when we travel abroad and project what we learn "at home" onto others.

Before entering into a business relationship with persons from another country, it is helpful to do your homework. Acquaint yourself with the country's culture, and not just the business, technological, and political sectors. All social institutions, such as education, family, and religion, impact how we interact and conduct business. For instance, a country's religious philosophy or spirituality can further one's understanding of why people behave the way they do. When doing business with an organization, it is important to understand its culture, including its values, norms, beliefs, language, and symbols. Information should be current since organizations change constantly.

Culture-specific information may be obtained from intercultural business consultants as well as foreign chambers of commerce, embassies, or other respected representatives of a particular country or group. Avoid quick and easy guides to travel in foreign countries. Often, information of this nature is full of sweeping generalizations that promote misunderstandings.

Go online to search for information about music, literature, history, and anything that might provide you with insight into a country's values, beliefs, and language(s).

For those interested in educational opportunities, international education programs are offered at the high school and college level. Additionally, there are internship exchanges, study tours, and training seminars and conferences available through a variety of government, business, and educational organizations worldwide. Some opportunities include scholarships, internships, and volunteer positions.

According to a recent survey on global relocation of workers, 81% of organizations offered cross-cultural training before assignments took effect. Interestingly, only 20% said this training was required. A sizable majority (73%) indicated cross-cultural training programs had high value. However, only 29% reported that CD-based and Web-based programs had high value.[9]

TO LEARN MORE

Access the Global Policy Network (GPN) Website at **http://gpn.org/main1.html.** GPN provides information to the public on working people in the global economy. In particular, it provides up-to-date statistical information and analysis on a growing number of countries. View the information on a country about which you know very little. How might this information help you as a business traveler to this country?

THE BOTTOM LINE

Globalization is infusing cultural differences into our everyday existence. This is even true for those of us who will live most if not all of our lives in the vicinity of our place of birth. Consequently, global consciousness is a necessary megaskill, in that it represents one of the most important and fundamental abilities we will have to develop in the 21st century. In addition to enabling us to cross cultural boundaries with ease, work with others, and see the value of multiple perspectives and experiences, global consciousness will allow us to pursue exciting and well-paying employment opportunities.

As previously discussed, lack of attention to cultural differences can have dire consequences, both at home and abroad. Research shows that international business ventures fail more because of a lack of global consciousness than professional or technical incompetence. With the emergence of an information economy in the United States, there is a need for culturally sensitive knowledge workers. White-collar jobs now place a premium on understanding cultures, languages, business practices, and world affairs. If workers cannot appreciate how our way of life is intertwined with the economic fortunes of the rest of the world, they become a liability.

By enhancing our awareness, understanding, and skills, global consciousness impacts the bottom line. As one key component of cultural intelligence, global consciousness allows us to excel in new and emerging environments that require flexibility, understanding, and the ability to appreciate the talents and contributions of all people and cultures.

A Look Back: I Have Learned

✓ _____ What is meant by globalization.

✓ _____ How globalization is changing our lives.

✓ _____ Why global consciousness is a megaskill today.

✓ _____ The value of becoming a global communicator.

✓ _____ How we can develop our global consciousness.

✓ _____ How to question our assumptions.

✓ _____ How to recognize ethnocentrism.

✓ _____ What is meant by critical cultural relativism.

✓ _____ How to show respect for diverse worldviews.

✓ _____ How global teamwork offers challenges and opportunities.

✓ _____ How to avoid or minimize culture shock.

✓ _____ How and why global consciousness impacts the bottom line.

Individual Action Plan

Think about one specific thing you can do to improve your skills in the area of global consciousness. Then complete the following plan during the next _____ (state time period).

Specific skill I want to improve first (refer to list of Performance Skills at the beginning of the chapter):

_____

My strategy:

_____

_____

_____

_____

_____

In order to develop this skill, I will:

_____

_____

_____

_____

Possible obstacles include:

_____

_____

_____

_____

Resources I need:

_____

_____

_____

_____

I will measure my progress by:

_____

_____

_____

_____

Answers

Your Turn (see p. 77)

_____ 1. Many perceptions of the United States throughout the world come from movies and television shows shown abroad. (*True*) For example, American women are perceived to be uniformly glamorous, sexy, and promiscuous. Women working abroad might need to counter this image by dressing conservatively and acting professionally in all business dealings. In general, the more women know, the less important gender becomes.

_____ 2. Outside of the United States, describing yourself or another person as a "foreigner" is typically a compliment. (*False*) Actually, it is a good idea to avoid using the term altogether. In many languages, such as French and Spanish, the word *foreigner* suggests something strange or alien. A better word to use is *international*.

_____ 3. Business cards are used more frequently in the Unites States than in other parts of the world. (*False*) Business cards, which are almost ritually exchanged in many countries, provide a record of the people you meet and how to contact them. In some countries, there is formal protocol regarding exchanging cards.

_____ 4. Good business is good business; if a business practice is successful in New York City or Los Angeles, it will be successful elsewhere. (*False*) Numerous examples show this line of reasoning to be faulty. Ignoring cultural differences may very well jeopardize business transactions abroad. Greeting others by shaking hands, holding eye contact, avoiding social chit-chat, and observing the importance of punctuality are typically the norm in New York City. These behaviors might be deviant and even offensive in cities in the Middle East, China, and other parts of the world.

Your Turn: Cultural Rules of Etiquette for Women (*see p. 84*)

1. In France, cheek-kissing is an acceptable way for a Frenchman to introduce himself to you. (*False*) Cheek-kissing is normally limited to good friends. If you shake hands with a Frenchman, however, he may slowly draw you closer and give you an "air kiss" to the one or both cheeks.

2. In Russia, when walking into a place with theatre-type seating, it is inconsiderate to enter facing the stage. (*True*) Enter with your back to the stage. By doing this, people you are passing will not see your rear.

3. In Italy, it is perfectly OK for two women to walk arm in arm in public. (*True*) This is simply a sign of friendship. It is not uncommon to see two men walking arm in arm as well.

4. In Switzerland, punctuality is not the norm. (*False*) You are expected to be on time. A widely known joke states that someone who arrives late does not wear a Swiss watch.

5. In Japan, you should avoid showing strong emotions such as anger. (*True*) Japanese are taught to control their emotions. Therefore, gesturing wildly or losing one's temper is viewed as impolite.

Your Turn: Analysis of Values Exercise (*see p. 85*)

1. "Pick yourself up by your own bootstraps" is a popular saying in the United States. It emphasizes independence and individualism. Contrast this saying with an African proverb, "It takes a whole village to raise a child."

2. "A rolling stone gathers no moss" emphasizes the U.S. preoccupation with mobility and speed. The Japanese have a similar saying, but the meaning is quite different. Moss represents important traditions. If people are constantly on the move, they will not appreciate those traditions and consequently they lose something of great value in the process.

3. "The nail that sticks up gets hammered down." This is a Japanese proverb. Contrast it with the popular saying in the United States, "The squeaky wheel gets the grease."

4. "I scratch your back, you scratch mine." In the United States, this means if you help me, I'll help you. Contrast this saying with the concept of giving in other cultures, in which nothing is expected in return. This even applies to giving something priceless to a total stranger.

Notes

1. CIA – The World Factbook. Online 7/18/2005. Available at **http://cia.gov/cia/publications/factbook/geos/xx.html**.

2. Dennis O'Brien, "Americans, Canadians Really Are Like Two Peas in a Pod," *Baltimore Sun*, October 21, 2005, pp. 1D + .

3. W. Barnett Pearce and Kimberly Pearce, "Extending the Theory of the Coordinated Management of Meaning (CMM) through a Community Dialogue Process," *Communication Theory*, *10*(4), 2000, pp. 405–424.

4. Shankar Vedantam, "Psychiatry Ponders Whether Extreme Bias Can Be an Illness," *Washington Post*, December 10, 2005, pp. A1 + .

5. W. J. Lederer and E. Burdick, *The Ugly American* (New York: Norton, 1958).

6. Stephanie Shapiro, "Medicine and Modesty," *Baltimore Sun*, March 11, 2005, pp. 1E + .

7. Lindsley Boiney, "Gender Impacts Virtual Work Teams." Online 7/25/2005. Available: **http://gbr.pepperdine.edu/014/teams/html**.

8. John Yunker, *The Web Globalization Report Card 2005* (San Diego, CA: Byte Level Research, 2005).

9. GMAC Global Relocation Services, *2006 Global Relocation Trends Survey* (Woodridge, IL: 2006).

CHAPTER 5

CQ MEGASKILL: SHIFTING PERSPECTIVES

Performance Skills

- *Taking the role of the other*
- *Shifting cultural perspectives*
- *Showing we are trying to understand*
- *Listening and responding effectively*
- *Developing multiple consciousness*
- *Interpreting symbols*

- *Stepping outside of our comfort zones*
- *Applying ethnorelative ethics*
- *Getting up close and personal*
- *Understanding the bottom-line benefits of shifting perspectives*

 REFLECT BEFORE READING

In the video *Blue-Eyed,* we join a racially diverse group of 40 men and women. They are participants in a workshop conducted by Jane Elliott, a diversity trainer. She opens the workshop with an exercise designed to force participants to step outside of their skin color for a period of time. The group of teachers, police, school administrators, and social workers is divided into "blue eyes" and "brown eyes." In order to easily distinguish them, Elliott places a paper collar around the neck of each blue-eyed participant.

Over the next hour, she subjects the blue eyes to verbal abuse, culturally biased IQ tests, and blatant discrimination. Meanwhile, she praises and coddles the brown eyes. On the walls are posters with slurs such as "Catch a blue-eyed by the toe." Elliott addresses blue-eyed men as "boys." Her behavior toward the blue eyes as a group is marked by extreme rudeness and condescension, hurried speech, self-contradiction, and bullying. At one point, a blue-eyed woman and man break down under the pressure and begin to cry.

This experience, according to Elliott, gives blue-eyed Whites a taste of what it is like to be a person of color. It creates a new cultural reality for them. During this workshop, these Whites realize that they have no control over what is happening to them. Elliott's intent is to force the blue eyes to shift perspectives or to walk in another person's shoes.

INTRODUCTION

As you enter the museum, to your right is "The Human Race Machine," a photo booth designed by Nancy Burson.[1] Once you sit down inside the booth, you can morph yourself into the race of your choice (see Figure 5.1). If you are Caucasian, you can see what you might look like as an Asian or African American. If you are African American, you can see what you might look like as a White or Hispanic. Burson, a multimedia artist and photographer, created this interactive machine to encourage conversation, questions, and reflection about race and identity. By seeing ourselves with someone else's race, we may alter our perspective of ourselves and others to some degree.

Imagine how you might look if you were of another race. You can find more information on "The Human Race Machine" on Nancy Burson's Website at **http://nancyburson.com**.

Developing **empathy**, the ability to understand another person's perspectives, feelings, and beliefs, is one of the most important skills we can develop. In order to develop and show this skill, we need to alter how we look at people, events, and our way of life. We do this by constantly **shifting perspectives**, meaning we examine the world from different vantage points.

Whenever we interact, it is important to shift perspectives, even for something as mundane as arranging a time for employees to meet. Take, for instance, a manager who suddenly called a mandatory meeting at 6:30 A.M. to deal with a pressing issue. The CEO of the company called the manager shortly thereafter. One employee, who could not attend the meeting, explained to the CEO that he had to take his children to day care that morning. This incident, according to the manager, was a wake-up call. He had not even considered the fact that one of his employees might have to miss the meeting for family obligations. Why? Because when he had children who needed to be driven to the babysitter or day care, his wife always handled this responsibility. Before making this meeting, he did not shift perspectives. Now, prior to

Figure 5.1 • The Human Race Machine

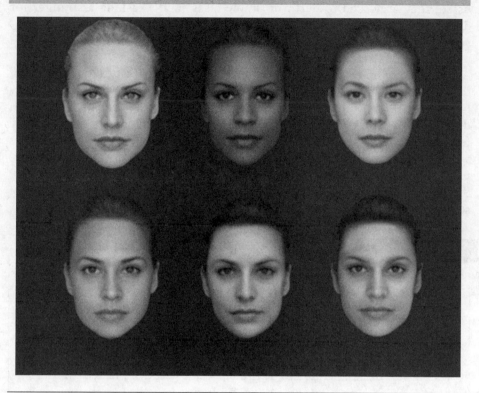

Copyright Nancy Burson, 2003.

scheduling meetings, he tries to anticipate possible work and family issues that may interfere with attendance at meetings.

TAKING THE ROLE OF THE OTHER

To shift perspectives with individuals whose ideas and experiences are different from our own, it helps to "put ourselves in their shoes." We call this **taking the role of the other**, meaning we try to put ourselves in somebody else's place. This might mean taking the role of someone who looks, thinks, talks, or acts differently than we do. We can do this by actually changing places with someone, but more often than not, we simply imagine doing this.

By taking the role of the other, we are further developing our cultural intelligence. Thus, it is a key competency whenever we deal with the general population. As an example, police officers may not know what to expect when they respond to incidents involving the mentally ill. In one large city, officers attend a workshop in which they strap on headphones and listen to tapes that simulate the voices someone with a mental illness might hear. While they listen, they are asked to perform simple tasks such as asking a stranger for directions or completing a reading test. After a while, the frustration, confusion, and fatigue experienced by the officers gives them a taste of what the mentally ill might feel when they interact with police.

A friend of mine, a police officer who works in a small city, takes the role of the other on a daily basis. As a White officer, he deals with many youth who view him as part of the White power structure. His ability to connect with these youth depends on whether he can put himself in their place and understand why they feel and react the way they do. For example, have they had negative encounters with police in the past? Are they viewing all officers, or all White officers, in a certain way? Are they simply trying to con him or do they have genuine concerns? Taking the role of racially diverse youth makes him better prepared for a variety of scenarios that he might encounter in possible life-and-death situations.

YOUR TURN • • • • • •

As the workweek for many people comes to an end, one common phrase employees may hear is "TGIF" ("Thank God It's Friday"). For some, this may be their reality as they look forward to relaxing and enjoying themselves over the weekend. For others, "TGIM" ("Thank God It's Monday") may be more appropriate. Try to take the role of the other. What might cause someone to relate more to TGIM than TGIF? Explain.

_____

_____

_____

_____

SHIFTING CULTURAL PERSPECTIVES

YOUR TURN • • • • • •

Describe a personal experience in which you could have benefited by shifting perspectives and looking at something through the eyes of a person of another culture. What might you have learned from this experience?

_____

_____

_____

_____

Regardless of where we live or the work we do, we will have to interact with people who do not share our cultural background. When we attempt to do this, the process of shifting perspectives becomes more complex and challenging. But as we develop this skill, we are better able to relate to each other's concerns and needs, even when cultural differences are the last thing on our mind.

While leaving a shopping center, Adam noticed an elderly lady carrying a big bag of groceries. Almost instinctively, he went up to her and said, "Can I help you?" The lady responded, "Go away." Since Adam could see her discomfort, he proceeded to offer an explanation, "In my culture, it is rude not to help." She countered, "Where are you from?" He answered, "Ethiopia." At that moment, prejudgments turned to empathy. She went on to explain why she was reluctant to accept his offer of help. Rather than clinging to their initial assumptions, both learned something by opening up and sharing their points of view.

Shifting cultural perspectives requires awareness of our own cultural lenses as well as an openness to learning. An oft-forgotten component of cultural awareness is the realization that our point of view is shaped by our culture. At times, we may look through our own cultural lens without realizing that our lens is affecting what we see.

As an example, suppose English is your native language but you are communicating with a customer who speaks English as a second language and cannot speak it fluently. Looking through your cultural lens is apt to make you impatient and perhaps even intolerant. But if you were to switch places with that customer, how would you want to be treated? Specifically, would you want the salesperson to

- Talk at a fast or slow rate? Why?

  _____

  _____

- Use basic or extensive vocabulary? Why?

  _____

  _____

- Use or avoid slang? Why?

  _____

  _____

- Enunciate clearly or slur words together? Why?

  _____

  _____

- Say something once or repeat it? Why?

  _____

  _____

- Assume you understand, or ask questions to make sure you understand? Why?

  _____

  _____

When we anticipate, recognize, and attempt to meet the needs of diverse customers by shifting cultural perspectives, everyone benefits.

THE CULTURAL DIMENSION OF EMOTIONS

Emotions or feelings are difficult to evaluate because they often remain hidden. For cultural or personal reasons, people may not voice how they really feel. Consequently, it may be necessary to assess a person's emotions by asking questions, reading nonverbal cues, or just thinking through the possibilities. Taking the role of the other can help, but this can be challenging when interacting cross culturally.

According to researchers, people throughout the world display basic emotions such as happiness, sadness, fear, anger, and surprise.[2] Although certain emotions are universal, how we show these emotions vary from culture to culture. The face, called the organ of emotion, may provide us with insight into people.

Verbal and nonverbal expressions provide us with valuable cues. However, cultural differences can make it difficult to ascertain what someone else is feeling. For example, openly showing affection by kissing, hugging, or even holding hands in public places is strictly forbidden among Orthodox Jews. In Brazil, loud displays of temper and anger in public may be frowned upon and viewed as impolite. If we lack this knowledge, it might be easy to ignore or misinterpret feelings based on behaviors such as these.

Understanding the cultural dimension of emotions provides us with a clearer picture of why people behave the way they do. For example, consider

- _Where we show emotion._ In the United States, we are more apt to openly display our emotions at home than at work.

- _How we display and interpret emotion._ Many cultures, including the United States, expect women and men to display emotions in different ways. In the United States, male workers who are very emotional may be seen as weak and unstable. Similarly, a man who is very empathetic may be viewed as "too soft." Women, on the other hand, are expected to show empathy.

- _How we value emotion._ Generally, places of work in the United States attach little value to what we feel. Workers are encouraged to focus on the task, be objective, and keep their emotions in check. In personal relationships, we attach much more importance to acknowledging and expressing our feelings.

EMOTIONAL INTELLIGENCE

Shifting cultural perspectives heightens our EQ, an important component of cultural intelligence. **Emotional intelligence, (EQ)** is the ability to recognize, interpret, and appropriately respond to feelings in others and ourselves. In his best-selling book *Working with Emotional Intelligence*, author Daniel Goleman analyzes data he collected from more than 150 firms.[3] His findings reveal EQ far outweighs IQ or technical expertise in determining who excels at any job.

Workers with high EQs are more able to *distinguish* and *manage* an array of emotions. Recalling his experiences aboard an airplane, Goleman cites an example. When the airplane encountered severe turbulence, the attendant kept her composure and did something a little out of the ordinary. By singing her instructions to the passengers, she succeeded in calming fears and putting everyone at ease.

In order to analyze the role EQ plays in interpersonal relationships, we need to look beyond the individual and examine the larger cultural context. We might ask, for example, how do cultural differences come into play when we attempt to recognize and respond appropriately to the emotions of others?

Emotional intelligence can be useful in the most unlikely of places. Imagine if you fought in the Iraq war along with other U.S. troops. You and your unit are outside one of the holiest mosques in all of Iraq. Suddenly, hundreds of Iraqis turn on you and your fellow soldiers, inspired by agitators who have spread the false rumor that the Americans are going to seize the mosque.

Lt. Colonel Chris Hughes found himself in this very situation at the beginning of the war in Iraq. He protected his troops and innocent civilians without even firing a shot. Lt. Hughes ordered his soldiers to not point their weapons at the Iraqis. Keeping his cool, he told them to smile, take a knee, and then relax. Next, Lt. Hughes told his troops to withdraw, keep smiling, and let the crowd defuse the tense situation themselves. By understanding what might trigger emotions in that situation and then defusing emotions through the body language of his troops, Hughes avoided a potential massacre.

TO LEARN MORE

What is your EQ? Psychologists John Mayer, Peter Salovey, and David Caruso created a test to measure one's EQ. To find out more about the test, go to **www.emotionaliq.org/MSCEIT.htm.**

YOUR TURN   · · · · · ·

Imagine you are afflicted with a disability. You are confined to a wheelchair. Since childhood, you have suffered from a disease that left you crippled. As a victim, you have to deal with able-bodied people who do not know what it is like to face each day as someone who is not normal.

To develop our EQ, we need to be more aware of the language that may alienate people with other frames of reference. Let's shift perspectives. In the prior paragraph I have used language that many people with disabilities find offensive. Underline the terms that you think might be perceived as offensive. How would you *feel* if these terms were used to describe you? Why?

_____

_____

_____

_____

_____

_____

_____

Words such as *afflicted, confined, suffer, crippled, victim,* and *normal* point to someone being defined and limited by his or her disability. For this reason, many people with disabilities see this language as making them out to be unidimensional, even pathetic. In other words, language such as this does not capture who they really are. Rather than emphasizing people's disabilities, use language that focuses on who they are as individuals, just like anyone else.

TO LEARN MORE

Go to the American Psychological Association's Website, "Removing Bias in Language Disabilities" (**www.apastyle.org/disabilities.html**). Scroll down to the numbered list for specific recommendations. Consider what language conveys inclusion, freedom, and respect when talking about or interacting with people with disabilities.

SENSITIVITY TO THE OTHER

Sometimes, we use the term **other** to refer to someone who is seen as different because of his or her appearance, culture, or some other trait. When we look at *others* as very different from us, it makes it difficult to relate to them and treat them as equals.

Arturo Madrid, a distinguished Latino activist and scholar, explains that his otherness lies in people's perceptions of him. He elaborates, "I am a citizen of the United States, as are my parents and as were their parents, grandparents, and great-grandparents . . . I do not, however, fit those mental sets that define America and Americans. My physical appearance, my speech patterns, my name, my profession, create a text that confuses the reader. My normal experience is to be asked, 'And where are you from?'"[4]

Being the *other* could make anybody feel different, isolated, stigmatized, and powerless. The *other* can frighten people, or at the very least make them feel uncomfortable or nervous. Often, people define the *other* on the basis of preconceived notions, which often have little or no basis in reality. If you are perceived as an *other* in a particular environment, people have a tendency to perceive you stereotypically. For this reason, you might feel as if you are constantly under a spotlight. You might feel this way because people cannot see beyond one or more of your differences, such as your name, appearance, gender, disability, accent, skin color, or religion.

YOUR TURN   · · · · · ──────────

Describe a situation in which you feel like an *other*.

_____

_____

_____

How does feeling like an *other* affect you?

_____

_____

_____

By shifting cultural perspectives, we sensitize ourselves to what otherness means. Sometimes we may feel like an *other* when there is only one of "us" and many of "them." We may be the only woman in the office, the only Filipino American student in a classroom, or maybe we feel like our dress or our age makes us stand out.

Others may feel different and uneasy or even afraid due to events beyond their control. During the aftermath of the terrorist attacks on September 11, 2001, I found myself reading about the fears and concerns of Arabs and Muslims living in the United States. Some of them were taking precautions, such as not wearing a head covering known as a *hijab*. Some Sikhs, who ran the risk of being mistaken for terrorists, weighed the consequences of wearing a turban. One Sikh carried around a sign that read, "I am not a Muslim."

Two weeks after the terrorist attacks, I began to wonder how I might feel if I were viewed as a threat because of my looks, religion, or heritage. One day, I briefly considered wearing a turban on my head. However, I started to think through what might happen, based on news reports I heard almost daily. Someone driving alongside my car might fire a gun at me. In all likelihood, some people would avoid me on the sidewalk, in restaurants and offices, and in shopping malls. I might put members of my family in danger. For a brief moment, I felt the powerlessness that comes from being perceived as an *other*.

The growth in cultural intelligence that comes with shifting perspectives allows us to see beyond the labels that define certain persons as *others*. We are better able to understand how being a cultural *other* can interfere with interpersonal relations and self-esteem. Specifically, we sensitize ourselves to the power of perceptions, and how people can be denied a voice, validity, or even visibility because of their looks, mannerisms, dress, or speech.

Recently, a White student shared her feelings with me about being an *other* at a historically Black college. "Because I am one of the only White people at this college, my classmates look to me to get the 'White perspective.' I don't enjoy having to sometimes be the spokesperson for my race because it puts a lot of pressure on me to say the right thing, whatever that is."

YOUR TURN · · · · · ·

Imagine waking up tomorrow and being of a different sexual orientation. Consider how your life will be different. Consider what adjustments you will need to make. More specifically, as this new person, will

*   You have more or less prestige and power? Why?

_____

_____

*   You have more or less difficulty finding the job of your choice? Why?

_____

_____

*   You be open and honest with others regarding your new identity? Why or why not?

_____

_____

*   Your close circle of friends remain the same? Why or why not?

_____

_____

SHOWING WE ARE TRYING TO UNDERSTAND

By shifting perspectives, we become much more sensitive to what others are thinking and feeling. Whereas this skill allows us to communicate more effectively, it is not sufficient. Too often we assume people know we are trying to understand them. If we do not show we care and are at least trying to empathize, others are likely to become much less communicative.

By showing our desire to understand, we open up lines of communication, build trust, and strengthen relationships. But it is not enough to simply say we understand, or we know what someone is feeling. If we say this, we might very well be seen as showing a total *lack* of empathy. Many times, we do not understand and it may be important to acknowledge that at the outset. For instance, we might preface what we say with, "I don't know what you are feeling," or "I do not know what it is like to . . . "

How can we show we want to understand? First, we need to be aware of body language as we listen. What messages are we sending? Are we rejecting, showing indifference, acting judgmental, or simply ignoring? Acknowledging, even without any show of empathy, is better than ignoring people's feelings. Leaning toward the speaker, focusing, and nodding your head are easy ways to show you are trying.

You can also show understanding or at least a desire to understand by constantly checking for understanding. If you are not sure of the message, ask questions until you do understand. As you ask questions, listen to yourself by taking the role of the other. In doing this, you carefully consider whether you are interpreting verbal and nonverbal communication correctly, both in terms of content and feelings.

CQ Applied · · · · · ·

Years ago, my son's pediatric neurologist asked me to imagine how it might feel to be a child, and see that not even the adults around you could keep you under control. In essence, he was asking me to trade places with my son Jimmy, who has autism.

When most doctors interacted with my son, Jimmy's behaviors would rattle them and even "hype" them up. This made Jimmy's behaviors that much worse. Dr. Weiner, on the other hand, had this calm, "I'm in control, I care about you" attitude. Dr. Weiner conveyed his understanding through his actions. Even the scheduling of an appointment showed something. He always scheduled Jimmy's appointment last. He knew that Jimmy would take a lot more time and energy than his other patients. As a result of this doctor's empathy, Jimmy became a calm and cooperative patient.

YOUR TURN   · · · · · ·

When you communicate with someone, how do you show you are trying to understand?

_____

_____

_____

_____

AWARENESS OF HISTORY

When we shift perspectives, we tend to think in terms of the present. But what if we go back into history? What if we shift historical perspectives? And why might it be important to do this?

Imagine you are living in Tuskegee, Alabama, in the mid-1900s. You are a very poor sharecropper. You haven't been feeling well at all for a while but cannot afford a doctor. One day, you are offered free physical examinations nearby, at Tuskegee University. On examination days, transportation to and from the clinic is provided, as well as free meals and treatment for minor ailments. For the first time in a while, you have reason to hope you will get better soon.

What you don't know is that you and approximately 400 other Black sharecroppers are part of an experiment conducted by the U.S. Public Health Service. All you have been told is that you suffer from "bad blood." Over a period of 40 years, during which time penicillin was discovered as an effective treatment, you and the other "experimental subjects" were never informed that you suffered from syphils, nor were you ever treated. Medical doctors simply used you to observe the effects of the disease, which ranged from dementia to blindness to death. Without knowledge of the Tuskegee experiment and other historical examples of the medical profession using minorities as guinea pigs, it is difficult to appreciate why some people of color are distrustful of health-care practitioners, and especially those who are not of their race.

When I talk to medical students about their field and the relevance of cultural intelligence, I ask them whether wearing a white coat erases one's prejudices. We talk about a mythical condition invented by the medical profession in the mid-1800s called _drapetomania_, the irrational and pathological desire of slaves to run away from their masters. Years ago, some medical schools even taught their students that African American women were more susceptible to cervical cancer because of their sexual promiscuity. Clearly, shifting historical perspectives can enhance our ability to relate to each other in contemporary society.

LISTENING AND RESPONDING EFFECTIVELY

 ## Where Am I Now?

DIRECTIONS: For each statement, mark **M** (most of the time), O (often), S (sometimes), R (rarely), or N (never).

1. _____ When I interact with people who look at things very differently from me, I tend to stop listening to what they are saying.
2. _____ I suspend judgment until I understand another person's point of view.
3. _____ When interacting in a multicultural environment, I am mindful of people's backgrounds.
4. _____ When I communicate with people who have difficulty speaking my language, I try to put myself in their shoes.

Shifting perspectives allows us to listen more effectively. This, in turn, enhances our understanding and our ability to respond appropriately. But how do we listen, especially when we find it difficult to relate to the speaker? Lee Mun Wah, author of *The Art of Mindful Facilitation*, suggests three basic techniques:

1. *Reflective listening.* Repeat back to the speaker as much as you can. For instance, you might say, "What I heard was . . . Is that correct?"
2. *Empathetic listening.* Show compassion for what the speaker is feeling. You might say to the speaker, "I can only imagine how difficult and painful this was for you."
3. *Nonverbal listening.* Closely observe physical messages as well as those matters that might be relevant but were not discussed. Sharing some of your observations with the speaker may lead to a more open, honest, and fruitful discussion. For example, you might say, "I happened to notice how you looked away from me every time you mentioned your relationship with your supervisor."

In addition to these techniques, another key is listening without judging. People feel affirmed and validated when people take the time to understand them. We can understand without necessarily agreeing. Phil Jackson, a highly successful basketball coach and a former player in the NBA, shares his approach to communication in his book, *Sacred Hoops*. As a coach, he tries to listen to his players without judgment, or what Buddhists call *bare attention*. Many of his players, according to Jackson, come from troubled families and desperately need support. When he listens, Jackson tries to be open, impartial, and extremely attentive, so he can develop a real feel for each player and his concerns.

Instead of listening, many of us are more interested in waiting for a break in the conversation in order to make our point. Or, we decide ahead of time what is worth listening to. Being an effective listener means assuming we need to listen. From there, we need to get information, clarify, and affirm. These processes require us to shift perspectives.

DEVELOPING MULTIPLE CONSCIOUSNESS

W. E. B. Du Bois, the first African American to earn a doctorate at Harvard University, spent a lifetime studying race relations in the United States. In his book *The Souls of Black Folk*, Du Bois discusses the term, **double consciousness**, a person's awareness of his or her own perspective and the perspectives of others. To Du Bois, double consciousness enabled people to move back and forth between two different worlds. These worlds might be differentiated by race, culture, or social class.[5] While double consciousness is a critical part of developing our cultural intelligence, it is no longer adequate. Rather, we must develop **multiple consciousness**, the ability to adopt multiple cultural perspectives or lenses regardless of the situation.

Developing multiple consciousness will allow us to shift gears, both intellectually and emotionally. Depending on the lens we are wearing, we might need to take someone's age, sensitivity, disability, and cultural background into account. This might mean changing our language slightly, being more reserved, asking certain questions, or listening very, very carefully.

YOUR TURN   · · · · · · ▬▬▬▬▬▬▬▬

Think of a setting in which you interact with older and younger males and females whose values and beliefs seem very different from yours. When interacting with these people, do you exhibit multiple consciousness? Why or why not?

_____

_____

_____

_____

When we interact with an individual or group, our ability to exhibit multiple consciousness depends on certain skills. Three of the most important are:

1. *Actively listening and observing.* By asking probing questions, being attuned to body language, or just being quiet for a while, we increase our ability to "simulate" a variety of feelings and behaviors as we interact with others.

2. *Being knowledgeable.* Taking advantage of opportunities to expand what we know about different cultures, histories, and perspectives allows us to be more sensitive and open to diversity.

3. *Drawing on a wide range of experiences.* Once we experience something, we are better able to relate to someone who has had a similar experience. For instance, if you rarely encounter discrimination, you may find it difficult to believe people who say they experience it every day. As you open yourself up to more diverse life experiences, you will be able to identify with more situations.

 **Applied** · · · · ·

At a large auto company, a team of engineers regularly participate in each other's religious activities. When anyone from this group celebrates Christmas, the New Year for Jews or Hindus, or Ramadan for Islam, the entire team is invited to that person's home. By interacting with others with diverse religious views, the group has learned to respect their different doctrinal views and affirm their common bonds, such as virtuous living, high morals, and the importance of family life.

INTERPRETING SYMBOLS

A **symbol** is something that carries a particular meaning for members of a group. Symbols, which can take the form of words, gestures, or objects, are the basis of communication. To interpret symbols correctly, we need to view them as **culturally specific,** meaning they can only be understood within the context of a particular culture. Depending on one's cultural lens or perspective, the same symbol may have positive or negative connotations.

Most symbols have multiple meanings. Consider the confederate flag, for example. Historically, it has been seen as a symbol of White supremacy. Yet, to many others, the flag signifies pride in one's heritage. Unless we understand the historical significance of this symbol, we will find it difficult to fully comprehend diverse perspectives.

Depending on how they are interpreted, symbols can either unite members of a group or create divisions. To evaluate the meanings and effects of symbols, we need to be open to and anticipate interpretations that are different from ours. This will help us communicate more inclusively, and reduce the risk of being misinterpreted.

YOUR TURN

Examine the three symbols in Figure 5.2. For each symbol, what are at least two different interpretations?

Figure 5.2 • Symbols and Their Meanings

Buddha Bash Tee ("Get your Buddha on the floor")

_____
_____
_____

_____

Lawn Jockey

_____
_____
_____
_____
_____

National Football League Mascot

_____
_____
_____
_____
_____

By shifting historical and cultural perspectives, we are better able to appreciate why each of these three symbols has triggered intense public dialogue and debate. The term *redskin* and the image of the Black servant holding a lantern may have negative connotations because of their historical significance. The T-shirt, in the eyes of some, is not humorous. Rather, it is racist and stereotypical.

Eaton High School in Greeley, Colorado, calls their sports teams the Reds. Their mascot is an American Indian wearing a loincloth. Nearby is the University of Northern Colorado (UNC). One UNC intramural basketball team has created quite an uproar by calling themselves the Fighting Whites (see Figure 5.3). Ryan White, one of three Native Americans on the Fighting Whites, says the name is intended to send a strong statement. If you could summarize that statement in one sentence, what would it be?

_____

_____

Figure 5.3 • UNC Intramural Basketball Team's Mascot

Every thang's gonna
be all white!!!

> **TO LEARN MORE**
>
> Access the Anti-Defamation League's website, "A Visual Database of Extremist Symbols, Logos, and Tattoos" at **www.adl.org/hate_symbols/default.asp.** The Website provides an overview of the signs, logos, and other symbols used by neo-Nazis, the Ku Klux Klan, racist skinheads, and other extremist hate groups. By increasing our awareness and knowledge of symbols such as these, we are better able to recognize and fight bigotry.

STEPPING OUTSIDE OF OUR COMFORT ZONES

Keeping comfortable or "playing it safe" might mean avoiding controversy, avoiding difficult dialogues such as those surrounding race and inequality, or interacting only with our "own kind." Whoever we are, moving beyond our comfort zones is a challenge. Yet, one of the best ways to develop our cultural intelligence is to expose ourselves to different perspectives.

 **Applied** · · · · · ──────────────────────

David Duke is a former leader of the Ku Klux Klan. Shortly after his gubernatorial bid in Louisiana, a New Orleans newspaper called Times-Picayune *began to plan a 6-month series titled "Together Apart: The Myth of Race." The series examined race relations through stories dealing with diverse personal experiences, histories, and perspectives on racism. Both during and prior to the series, the entire newsroom staff participated in diversity training in which they examined their own views on race, and tried to speak honestly about their roles and responsibilities as journalists. Controversial and volatile questions were addressed, such as when is the mention of race in a news story appropriate and when is it not?*

For the newspaper staff, it was a humbling experience. They were used to dealing with statistics, interviews, books, and the like, not definitions of racism. Keith Woods, the city editor in charge of the project, stated, "We were not that well equipped in the first place, so it was very clumsy to handle. There were a lot of trampled feelings [about race] . . . There was in fact a tremendous amount of strife that emerged as a result of diversity training and the race project. A lot of emotions because people were feeling put upon—every time you turned around, somebody was talking to you about this." Woods continues, "We didn't all emerge singing 'Kumbaya' and holding hands. But I think we are wiser, and, I daresay, a little better at handling race in [our newspaper] pages. I shudder less often when I read our newspaper." [6]

For each of us, there are different pockets of comfort and discomfort. Imagine you are an Asian American female who has been raised to defer to older males and always show them respect. Because of your Chinese heritage, you avoid confrontation. You are someone who does not want to "rock the boat." Now you find yourself seeking a leadership position at work, but you wonder whether your reluctance to be more assertive will hold you back. Indeed, you believe that your cultural norms help explain why there are not more Asian American females in upper-level management. But at the same time, you think that if you were more assertive, you would not be true to your cultural upbringing.

Examining our own assumptions may make us feel emotionally vulnerable. Furthermore, sharing how we feel, understanding what we feel, and learning

YOUR TURN · · · · · · ──────────────────

Briefly describe a time when you stepped outside of your comfort zone. What did you learn by doing this?

_____

_____

_____

_____

_____

about ourselves and others is not easy. One CEO of a large U.S. textile manufacturing company requires his top officers to join organizations in which they are the minority. As he sees it, the only way to break out of our comfort zone is to dialogue with others who might otherwise be invisible or seem much more different from us than they really are. The risk of engaging in "courageous conversations" such as these is real but worth it.

APPLYING ETHNORELATIVE ETHICS

Ethics is the study of what is considered right and wrong conduct. When it comes to dealing with people from different cultures, what is right is not always clear. There are many gray areas.

Many assume that being culturally sensitive means "anything goes." Since there is no one set of moral guidelines on which we can all agree, there are no universal ethical standards. This position, while it allows for more than one equally valid way of thinking, is problematic in the workplace. Regardless of their cultural values, workers must be held to certain standards of conduct. This is the position taken by **ethnorelative ethics**, understanding and evaluating behavior in its cultural context. Ethnorelative ethics requires us to step outside of ourselves and our culture in order to weigh how our actions affect others.

At the end of his seminars, one well-known author and speaker on the subject of ethics asks, "Why should we be ethical?" More often than not, the answer he hears is something along the lines of, "So I can have peace of mind," or "So I can look in the mirror and like what I see." Most of these answers focus on one's self instead of on the well-being of others. Perhaps this says something about cultural perspectives. Instead of only focusing on w.i.i.f.m. ("what's in it for me?"), doing what is ethical may require us to shift our cultural perspective. For example, we might ask what is the right or ethical thing to do from a group or organizational or even a global point of view?

Imagine being an editor of a magazine. One of your jobs is to decide what should be included in your publication and what is not appropriate. Recently, you and your staff debated whether to include a cartoon of the prophet Mohammed. The cartoon depicts Mohammed wearing a turban in the shape of a bomb. Reaction from your staff is mixed. Most of your staff sees it as appropriate social commentary while one staff member considers it insulting and even blasphemous. She points out that Muslims are absolutely forbidden from drawing images of the Prophet Mohammed, let alone images that depict him as a terrorist. As with many ethical questions, looking at this issue from different cultural perspectives makes this decision extremely difficult. Regardless of what you decide, people will accuse you of being biased.

If we do not apply ethnorelative ethics, we limit our understanding. In each of the following real-life situations, consider at least one perspective other than your own:

- A patient will not allow a Black doctor to operate on him.
- An employee refuses to sign a diversity policy statement requiring him to respect the beliefs of others, including gays and lesbians.
- A woman wonders if she should quit her job in order to have more time to "serve" her husband.

What is offensive or inoffensive, acceptable or unacceptable, and moral or immoral may be hard to determine. For instance, while some behaviors are clearly out of line at work, determining the appropriateness of other behaviors requires more information, deliberation, and perhaps advice from those in positions of authority. In these instances, reflecting on how cultural expectations interrelate with definitions of right and wrong can only help matters.

YOUR TURN   . . . . .

Ethical questions may arise in our dealings with the public. For example, imagine you are a phone operator who speaks fluent English with a noticeable accent. After working on the job for three months, you talk to a customer who refuses to talk with you or in her words, "any other operator who has an accent." She requests that you transfer her call to someone who "speaks good English." Should you accommodate the customer's bias, even though you know you are perfectly able to answer her question? Why or why not?

_____

_____

_____

_____

GETTING UP CLOSE AND PERSONAL

Our ability to learn from others, understand their reality, and shift perspectives with them is influenced by a number of variables. One of the most important is the closeness or intimacy of our interaction. Years ago, a sociologist by the name of Emory Bogardus developed a scale designed to measure this aspect of human relations.

As defined by Bogardus, **social distance** is a person's willingness to accept people of various racial and ethnic categories in various situations. According to research by Bogardus, we have a harder time accepting people we perceive as socially distant from us. For instance, Whites in his study were more apt to distance themselves from African Americans than from Europeans and Canadians.[7]

 ## Where Am I Now?

DIRECTIONS: In Table 5.1, place an X for each situation in which you would accept a group member.

Table 5.1 •

Relationships		Groups						
		Muslims	South Africans	Canadians	Mexicans	French	Cubans	Jamaicans
Social Distance	Accept as a close friend outside of work							
	Accept as a close friend at work							
	Accept as a mentor at work							
	Accept as a casual acquaintance at work							

YOUR TURN   • • • • • •

Examine your answers in the preceding exercise. Do you have a tougher time shifting perspectives with people you keep at a distance? Explain.

_____

_____

_____

_____

_____

With greater cultural diversity, it is difficult to shift perspectives, especially with people from whom we feel very distant. Social psychological research points to our tendency to gravitate to those whose experiences, values, and beliefs seem similar to ours. Increasingly, we need to put ourselves in situations where we expand our social circle. As we do, we will develop our ability to relate to and identify with those nationalities, religions, histories, and ways of life that may now seem "worlds apart" from us.

 Applied · · · · · · ──────────────

In The Scalpel and the Silver Bear, *Dr. Lori Arviso Alvord discusses how her medical school training made it difficult for her to relate to her Navajo patients. By talking with her patients, observing them, and listening closely, she developed better ways to respect their traditional beliefs and customs. Navajo patients did not respond well to the impersonal clinical manner of Western doctors. It was not acceptable to walk into a room and immediately ask probing questions, or to quickly examine patients by sticking something in their mouths or listening to their hearts with a stethoscope. Once Dr. Alvord learned to reach out to her patients as individuals, help them become more comfortable, and shift her own perspective regarding effective medical practices, she noticed something remarkable. She discovered that her patients were more trusting and had fewer operative or postoperative complications.*[8]

THE BOTTOM LINE

By shifting perspectives, we gain information. More information helps us understand others and move past first impressions. As our cultural intelligence increases, we develop a deeper, more accurate understanding of people's priorities and concerns.

Equally important, shifting perspectives helps us empathize, communicate, and connect. Developing this skill is a fluid, incremental, and cumulative process. Simply put, it takes time, lots of work, and plenty of practice. But the bottom-line benefits are substantial. Shifting perspectives nourishes and strengthens relationships, improves cross-cultural teamwork and communication, deepens our understanding of issues, improves decision-making ability, and allows us to adapt to cultural differences much more effectively.

A Look Back: I Have Learned

✓ _____ What shifting perspectives entails.

✓ _____ How shifting perspectives relates to taking the role of the other.

✓ _____ How people benefit from shifting cultural perspectives.

✓ _____ How culture and emotions interrelate.

✓ _____ How to show we are trying to understand.

✓ _____ Why awareness of history helps us to shift perspectives.

✓ _____ Techniques for listening and responding effectively.

✓ _____ What is meant by multiple consciousness.

✓ _____ How shifting perspectives allows us to interpret symbols.

✓ _____ Why we need to step outside of our comfort zones.

✓ _____ What is meant by ethnorelative ethics.

✓ _____ Why social distance is relevant to shifting perspectives.

✓ _____ How shifting perspectives addresses the bottom line.

Individual Action Plan

Think about one specific thing you can do to improve one of your skills in the area of shifting perspectives. Then complete the following plan during the next _____ (state time period).

Specific skill I want to improve first (refer to list of Performance Skills at the beginning of the chapter):

_____

My strategy:

_____

_____

_____

In order to develop this skill, I will:

_____

_____

_____

Possible obstacles include:

_____

_____

_____

Resources I need:

_____

_____

_____

_____

I will measure my progress by:

_____

_____

_____

_____

Notes

1. Jonathan Pitts, "Beauty That Is More Than Skin Deep," *Baltimore Sun*, September 25, 2005, p. 1E.

2. Paul Ekman, *Face of Man: Universal Expression in a New Guinea Village* (New York: Garland Press, 1980); Catherine Lutz, *Unnatural Emotions: Everyday Sentiments on a Micronesia Atoll and Their Challenge to Western Theory* (Chicago: University of Chicago Press, 1988).

3. Daniel Goleman, *Working with Emotional Intelligence* (New York: Bantam, 1998).

4. Arturo Madrid, "Missing People and Others: Joining Together to Expand the Circle," *Change*, 20, May/June 1988, pp. 55–59.

5. W. E. B. Du Bois, *The Souls of Black Folk: Essays and Sketches* (Chicago: McClurg, 1903).

6. "Topics: Civic Communication." Online 7/27/03. Available: **www.cpn.org/topics/communication/neworleans.html.**

7. Emory Bogardus, "Social Distance and Its Origins," *Sociology and Social Research*, vol. 9, July/August 1925.

8. Lori Arviso Alvord and Elizabeth Cohen Van Pelt, *The Scalpel and the Silver Bear* (New York: Bantam, 1999).

CHAPTER 6

• • • • • • • •

CQ MEGASKILL: INTERCULTURAL COMMUNICATION

Performance Skills

- *Understanding the process of communication*
- *Recognizing different forms of nonverbal communication*
- *Understanding communication styles*
- *Evaluating our intercultural communication skills*
- *Recognizing cultural misunderstandings*
- *Avoiding barriers to intercultural communication*
- *Learning to listen*
- *Tuning in to conversational gender gaps*
- *Using electronic communication effectively*
- *Understanding intercultural communication as a bottom-line issue*

REFLECT BEFORE READING

Answer true or false (answers are given at end of chapter).

_____ 1. When people raise their voices, we can assume that a heated argument has begun.

_____ 2. In comparison with European Americans, Asian and Hispanic cultures tend to place more emphasis on developing relationships before focusing on the task at hand.

_____ 3. In many Southern European and Latin American countries, there is a strong reluctance to assign decision making to a subordinate.

_____ 4. Regardless of one's cultural background, it is important to be open and honest about the reasons behind a misunderstanding.

• • • • • • • ━━━━━━━━━━

INTRODUCTION

Culture and communication are closely interwoven. Our culture influences the way we view communication, as well as when, where, and how we communicate. Moreover, culture shapes how we view problems, participate in groups and organizations, and view our coworkers and customers.

Understanding and appreciating the connection between communication and culture enhances our ability to communicate effectively. By building our cultural intelligence, we gradually become more sensitive to cultural cues and how to adapt to make ourselves better understood. Considering the frequency of cultural misunderstandings and conflict, it is abundantly clear that this is not easy by any means. By opening ourselves up to cultural differences, increasing our knowledge of how culture is acting on us, and finding common ground, we will grow in our ability to express ourselves, listen, and learn from others.

THE PROCESS OF COMMUNICATION

❓ Where Am I Now?

1. When I think about how well I communicate, I tend to focus almost exclusively on what I say rather than on my body language. Does this statement apply to you? Explain.

   _____

   _____

   _____

   _____

2. Does the way I communicate differ from those around me at work, at home, and in other settings? Explain.

   _____

   _____

   _____

   _____

3. Think of someone who knows you very well. Explain how that person would describe the way you communicate.

   _____

   _____

   _____

   _____

4. What might I do differently to communicate more effectively with people from diverse cultural backgrounds?

_____

_____

_____

_____

_____

Communication refers to the process by which we exchange ideas, feelings, and symbols of all kinds in a way that can be understood by others. When done effectively, communication can build trust, empathy, and respect. But when ineffective, it can create misunderstandings, build walls of mistrust, and make any group activity that much more difficult.

Communication is **socially constructed**, meaning it is learned through interaction with others. Moreover, it shapes our cultural lens or our perception of reality. Misunderstandings develop because we fail to understand and acknowledge that our cultural lenses vary. At times, we may assume that "I am the world." Consequently, we find it difficult to step outside of ourselves and respect people who do not communicate the same way we do.

As a process, communication is ongoing and always changing. In addition, it is **systemic**, meaning communication involves a number of interrelated parts. We cannot fully understand communication without examining the larger context or system in which it takes place. This examination includes the **organizational culture:** the behaviors, values, rules, and social relations found within an organization.

Consider communication at a financial consulting firm. Within this organization is an unwritten code of conduct. More specifically:

- Organizational values are not backed up by time, commitment, or money.
- Feedback from supervisors is intermittent at best.
- Unethical practices are widely ignored by senior-level managers.
- Training and development is only offered to a select few.
- Community outreach is not a priority.

Clearly, this organizational culture will not only negatively influence communication among employees and managers, but will also affect communication with customers and the surrounding community.

RECOGNIZING DIFFERENT FORMS OF NONVERBAL COMMUNICATION

YOUR TURN   · · · · · · ━━━━━━━━

List the different ways of communicating nonverbally.

_____

_____

_____

_____

_____

According to noted social anthropologist Edward T. Hall, communication is not simply *saying* what we mean. Rather, more than half of our communication is nonverbal. **Nonverbal communication** embraces all of the ways in which we communicate other than words themselves. Although nonverbal communication is commonly referred to as "body language," it is much more than that. Eye contact, gestures, stance, facial expressions, use of space, and even personal images such as dress and jewelry are just a few examples. Our nonverbal communication frequently reveals something about our feelings and attitudes. But because of its subtlety, we may not be aware of the messages we are sending or receiving.

We learn to express ourselves nonverbally just as we learn language. Because it is acquired, nonverbal communication is relative, meaning it varies from person to person, situation to situation, and culture to culture. Linguist Ray Birdwhistell noted that "we have found no gesture or body motion which has the same social meaning in all societies."[1]

YOUR TURN   · · · · · · ━━━━━━━━

On a scale of 1 to 10 (1 = poor, 5 = average, 10 = excellent), how would you rate your nonverbal communication skills as a receiver? Explain.

_____

_____

_____

As a sender? Explain.

_____

_____

_____

UNDERSTANDING COMMUNICATION STYLES

When we practice something important to communicate, we usually rehearse what we will *say*. Yet research shows that what we *say* may not be nearly as important as *how* we say it. Differences in how we express ourselves are called **communication styles**.

Communication styles can differ depending on any number of cultural variables. These include nationality, geographical region, ethnicity, gender, race, economic status, and age. Even though we may be initially surprised by differences in communication styles, understanding them will help us work through these moments and ascertain what is happening.

Because of cultural and individual differences, there is a tremendous variety in the way we send and receive messages. For instance, some of us may talk in circles or loops and repeat ourselves for emphasis. Or we may tend to line up our thoughts sequentially and repeat ourselves very little if at all. To illustrate further, communication styles may be

- Indirect or direct.
- Emotionally charged or emotionally flat.
- Personal or strictly business.
- More or less confrontational.
- More or less connected to personal relationships.
- More or less connected to accomplishing a task.
- Varied in many other ways.

Owing to the complexity of the number of variables making up communication styles, there is no definitive and comprehensive list. However, given this complexity, it is clear that friction and misunderstandings are inevitable when people with largely varying styles attempt to communicate.

Where Am I Now?

Below you will find several communication styles. Each style represents a range or continuum extending from one extreme to another. On each of the following continuums, place an **X** on the line to represent where you see yourself.

To communicate ideas, I emphasize:

Opinions and .... Logic and facts
personal
experiences

I tend to communicate by:

Lining up my .... Expressing my
thoughts   ideas in loops
step-by-step

Most of the time my messages focus on:

My concern .... Accomplishing
for others   a task

As we become more knowledgeable about various communication styles and their prevalence in certain cultural settings, we must be careful not to over-generalize or stereotype. Cultural norms do not apply to every individual in a given culture. For example, research shows that Hispanics tend to focus more on relationships when they communicate and are less preoccupied with just getting a job done. Of course, this style does not apply to every individual who is Hispanic.

TO LEARN MORE

Using google.com or another search engine, key in "communication styles." Click on some of the links returned for your search. How many different communication styles can you find? List three things you have never thought of before.

_____

_____

_____

_____

_____

THE NATURE OF INTERCULTURAL COMMUNICATION

YOUR TURN · · · · · ·

Describe an experience in which you had an extremely difficult time communicating with someone from another culture. What made this experience so challenging?

_____

_____

_____

_____

As the workplace and marketplace become more multicultural, understanding managers, coworkers, or clients who speak a different language or share a different perspective becomes more of a challenge. **Intercultural communication** is the process by which people from different cultures relate or "connect" with each other by exchanging ideas and feelings and creating meanings. Regardless of who we are, where we live, or what we do for a living, communicating with people who do not share our cultural lens and life experiences is becoming an everyday experience. Consequently, intercultural communication, also referred to as cross-cultural communication, is no longer a nice skill to have; it is a necessity.

Different cultures may have different meanings for the same word or symbol. Many words and symbols have no direct translation. Vocabulary, slang, and dialects can also be problematic. What is needed goes far beyond word-for-word translation. If we are going to relate effectively to customers who do not speak our language, we must develop our ability to communicate across cultures.

In order to understand intercultural communication and appreciate its importance, we need to develop an awareness of how cultural perspectives can shape interaction. For example, cultures have different ideas about personal space, eye contact, and touching. Thus, these behaviors are **culturally specific**, meaning they can only be understood in the context of a particular culture.

Consider how we introduce ourselves. Without thinking, many of us shake hands. According to Robert Axtell, a retired U.S. businessman and author of _Gestures: The Do's and Taboos of Body Language Around the World_, this gesture is not universally accepted. In Japan, for example, friends and business associates greet each other with a polite bow. And in a business setting, the person with the least status bows first and deepest. Whereas many U.S. citizens may view a bow as a sign of subservience, Japanese view this traditional greeting quite differently; to them it shows respect.

EVALUATING OUR INTERCULTURAL COMMUNICATION SKILLS

True or False? The first step in developing our intercultural communication skills is to become familiar with the rules, values, and customs of other cultures.

Typically, when we think about promoting effective communication in the workplace, we start with other people such as the custodial worker who never smiles, the secretary who seems unaware of her body language, or the supervisor who comes across as insensitive and uncaring. Although the behavior of others is important, any assessment must start with us.

You might start this process by answering the following questions:

? Where Am I Now?

DIRECTIONS: For each statement, mark M (most of the time), O (often), S (sometimes), R (rarely), or N (never).

1. _____ When I find myself in a culturally diverse group of people, I change the way I communicate depending on the group.

2. _____ When I communicate cross-culturally, I pay close attention to nonverbal communication.

3. _____ I am mindful of how my own culture impacts my ability to communicate cross-culturally.

4. _____ I am mindful of the potential for misunderstanding when I communicate cross-culturally.

5. _____ When I communicate electronically, I am aware of cultural differences.

Initially, we need to examine all of the ways in which *we* communicate as well as the rules, values, and communication patterns of *our* culture. Rather than just paying attention to what words we and others use, we need to be mindful of the context of the situation and who is communicating. Furthermore, examine how cultural influences shape our ability to communicate cross-culturally. For example, when we ask a question of someone, how long do we wait for a response? We refer to this as **wait time**. Research shows that wait time varies significantly from one culture to another.

As we communicate, cultural intelligence requires us to look at ourselves through the perspectives of others, and then reflect on

- What was communicated
- What assumptions are we and others making
- What cultural differences might exist

This is not easy to do, since at any given moment, we are sending, receiving, *and* interpreting messages.

RECOGNIZING CULTURAL MISUNDERSTANDINGS

Due to the complexity of intercultural communication, it is easy to be misunderstood. For instance, misunderstandings can result from differences in the meanings cultures attach to the volume and animation of our speech, our closeness when standing, the directness of eye contact, and even the amount of silence. In order to identify and understand different styles or ways of communicating, we need to be aware of some of the "mixed meanings" that may emerge in the workplace and elsewhere. A few examples follow.

Disagreement

Many Asians avoid raising controversial issues, showing anger, or even disagreeing, particularly with superiors. In particular, they avoid saying *no* in order to save face and maintain people's dignity. The concept of saving face is very important in Asian cultures; and it may very well mean repressing one's own feelings and thoughts to maintain harmonious relationships. For example, a response of *yes* to the question, "Do you understand?" may not indicate the person understands. Rather, it might mean, "Yes, I hear you," "Yes, I will try," or "Yes, I will do my best."

Silence

> **YOUR TURN** · · · · · ——————
>
> In professional settings, do you ever consider how you and others around you perceive silence differently? How might this affect your ability to communicate effectively?
>
> _____
>
> _____
>
> _____

European Americans tend to be uncomfortable with silence, and therefore avoid silence for any length of time by being talkative. Native Americans, on the other hand, are apt to view silence quite differently. One of the skills they value most is the individual's ability to remain silent. Similarly, many Asians believe in the importance of listening to what is verbalized *and* what is not verbalized.

Space

YOUR TURN   · · · · · ·

When you are talking to strangers in a public setting, how far away do you generally stand? What about friends? Does gender, race, sexual orientation, or the topic of conversation make a difference?

Why? _____

_____

_____

_____

_____

While advising students at Harvard Business School, anthropologist Edward Hall developed the concept of **proxemics**, the cultural use of space. In *The Hidden Dimension*, Hall outlines proxemic theory.[2] The way we perceive space and the distance we maintain between ourselves and others is molded and patterned by our cultural backgrounds and the social setting. While Hall feels that space sends a message just as much as the words we use, it is not something we think about; hence the title of his book.

As an anthropologist, Hall observed that when talking to each other, North Americans kept further apart than either Arabs or Latin Americans. In these latter cultures, keeping a greater distance apart from someone may be viewed as a sign of unfriendliness or even disdain. Besides physical distance, proxemics includes variables such as vocal volume, eye contact, and the degree of touching.

Other proxemic researchers have tested Hall's theory. In general, they have found that a host of factors may impact conversational distance. While culture is certainly important, so too is the topic of conversation, an individual's status, and surrounding noise. Burgoon and Hale, both communications professors, remind us that individual differences within a culture must be taken into consideration as well.[3]

Eye Contact

YOUR TURN   · · · · · ·

When talking to an acquaintance at work or school, how much eye contact do you make?

_____

_____

For European Americans in the United States, eye contact generally symbolizes sincerity, interest, and respect. However, in many Asian cultures such as Japan, Korea, and Thailand, it is avoided and seen as threatening and rude. Similarly, closing one's eyes in the United State is apt to be construed as a sign of boredom. In Japan, however, it is seen as a way to concentrate on listening.

Touch

YOUR TURN • • • • • •

Under what, if any, conditions might you physically touch someone when talking in a public setting?

Devout Muslims and Orthodox Jewish men refrain from any physical contact with women outside of their family. This even includes shaking hands. In many cultures, it is taboo to touch certain areas of the body. Many Chinese, for instance, do not want to be touched on the head. Korean store owners may avoid putting change in a person's hand because they think it is rude to touch someone they do not know. To those who expect change to be placed in their hands, this behavior may be misconstrued as disrespectful.

AVOIDING BARRIERS TO INTERCULTURAL COMMUNICATION

YOUR TURN • • • • • •

Picture yourself speaking on the phone to a potential client. The client's accent makes it very difficult for you to communicate. What assumptions, if any, might you make about this person because of his or her accent?

Figure 6.1 • What Does a Smile Communicate?

SOURCE: DILBERT: © Scott Adams/Dist. by United Feature Syndicate, Inc.

Cultural misunderstandings in the workplace result from a variety of factors that we can control and correct. These include:

- *Misreading nonverbal communication.* Nonverbal communication is **symbolic**, meaning it represents something. Consequently, it is often ambiguous (see Figure 6.1). What does a smile represent to you? In an effort to improve customer relations, one large chain of stores required all of their employees to smile when they established eye contact with a customer. However, they had to discontinue this policy after a short period of time. A number of female employees complained that male customers were harassing them, reading something quite personal into this behavior.

- *Stereotyping.* **Stereotypes**, those overgeneralizations applied to every person in some group, distort our perceptions and, in turn, undermine our ability to connect with others. If we stereotype, we may be less prone to hear people or value what they say. People who are frequently targets of stereotypes are affected as well. For example, women, people with disabilities, the elderly, and other minorities may hesitate to ask questions, not wanting to reinforce stereotypes that portray them as less intelligent.

- *Lack of awareness of different communication styles.* For instance, coworkers who emphasize logic and accuracy may be seen as cold, aloof, and manipulative, while those who are more personal and animated can be viewed as unstable and argumentative. When differences such as these emerge, misunderstandings may be more attributable to style than substance.

- *Lack of empathy.* **Empathy** is the ability to develop an intimate understanding of another person's feelings, motives, and thoughts. In *The Seven Habits of Highly Effective People,* Stephen Covey addresses empathy when he discusses Habit Five: "Seek first to understand and then to be understood." Failing to observe messages that are not necessarily communicated through words will limit our ability to be empathetic.

- *Poor listening skills.* In many cases, the key to customer or client service and satisfaction is **listening,** an interactive process that involves receiving and organizing information as well as interpreting, responding, and remembering. According to a recent Gallup poll, more than 45,000 patients gave their doctors high ratings for care and compassion but much lower ratings for communication skills. Many patients questioned the accuracy of diagnoses by doctors who did not take the time to listen to them. When patients did speak, doctors interrupted them before they could finish.[4]

- *Ethnocentric perceptions.* When we encounter a situation we do not understand, there is a tendency to assume it is wrong or weird rather than just different. This is called **ethnocentrism,** the assumption that our way of doing things is naturally superior. Anthropologist Mary Catherine Bateson (1968) has noted that when we first encounter others who seem different, our reaction is typically ethnocentric.[5] Because of this, we will tend to devalue what they say. This can short-circuit communication and make any kind of meaningful dialogue impossible.

YOUR TURN   · · · · · ·

Which of the aforementioned cultural misunderstandings do you encounter most often? Explain and give an example.

_____

_____

_____

_____

Recently, I found myself in an airport terminal seated next to a group of businesspeople who were meeting over breakfast. The group was made up of four men and one woman. It soon became clear that the oldest male was in charge. As the other men talked and made suggestions, the leader would look at them, nod his head, and ask follow-up questions. Every time the lone woman gave her input, the leader would look down or look at the other men and smile. His response to the woman was littered with short comments such as, "We've done that already" or simply "Yes. Well," and then he would proceed to address the men.

If I had shared my observation with the leader of this group, what do you think would have been his reaction? Developing cultural intelligence means questioning our own values, assumptions, and behaviors. Acknowledging personal barriers helps us reassess our own communication and move beyond denial. Only then can we look for specific ways to promote effective communication. Learning to listen is a good place to start.

YOUR TURN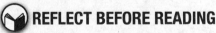

You are asked to head up a work group to discuss the need for cultural diversity training. You call a meeting with the idea of seeking input from team members. You make it clear that you want them to be open, honest, and even critical. Because of their cultural background, a number of people are hesitant to voice their concerns and question those in authority. What can you do to get the feedback you need?

_____

_____

_____

_____

LEARNING TO LISTEN

REFLECT BEFORE READING

Do you

- Hear only what you want to hear?
- Talk excessively?
- Jump to conclusions?
- Grow inattentive and passive as you listen?

Developing intercultural communication skills means becoming a two-way communicator. Do not think of communication as a one-way process in which the sender transmits information to the receiver. Through soliciting feedback, careful observation, and active listening, we enhance our communication skills by receiving and sending information contemporaneously.

Active listening is interactive. It requires diligence and practice. Three specific skills necessary for active listening are attending, summarizing, and clarifying.

1. *Attending.* Using nonverbal behaviors to show that you hear and are interested. These might include facial expressions, posture, and gestures, as well as listening noises such as "Hum," "OK," and "Ah-hah."
2. *Summarizing.* Restating the essence of what you hear. As you do this, be attuned to feelings as well as the facts.
3. *Clarifying.* Using open-ended questions to make sure you understand. You might ask "How did you feel when . . . ?" or "Do you have anything to add?"

YOUR TURN   · · · · · ———————————

Which of these three listening skills—attending, summarizing, clarifying—do you think you need to work on the most? Explain.

_____

_____

_____

Listening is an active process that requires just as many skills as speaking effectively. With intercultural communication, active listening is even more important. Why? Because it is difficult to be attentive and assign meaning to a message that may be difficult to understand. When you have a hard time relating to a speaker, it requires more discipline to put aside your own initial thoughts and focus on what the speaker is really thinking and feeling. Finally, we do not have the luxury of solely listening for content. We need to pay attention to all factors that may give us a better understanding of the message.

According to Hall, the context of a situation can significantly alter the meaning of a message. This is particularly true in cultures Hall identifies as high context cultures.[6] China, Korea, Greece, and many Arab countries are examples of *high context cultures*. In these countries, what is not said but is understood often carries more weight than what is said or communicated in writing. Personal relations and trust play a key role in negotiations and agreements. In *low context cultures*, the focus is more on the message itself, whether verbal or written. Scandinavian countries as well as the United States, Germany, and Switzerland, typify low context cultures. While handshakes and verbal agreements are common in these countries, they are not sufficient. Contractual agreements are viewed as "good business."

Of the total time spent communicating, 23% is devoted to speaking, 22% to reading and writing, and 55% of the time involves listening.

(Estimate by U.S. Department of Labor)

DID YOU KNOW?

TUNING IN TO CONVERSATIONAL GENDER GAPS

YOUR TURN   · · · · · · ────────────

Have you noticed differences between the way men and women communicate? If so, list some.

_____

_____

_____

_____

_____

According to Deborah Tannen, a Georgetown University linguistics professor, gender influences the way we communicate. Interestingly, she views talk between men and women as intercultural communication (see Figure 6.2). Take the simple phrase, "I'm sorry." Women, Tannen found, frequently do not say "I'm sorry" to apologize for something they did, but rather, to express concern or empathy.

Another source of confusion occurs when something needs to be done. A man is more apt to be straightforward, such as "Have this done by the end of the work day." A female, on the other hand, is more apt to say, "Do you think we could do this today?"

Tannen's book, *Talking from 9 to 5*, is based on data she collected by listening to tapes of the way men and women talk at work. Her extensive research on gender communication points to the importance of gender socialization. While growing up, boys learn to be more competitive and view relationships as hierarchical. Boys

Figure 6.2 • Intercultural Communication?

SOURCE: © Sally Forth © King Features Syndicate.

Table 6.1 • Men's and Women's Talk

Feminine Patterns: Talk tends to ♀	Masculine Patterns: Talk tends to ♂
• Be more expressive • Focus on feelings, relationships with subordinates and peers • Be more cooperative • Establish and nurture connections • Be more inclusive and tuned in to others • Provide feedback when others are talking • Be more indirect when making requests	• Focus on accomplishing tasks • Be more competitive • Be a means of exhibiting knowledge • Be more assertive • Establish one's expertise and identity • Be more indirect when admitting a fault or shortcoming

emphasize their status by giving orders and "taking center stage." On the other hand, girls are encouraged to be more cooperative. They learn to downplay ways in which one person is seen as better than another. Therefore, girls are apt to converse in ways that "save face" for others, even if this means putting themselves in an inferior position relative to another person. In effect, females look out for everybody's welfare during a group conversation.

Tannen argues that lessons learned in childhood carry over into the workplace. Male and female workers show different patterns of what Tannen calls **linguistic style,** meaning an individual's characteristic speaking pattern. A few examples appear in Table 6.1.

Not all men and women conform to these predictable communication behaviors. Male and female differences in linguistic style may not apply to the behavior of particular individuals. And factors such as personality, education, and other cultural variables may be more important than gender in explaining why we converse the way we do. Even Tannen would agree that a great variety of factors influence the way we communicate.

TO LEARN MORE

Go to Deborah Tannen's Web page at **www.georgetown.edu/faculty/tannend** to learn more about her work.

MULTILINGUAL SKILLS

YOUR TURN   · · · · · ·

Imagine you are interacting with coworkers from diverse cultural backgrounds who speak a multitude of languages. Although you speak English fluently, many of them speak very little English. What are two specific things you could do to promote intercultural communication in this situation?

(continued)

1. _____
   _____
   _____
   _____

2. _____
   _____
   _____
   _____

Learning more than one language will provide you with a tremendous edge in the job market today. As social and geographic boundaries continue to blur, companies are increasingly looking for employees with **multilingual skills**, meaning they are able to think and speak in a number of languages. Contrary to what we might think, the vast majority of the world does not speak English.

In a survey of nearly 1,500 U.S. business executives by TheLadders.com, a majority indicated Spanish was the most useful second language in business, followed by Chinese.[7] TheLadders.com is the world's leading Website for professionals and executives earning and seeking $100,000+ jobs. With the buying power of African Americans, Hispanics, Asians, and Native Americans almost tripling since 1990, the demand for multilingual employees has sky-rocketed.[8]

In some cases, U.S. businesses are paying for their customer service employees to take language courses. Proficiency or even minimal familiarity with foreign languages such as Spanish, Mandarin Chinese, and French is increasingly a money-making attribute at work. As an example, utility employees in the southeastern United States are taking four- to six-hour courses in Spanish to serve their customers better. A large national department store chain offers courses in Spanish on the company's intranet. Courses such as Conversational Spanish or Situational Spanish are proliferating. Although not designed to make employees fluent in Spanish, they do help employees learn specific information and key phrases and words to help them get started. And some companies, such as Marriott International, provide or pay for English courses for employees who have yet to master this language.

You do not have to master the language for it to be useful. *Hola, guten tag, namaste, nin hao, konnichi wa, ahlen.* This is just a sampling of the many ways in which we might greet someone in different languages. It is a good idea to learn some key phrases such as hello, good day or good morning, good-bye, how are you, thank you, and please. Phrases such as these show people you are trying and open the door for communication. Even if a translator is present, people will be more receptive to you if you can converse, even a small amount, in their native language. You can start by learning one word or catchphrase each day.

> **DID YOU KNOW?**
> According to the most recent census, almost 20% of the U.S. population speaks a language other than English at home. Of these people, 60% speak Spanish, 15% speak an Asian language, and the remaining 25% communicate in some other language. The U.S. Census lists 25 languages.

 Applied · · · · · ·

Imagine what it might be like to desperately need medical treatment but not be able to communicate what is wrong. Given the linguistic diversity of the U.S. population, doctors, nurses, and other health-care professionals encounter this situation more and more.

Dr. Francesca Gany, executive director of the New York Task Force on Immigrant Health at New York University's School of Medicine, recalls meeting a patient from Senegal in West Africa. The patient, who had Hansen's disease, formerly known as leprosy, agreed to be admitted to the hospital where Dr. Gany worked. Even though the patient was very nice and cooperative, he refused medication. Unfortunately, no one in the hospital spoke the patient's language. However, both Dr. Gany and the patient did speak some French. Dr. Gany discovered that he had already contacted his family in Senegal, who told him that the spirits were upset with him because he had left his family and country to come to the United State. The only way he was going to get better was through a healing ceremony. Since the patient was too sick to travel home, Dr. Gany asked the healer if he could conduct the ceremony over the telephone. The healer agreed and soon thereafter he performed the ceremony. After the ceremony, the patient took his medicine and his health quickly improved. This outcome was only possible because of Dr. Gany's ability to put herself in her patient's culture, adjust her language, respect his cultural beliefs, and tailor the treatment to fit his needs.

USING ELECTRONIC COMMUNICATION EFFECTIVELY

Electronic communication, the interchange of ideas and information through technology, expands the bounds of cultural diversity. More and more Web pages are being posted in multiple languages. Satellites as well as the Internet have the potential to transcend geographical and political boundaries and bring together businesses and customers throughout the world.

> **DID YOU KNOW?**
> According to a new survey by Simmons Graduate School of Management, a majority of working women think they are more apt to be heard and appreciated when they communicate online.

 **Applied** · · · · · ——————————————

As e-mail and electronic bulletin boards become a staple of communication in today's workplace, **master statuses,** or those positions that "stand out" in the eyes of society, tend to become less important. In other words, because of the anonymity of electronic communication, a person's age, disability, job classification, or rank may remain unknown. This, in turn, "levels the playing field" and makes it easier to move beyond labels.

However, electronic communication comes with significant risks. The casual or "quick and dirty" nature of e-mail appears more simple and inclusive than it really is. Because it is not face to face, we may be less sensitive to various communication styles and cultural nuances. In interactions on the Net, we can log off or initiate a conversation at will. The ease and speed of computer technology may make us less prone to think through the receiver's mood, vocabulary, personality, or cultural background.

When we communicate electronically, we can ill afford to ignore the influence of culture. People may not be familiar with the meaning of certain **emoticons**, culturally defined symbols that refer to emotions and thoughts such as :-x ("My lips are sealed"). Also, shorthand language such as *brb* ("be right back") and *LOL* ("laugh out loud") can cause confusion. Text is not likely to capture the intricacies of many emotions.

If we use bulletin boards or instant messaging, remember that someone who is not fluent in a language may have a hard time keeping pace and contributing as much as he or she would like. Furthermore, we should be open to the fact that some individuals and cultures prefer meeting in person if at all possible.

With cell phones, people can easily connect with each other, any time and any place. It is tempting to call without thinking through what we are going to say and how we are going to say it. And when thinking about cell phone etiquette, do not ignore your audience or the environment. In some cultures, people may expect greater sensitivity to cell phone use. For example, out of courtesy, Japanese may be more apt to cover their cell phones with their hands to minimize the noise level when they ride on public transit.

Since we do not have the luxury of immediate face-to-face feedback while communicating electronically, we should anticipate and be mindful of language issues. Even people who share a language may encounter problems, just as they might in face-to-face communication. People from Australia, Britain, and the United States may all speak English but use different vocabularies and slang. Moreover, the speaker may use the dictionary definition of a term while the receiver uses a different, more personal meaning. As a general rule of thumb, do not assume. Ask questions and seek clarification if in doubt.

TO LEARN MORE

Using google.com or some other search engine, find out the name of a company in your area. Visit that company's Website. Does this Website reach out to a multilingual audience? Explain why or why not.

_____

_____

_____

_____

THE BOTTOM LINE

Often, we exclude certain people by the way we communicate. While sometimes this is a conscious effort on our part, typically we are unaware of doing this. Examples of exclusive communication range from the blatant to the subtle. Perhaps we only hear what we want to hear because of our cultural bias. Using one style as opposed to a variety of communication styles may also limit who and what is heard.

Developing cultural intelligence makes us more aware of the payoffs of effective intercultural communication. Besides promoting understanding, intercultural communication builds and strengthens relationships. In the process, we discover common ground and shared interests. Use of good intercultural communication skills triggers the creativity of everyone. When we feel we are part of the process, we are more apt to be open to new approaches. By-products of effective intercultural communication are teamwork, diversity of imagination, productivity, and a sustained commitment to a common goal.

It is important to realize that individual and cultural differences do not have to be a source of divisiveness when we communicate in diverse settings. Nor do we need to feel as if we are constantly "walking on eggshells," out of fear that we might offend someone. By increasing our intercultural communication skills, we increase our comfort level in dealing with people who are different from us. Furthermore, the connection between intercultural communication and the bottom line becomes clearer.

• • • • • • • •   ━━━━━━━━━━━━━━━━━━━━━

A Look Back: I Have Learned

✓ _____ What is meant by communication.

✓ _____ Why communication in today's diverse workplace is so challenging.

✓ _____ To identify different communication styles, including my own.

✓ _____ What nonverbal communication encompasses.

✓ _____ What is meant by intercultural communication.

✓ _____ How to evaluate my own intercultural communication skills.

✓ _____ How cultural differences may lead to misunderstandings.

✓ _____ How male and female linguistic styles differ.

✓ _____ How electronic communication impacts our ability to communicate across cultures.

✓ _____ What I can do to improve my ability to communicate across cultures.

✓ _____ Why intercultural communication is a bottom-line issue in the workplace.

Individual Action Plan

Think about one specific thing you can do to improve your skills in the area of communicating across cultures. Then complete the following plan during the next _____ (state time period).

Specific skill I want to improve first (refer back to Performance Skills at the beginning of the chapter):

_____

My strategy:

_____

_____

_____

_____

In order to develop this skill, I will:

_____

_____

_____

_____

Possible obstacles include:

_____

_____

_____

_____

Resources I need:

_____

_____

_____

_____

I will measure my progress by:

_____

_____

_____

_____

Answers

Reflect Before Reading (see p. 127)

1. When people raise their voices, we can assume that a heated argument has begun. (*False*) Among many groups, including some Arab Americans, African Americans, Italian Americans, and Jewish Americans, an increase in volume is no cause for alarm. It simply means that friends or acquaintances are having an exciting or intense conversation.

2. In comparison with European Americans, Asian and Hispanic cultures tend to place more emphasis on developing relationships before focusing on the task at hand. (*True*) Different cultures approach tasks differently. European Americans are more inclined to focus immediately on the task at hand, and let relationships develop as people work together over time. Other cultures

may view this task-oriented focus as impersonal and even disrespectful. For them, the emotional exchange or the process of coming together should take place before getting down to work.

3. In many Southern European and Latin American countries, there is a strong reluctance to assign decision making to a subordinate. (*True*) The role individuals play in decision making varies. In the United States, for example, people often delegate decision making. For example, someone in authority assigns responsibility to a subordinate. In certain Latin American and Southern European countries, individuals tend to retain this responsibility. When groups are making decisions, differences emerge as well. Majority rule is commonplace in the United States, while in Japan consensus is more likely to prevail.

4. Regardless of one's cultural background, it is important to be open and honest about the reasons behind a misunderstanding. (False) Different cultures have different attitudes toward disclosure. Therefore, when communicating, it is important to remember that others may not share your feelings regarding what they are comfortable revealing. For instance, questions that focus on conflict in the workplace—what brought it about, the role of different people, how people are dealing with it, may seem completely OK to some but intrusive to others.

Notes

1. Ray Birdwhistell, *Kinesics and Context: Essays on Body Motion Communication* (Philadelphia: University of Pennsylvania Press, 1970), p. 35.

2. Edward Hall, *The Hidden Dimension* (Garden City, NY: Doubleday, 1966).

3. Judee Burgoon and Jerold Hale, "Nonverbal Expectancy Violations: Model Elaboration and Application to Immediacy Behavior," *Communication Monographs*, 55, 1988, pp. 58–79.

4. Mike Anton, "Aspiring Doctors See More Through Art," *Baltimore Sun*, 5/25/03, p. A10.

5. Mary Catherine Bateson, "Insight in a Bicultural Context," *Philippine Studies 16*, 1968, pp. 605–621.

6. E. T. Hall, *Beyond Culture* (Garden City, NY: Anchor, 1976).

7. PRWeb Press Release Newswire, "Memo to Global Executives: Learn Spanish," 4/12/05.

8. Jeffrey Humphreys, "The Multicultural Economy 2003," Selig Center for Economic Growth, University of Georgia, 2003.

CHAPTER 7

CQ MEGASKILL: MANAGING CROSS-CULTURAL CONFLICT

Performance Skills

- *Knowing ourselves first*
- *Recognizing clashing cultural realities*
- *Acknowledging differences without stereotyping*
- *Gaining cultural insight during conflict*
- *Tuning in to communication styles*

- *Avoiding ritual conversations*
- *Seeing conflict as an opportunity*
- *Achieving a win-win solution*
- *Embracing cultural dilemmas*
- *Recognizing the costs of conflict management*
- *Self-assessing*

 REFLECT BEFORE READING

Imagine a large expanse of water in which there are a number of icebergs. Most of each iceberg remains hidden beneath the surface of the water. When viewing the icebergs from above, they do not appear to come into contact with each other. However, at their bases, they often collide.

How might this analogy apply to conflict, and particularly cross-cultural conflict? In other words, does a similar dynamic occur in the workplace, at school, or in other areas of life?

- - - - - - - -

INTRODUCTION

Picture yourself working for a company. You are working on a team with someone who comes across to you as narrowminded and ignorant. Or perhaps you and your supervisor have very different values when it comes to the relative importance of family and work.

Imagine another situation in which you are being supervised by someone young enough to be your child. Your supervisor makes constant subtle references about your age, producing constant tension between the two of you.

Considering the innumerable ways in which we differ and the assumptions we make about each other, it is not surprising that conflict is rampant among employees today. Add to this the potential for conflict when employees interact with diverse customers and clients, and it becomes clear why it is difficult if not impossible to avoid conflict. Conflict is inevitable when people with different agendas, communication styles, languages, and interpersonal skills come together.

While conflict is a human universal, the way in which we deal with conflict varies from individual to individual and culture to culture. Having academic or professional credentials says very little about our skills in this area. In order to expand our cultural intelligence, we need to begin by understanding the dynamics of cross-cultural conflict. Then, we then need to equip ourselves with the necessary skills to deal with conflict in productive ways.

 **Applied** · · · · ·

The terrorist attacks of September 11, 2001, have increased the frequency of cross-cultural conflict in the workplace. In particular, people who are perceived to be Muslim, Arab, South Asian, or Sikh have increasingly been the target of intolerance. To help people understand their options, the U.S. Equal Employment Opportunity Commission (EEOC) Website provides questions and answers and describes various workplace scenarios. For instance, "I am a Sikh man and the turban that I wear is a religiously mandated article of clothing. My supervisor tells me that my turban makes my coworkers 'uncomfortable,' and has asked me to remove it. What should I do?"

Managing conflict means knowing our rights. If clothing, such as a turban, is religiously mandated, an employer has a legal obligation to grant this request if it does not impose an "undue hardship." If said clothing makes other workers feel uncomfortable, that is not an undue hardship. Contact the EEOC for more information (www.eeoc.gov/facts/backlash-employee.html).

THE MEANING OF CONFLICT

Conflict represents a clash between multiple realities or points of view. Specifically, we may clash or struggle over any number of things, including ideas, interests, values, agendas, and cultural misunderstandings. Our realities reflect a complex mixture of individual experiences and cultural backgrounds.

For example, people might experience conflict because they are vying for more money, power, fame, or prestige. Since these are scarce resources, people find themselves competing to get more of these things. Besides competition, people collide because of their diverse points of view. Human collisions may reflect underlying biases and cultural misunderstandings. Anytime people interact, the potential for conflict exists.

When we talk about parties in conflict, the word *parties* can refer to individuals, groups, organizations, communities, and societies. The primary focus in this chapter will be conflict among individuals. Regardless of who is involved, we need to examine how their cultural backgrounds might provide us with clues as to why the conflict exists and how to respond.

CONFLICT MANAGEMENT

Recently, employees at Kodak Corporation, a Fortune 500 multinational firm, received a controversial e-mail. The e-mail informed workers of an upcoming event, the Human Rights Campaign's Annual Coming-Out Day for people who are gay, lesbian, bisexual, or transgender. Further, the e-mail stated, "there are several things you can do to help that person feel comfortable in sharing his/her orientation in the workplace . . . Be supportive of the individual who wishes to share this information. Acknowledge his/her courage to publicly share this information." [1]

One employee, upset by the e-mail, responded to the entire Kodak workforce by writing an e-mail of his own. He wrote, "Please do not send this type of information to me as I find it disgusting and offensive. Thank you." Immediately, the company took action. The employee's supervisor wrote still another e-mail to the entire workforce apologizing for the individual's e-mail in question and reiterating the company's policy of creating an inclusive culture in which everybody is welcome. Additionally, he apologized to the firm's employees who were gay, lesbian, bisexual, or transgender.

This example illustrates **conflict management**, the ability to deal with conflict in an effective and constructive manner. Unlike conflict resolution, conflict management does not necessarily seek to terminate or even "solve" the conflict. The supervisor sought cooperation in the way the employee dealt with the conflict, with the understanding that the employee's values about this issue should have been kept private.

Although all parties at Kodak were asked to work together to find common ground, this did not occur. The employee who wrote the e-mail was eventually fired. He was fired not because of his views but because of the way he expressed them. Moreover, he refused to apologize for sending the e-mail.

YOUR TURN   · · · · · ——————

Think back to a specific situation in which you experienced conflict. How did you deal with the conflict?

_____

_____

_____

Did you manage it well?

_____

_____

_____

What could you have done better?

_____

_____

_____

CROSS-CULTURAL CONFLICT

 Where Am I Now?

DIRECTIONS: For each statement, mark M (most of the time), O (often), S (sometimes), R (rarely), or N (never).

When I experience conflict:

1. _____ I try to be constantly aware of my own cultural assumptions.
2. _____ I consider the possibility that cultural differences might have something to do with it.
3. _____ I try to tune in to other people's cultural assumptions.
4. _____ I "step back" and think about what is taking place before I react.

In order to make sense of conflict, we need to examine diverse perspectives, including our own. We might ask, "Did I misinterpret somebody's body language or what he or she said?" Or, "Is it possible he or she misinterpreted my actions or comments?"

People's socially learned behaviors, norms, values, beliefs, languages, and other components of their culture help us understand the causes of conflict and how we perceive and manage it. More specifically, different ways of communicating, leadership styles, gender roles, methods of getting work done, and orientations toward teaming are only a few of the cultural variables that we need to consider.

Cross-cultural conflict is conflict among people from differing cultural backgrounds. To some degree, all conflict is cross-cultural. But when people's backgrounds are significantly different, the likelihood of misunderstanding and mismanagement of conflict increases.

Consider what we value or consider important. Besides differences in values, all of us do not attach the same importance to what we value. As an example, people from different cultures might attach greater or lesser importance to religion, family, and work. If individuals are arguing over abortion or the importance of observing a religious holiday, their religious affiliation and the strength of their religious convictions are likely to influence their willingness to compromise or even listen to each other.

Beliefs about managing conflict vary a great deal. In certain cultures, people may discuss a conflict for days or however long it takes to arrive at a solution. Depending on one's cultural background, dealing with conflict may be more of a spiritual than a logical process.

The Japanese concept of *nemawashi* is an informal way of building consensus by first getting feedback and buy-in from everyone involved. Before the start of a meeting, for example, people already have an idea of what will be discussed. Giving people the opportunity to adjust their thinking ahead of time serves to minimize conflict and maintain harmony. *Nemawashi* may also be seen as a way of incorporating opposing views into a plan during prior consultation. While some may see *nemawashi* as artificial and undemocratic, it is important to respect the process. If conflict arises, move slowly. Confronting people and raising your voice is at odds with *nemawashi*.

YOUR TURN   · · · · · ·

Table 7.1 shows a number of workplace issues that often give rise to cross-cultural conflict. For each issue, place an X on the continuum where it best describes you.

Table 7.1 • Cultural Perspectives on Workplace Issues

Workplace Issue	Dominant Cultural Perspective in U.S.	Your Perspective	Another Cultural Perspective
Self-interest/ Collective Welfare	My own needs come first	....	Suppress my own interests for the good of the group
Family/Work Relationship	Keep work and family separate	....	Family and work are intertwined
Religion/Work Relationship	Religion should have no influence on business decisions	....	Religion has tremendous influence on business decisions
Criticism and Saving Face	To get the job done right, criticize people whenever necessary	....	"Saving face" and maintaining harmony are of utmost importance

THE DYNAMICS OF CROSS-CULTURAL CONFLICT

When cultural homogeneity or sameness exists, behavior is much more predictable. Communication is not as difficult. Mutual trust, social cohesion and cooperation are easier to develop. In contrast, cross-cultural interactions are more apt to lead to miscommunication, mistaken assumptions, and conflict.

All of us tend to be **culturally myopic** to some degree, meaning we are unable to see things and make connections beyond our own, limited world. Consequently, if conflict occurs, we see what *we* want and *our* reasons for wanting it. We have a much more difficult time seeing what *others* want and why.

Social scientists, including Gordon Allport, author of the seminal study *The Nature of Prejudice*,[2] have shown that without meaningful intergroup and intercultural contact, prejudice and conflict are likely. If we lack experience with culturally diverse populations, we are more prone to project our own assumptions onto others and assume similarity instead of dissimilarity. This can alienate people, shut down communication, and provoke conflict.

Historical Differences

Our histories are an important part of our culture. Whether a few years ago or generations ago, what took place in the past can shape who we are and how we interact at the present. Historical experiences between societies can also lay the groundwork for cross-cultural interaction among individuals.

As an example, knowledge of history can provide insight into the relationship between a patient and his doctor. For years, Dr. Kenneth Kipnis had ethic consultations at a number of hospitals in Hawaii; however, this case was different. An elderly Korean gentleman, suffering from a serious medical condition, refused medical treatment that promised a reasonably good chance of recovery. The patient gave no reason for his refusal. In spite of this, he indicated he wanted to be put on life support if he went into cardiac arrest. Dr. Kipnis's job was to make sense of this discrepancy. Why would the patient refuse possible life-saving treatment but request life support if his heart stopped beating?

The Korean patient and Dr. Kipnis talked for a long time. After being asked question after question, the patient asked if anybody had noticed that all of his doctors were Japanese. Suddenly, the patient's behavior began to make sense to Dr. Kipnis. During the early to mid–1900s, Imperial Japan had tyrannized Korea. As a result, many Koreans still harbored strong anti-Japanese feelings.

What surprised Dr. Kipnis was how he had not even considered this possibility, even though he had extensive experience dealing with other types of prejudices that were rooted in the past. For example, he had examined cases in which White racists did not want Black doctors, or Jewish patients who did not want to be treated by German physicians. But the history of Japan and Korea was far removed from his consciousness.

As an ethics consultant, he decided to honor the Korean patient's request and bring in a non-Japanese doctor. Otherwise, the patient would have died. Dr. Kipnis tries to treat patients in need with respect and understanding, even when their thinking is prejudicial and hateful.

Differences in Power

Power refers to a person's ability to control or influence others. In some cases, differences in power can lead to conflict. How we relate to each other may very well be impacted by how much power we have or how we view the unequal distribution of power. When we are treated a certain way because we are powerful or powerless, it can lead to conflict. Moreover, power can affect whether an open and honest discussion of conflict or differences is even possible.

Do you see power as a corrupting influence? While some cultures view power as problematic, others see it as a natural part of the social world. Many social relationships are hierarchical, meaning power defines how we relate to each other. Hofstede describes many Asian cultures as **large power distance cultures**, cultures in which people accept and do not question the fact that power is distributed unequally. In these cultures, it is assumed that certain people have more power because of their moral and ethical excellence. Additionally, there are any number of obligations that serve to unite people with varying degrees of power.

On the other hand, Hofstede found that other cultures such as the United States, Australia, and Israel view inequality differently. Because they are **small power distance cultures**, they seek to minimize differences in power as much as possible. Moreover, they view power as a source of abuse and work to "level the playing field." People in small power distance cultures see a disconnect between those with and without power.[3]

The implications for conflict between people from small and large power distance cultures are significant. Conflict can arise between those who are suspicious of power differences and those who accept them. For example, an individual from a small power distance culture might want to change the system and work for more egalitarian relationships between superiors and subordinates. But a person from a large power distance culture might disagree, and strive to keep things the way they are, expecting that those in power will help others in times of need.

KNOWING OURSELVES FIRST

Managing cross-cultural conflict starts with knowing ourselves — our culture as well as our skills in dealing with conflict. For instance, how might *my* values, beliefs, and ability to shift perspectives come into play? What groups do I identify with and how might they influence my orientation toward conflict? What are my statuses and roles and how do they affect the way I see myself and others?

As we try to understand conflict, we need to continually examine our thinking and behaviors. Conflict is relational; it involves you and at least one other person. Therefore, self-awareness is essential. Your responses to the following assessment will tell you something about your approach to people who think or act differently than you.

Where Am I Now?

Part of self-awareness is examining how we react to conflict. Below are six specific things you can do to deal with conflict effectively.

DIRECTIONS: For each statement, mark **M** (most of the time), **O** (often), **S** (sometimes), **R** (rarely), or **N** (never).

When I disagree with another person:

1. _____ I am open to looking at things differently.
2. _____ I work hard at keeping an open mind.
3. _____ I explore alternate ways of thinking or doing things.
4. _____ I focus on understanding the other person's values and needs as well as my own.
5. _____ I am aware of how my values influence the way I respond to conflict.
6. _____ I am aware of how my position and power influence the way I respond to conflict.

During disagreements, we should be making a conscious effort to do all of the things listed above. In assessing your answers, look at those statements to which you responded "rarely" or "never." Are you working on improving your skills in these areas?

RECOGNIZING CLASHING CULTURAL REALITIES

As our social experiences and knowledge change, so do our realities. Because the world in which we live is continually changing, people's realities are apt to differ and sometimes clash. Diverse histories, languages, positions and roles, family experiences, and people skills are apt to give rise to diverse impressions of the world. Therefore, our reality may not coincide with someone else's reality.

For example, different societies or different people within the same society may not agree on the "proper" roles of males and females. The norms of some societies make a sharp distinction between what males and females should and should not do. Traditional gender roles, such as men making the important decisions and women taking care of the home, predominate. In other societies, such as in the United States, males and females assume many of the same roles, and traditional roles are viewed by many as outdated and stereotypical.

When people from different cultural backgrounds interact, their realities regarding gender roles and decision-making can cause conflict. Imagine a woman in the United States who goes to a car dealer with the intent of making a purchase. After test-driving a new car that she likes very much, she is ready to negotiate with the salesperson. Following some discussion about the car's options and cost, the salesperson suggests to her that she consult with her husband before making a final decision. Offended by this suggestion, she decides to purchase the car elsewhere.

What we have here are clashing cultural realities. The salesperson lost a sale because he failed to recognize that his customer did not share his views regarding gender roles. Consequently, he had no idea why the customer never returned to finalize the deal. In this case, an opportunity was lost. The customer, a financially independent Hispanic woman, was clearly insulted by the salesperson's assumptions.

To deal with cross-cultural conflict effectively, we need to adapt and learn. In order to understand this conflict and avoid repeating this mistake, the sales representative needs to understand that his customers—male or female—may be offended by his assumptions about gender roles. Recognizing how and why our cultural realities may clash with those of other individuals allows us to anticipate and avoid costly conflict.

ACKNOWLEDGING DIFFERENCES WITHOUT STEREOTYPING

Acknowledging cultural differences without stereotyping can be a difficult balancing act. Additionally, what you interpret as cultural sensitivity might come across as stereotypical to another person.

For example, some African American college students at a liberal arts college in Virginia took exception to a textbook used in one of their communication classes. The book, written by Julia Wood, is titled *Communication in Our Lives.* Specifically, certain students found Wood's discussion of culture and its influence on communication to be stereotypical.

One example they cited has to do with a table the author refers to as "A Translation Guide." For example, Wood contrasts the European American meaning and the African American meaning for various terms such as *sister* and *brother.* To European Americans, sister and brother refer to family members. To African Americans, sister and brother refer to a Black woman and a

Black man. Another example offered by Wood is the phrase, "You call that dancing? My kid dances better." According to Wood, European Americans interpret that phrase to be an insult, whereas African Americans see it a little differently. They see it as a game of exchanging insults, sometimes called "slammin" or "jonin." The objective is to see who is more adept at putting the other person down.

Wood was taken aback by the students' criticism of her translation guide. After all, she addressed multicultural speech patterns in her book because speech patterns used by White males have traditionally been presented as if they are universal. Wood tried to show they are not and used research to back up her argument. But the students argued that they and their African American friends did not identify with these cultural differences and found them offensive.

Acknowledging differences without stereotyping is a difficult task. It is important to note that Wood mentions in the text that not all African Americans or European Americans communicate the same way. Yet, it is understandable that a table labeled a translation guide is apt to convey something quite different.

YOUR TURN   · · · · · ·

Can you think of a different, and maybe better, way to present this material on multicultural speech patterns?

_____

_____

_____

GAINING CULTURAL INSIGHT DURING CONFLICT

By reflecting on open-ended questions during conflict (see Table 7.2), you will gain cultural insight and understanding. These are sample questions that you may tailor to your particular situation. As you question and collect information, find time to step back and reevaluate, especially if communication is difficult and the process is not going smoothly. William Ury, author of *The Power of a Positive No*, refers to this as "going to the balcony:" taking a moment to slow down and analyze what is going on before you act.

When formulating additional questions, seek to understand rather than assign blame. Moving through this process does not necessarily require agreement. However, it does require you to understand other perspectives, and then be understood.

Table 7.2 • A Guide for Cross-Cultural Conflict Management

Defining the Conflict	Uncovering Communication Challenges	Coming to an Understanding	Analysis and Application
What is the conflict about? What cultural differences help explain the conflict?	Am I conscious of diverse communication styles? Am I demonstrating understanding of others' points of view? Are stereotypical assumptions interfering with communication?	How might cultural differences influence what parties are willing to do? Are cultural expectations influencing what parties want to happen?	Was I attuned to cultural differences throughout the process? What did I learn from this experience that will help me in the future?

TUNING IN TO COMMUNICATION STYLES

When people are confronted with cross-cultural conflict, communication is essential. Not only do we view conflict differently, but we also view the "right" way to communicate differently. Effective conflict management hinges to a large degree on being mindful that your communication style is one of many and that it is not better, just different (see Table 7.3).

Conflict can arise because differences in communication styles lead to misunderstandings. For instance, in the course of an argument we forget that

Table 7.3 • My Communication Styles

DIRECTIONS: Below are a variety of communication styles. For each style, place an **X** on the continuum to show where you think you are.

Only one person speaks at a time; you should not interrupt.	....	It's OK to talk over another person and break into a conversation.
Showing a lot of passion during an argument is positive because it conveys honesty.	....	Showing emotion should be avoided, because people might question your objectivity and self-control.
When arguing with someone, winning the argument is the primary goal.	....	Respecting the other person's feelings is most important.
It is best to deal with conflict directly, preferably through face-to-face meetings.	....	Conflict should be worked out privately, possibly through written communication.
It is important to be rational and stick to the facts.	....	Feelings and intuition should guide how you react.

people from different cultures show different levels of emotion and expressiveness. We might assume that someone who is task-oriented is not a caring person, or someone who is tuned in to others' feelings is not capable of making tough decisions.

Sometimes, conflict has more to do with style than substance. Consider what happens when one person insists on talking over another person. In a study of NASA astronauts, it was found that this could lead to conflict in emergency situations, especially if the other person does not understand that this might represent a cultural difference. In some cultures, it is just another way of inserting ideas into a discussion. According to the NASA study, "talk-overs" might be misdiagnosed as evidence of unclear thinking and a rush to judgment.[4]

When you start to argue with someone, perhaps your style of argumentation is based on giving the facts and being totally rational. Although you may consider this to be the correct approach, this communication style might be misinterpreted. For instance, many Saudis value the importance of intuition, and they avoid basing decisions solely on the basis of scientific research. To many Japanese, simply relying on data and logic is cold. To reach a decision, the feeling, or *kimochi*, has to be right.

Are you the kind of person who believes that conflict is best handled as openly and directly as possible? If so, how do you communicate with someone who thinks it is demeaning and embarrassing to air differences in face-to-face meetings? In some Eastern European countries, people believe conflict should be worked out quietly, possibly in writing.

AVOIDING RITUAL CONVERSATIONS

Ritual conversations are those traditional dialogues that occur over and over again and inhibit meaningful and productive communication. We fall into this rut because it is easier to relate to each other in ways that make *us* feel secure and comfortable. In effect, two individuals carry on a monologue and neither is willing to venture outside of his or her comfort zone. The result is that

- Information is collected and used to support prior views.
- Information that does not support one's views is dismissed.
- Personal biases reinforce one's position.
- Conflict is mismanaged.

Ritualistic conversations can revolve around the conflict between your own needs and the demands of your boss or coworkers. For example, cultural expectations may dictate who works over the holidays. Perhaps you find yourself being asked to work on a holiday because you are the only one in the office who is not married and does not have children. Whenever you raise this issue with the hope of finding an equitable solution for everyone, people tend to ignore what you are saying. Consequently, you no longer broach the subject even though there is an underlying tension between you and your coworkers around the holidays.

Or perhaps you have a boss who makes a habit of holding impromptu meetings at the end of the workday. Because of your child-care arrangements, you find it extremely difficult to stay for these meetings which can go on and on. You are experiencing **role conflict**, meaning the expectations associated with our multiple roles are pulling us in different directions. In this case, the expectations of your boss interfere with those of your family. You repeatedly suggest an alternative time for these meetings, but the response is always the same. In effect, you are told that other people have to sacrifice as well, and there is no single meeting time that is good for everybody. After a while, you hesitate to say anything more because no one else complains about the meeting time and you are relatively new on the job.

YOUR TURN   · · · · ·

Describe one argument about something important to you that always elicits the same response from you and another person. How might you respond differently?

_____

_____

_____

_____

_____

Avoiding ritual conversations takes practice. Remember, we choose how to respond. We can avoid a knee-jerk reaction by suspending judgment. This requires discipline, especially if we encounter a point of view that we see as incompatible with our own.

Peter Elbow, a professor at the University of Massachusetts, teaches his students to "try on" other perspectives through the Believing Game. Instead of routinely dissecting and criticizing another person's position and looking for flaws in his or her reasoning, Elbow asks students to (a) try to believe in the idea put forward by only looking at its strengths, and (b) not come to any conclusion until everybody has offered their reasons for supporting the idea. The Believing Game can be practiced in a group or individually.

By playing the Believing Game we are better able to understand issues from the other person's perspective. As an example, even though my coworker and I might not share family values or religious beliefs, we can still respect each other's position and needs. By engaging each other, thinking "outside the box," and exploring what we share in common, we are more likely to avoid the ritual conversations that make cross-cultural conflict more difficult to manage.

SEEING CONFLICT AS AN OPPORTUNITY

YOUR TURN   · · · · ·

Whenever conflict occurs, there is a winner and a loser. Do you agree? Explain.

_____

_____

_____

_____

Should we always try to avoid conflict? Whether we see conflict as positive or negative is apt to influence how we respond to this question. If the emphasis is on keeping order and maintaining the status quo, conflict is apt to be seen as destructive. In such an environment, we may avoid or smooth over conflict if at all possible.

Conflict can also be seen as something to acknowledge, regulate, and perhaps even cultivate. In the literature on conflict management, terms such as *creative conflict* and *creative contention* refer to the potential benefits of conflict. The Chinese pictograph for the word *crisis* comprises two symbols, one meaning danger and the other opportunity (see Figure 7.1). Conflicts, like crises, can spur innovation. Insofar as conflict tests the strength and viability of a position, it can lead to better decision making. Conflicts can uncover different perspectives and options for action. Also, conflicts afford the opportunity for greater cooperation and a sense of unity.

Figure 7.1 • Chinese Symbol for *Crisis*

Danger + Opportunity

Trying to always steer clear of any conflict can have negative consequences. It can stifle creativity and problem solving. People may feel compelled to think alike, even though they disagree. Avoiding conflict can also lead to denial. In reality, differences exist and will always exist. When deeply held values conflict, people can agree on solutions even though their values differ.

Peter Senge, author of the widely acclaimed book *The Fifth Discipline*, talks about how conflict becomes a positive in great teams and organizations. The exchange of conflicting ideas and feelings spurs creative thinking. In turn, this allows groups to think creatively, problem-solve more effectively, and generate better solutions.

With effective conflict management, our mindset shifts from who we can blame to what we can learn. Instead of simply conceptualizing conflict as a competition or a fight in which there is always a winner and a loser, we need to think of conflict in a different way.

> **DID YOU KNOW?**
>
> *Findings from surveys of 223 employees in four large companies reveal the value of conflict management when working on teams. Employees on teams who were able to manage their conflicts successfully were more apt to see their teams as effective. Further, there was a positive correlation between perceptions of team satisfaction and conflict management.[5]*

YOUR TURN · · · · · ·

What is one crisis that you have weathered during the past year? What good, if anything, came out of it?

_____

_____

_____

_____

ACHIEVING A WIN-WIN SOLUTION

A win-win solution to conflict requires us to think in terms of the best option for *us* rather than *me*. This is true whether the conflict is with a coworker, your boss, a customer, or anyone else you encounter. Win-win thinking requires (a) greater awareness of cultural commonalities and differences, (b) excellent communication skills, and (c) cooperative, integrative solutions.

All sides need to identify how their desired outcomes are similar as well as different. The solution, based on similar values, ethical beliefs, needs, and other points of agreement, represents the best or optimal way to address the conflict for everyone involved. If the parties cannot come to an agreement, then help can be sought in the form of a third party or mediator.

Reaching a solution that is agreeable and fair to everyone is not easy. To do this, you need to do the following:

1. *Start with the right mind-set.* Two or more perspectives are more productive than one. If you think that you have all the answers and know the best way to handle conflict, a win-win solution will be difficult if not impossible. A true dialogue in which everybody's perspective is shared, heard, and understood is absolutely necessary.

2. *Relate to each other as equals.* Collaboration involves equal respect for everyone, regardless of position, power, or cultural background. When we have a voice and people actively listen to us, we are more open to a win-win solution.

3. *Shift perspectives and show empathy.* Try to do more listening than defending or supporting your position. Specifically, you should be listening for similar concerns and goals.

4. *Question stereotypes.* If your image of the other person is overly simplistic or stereotypical, communication will suffer. Recognizing stereotypes allows us to move beyond labels and preconceptions. In doing so, we can communicate more effectively and make better decisions.

5. *Adapt your communication style.* Respect cultural differences in communication. This might mean questioning your assumptions. For instance, if you think someone is coming across as overly aggressive, might this represent a cultural difference? And if you believe in being open and honest when it comes to conflict, have you considered that others might view your behavior as intrusive and disrespectful?

6. *Recognize as many solutions as possible.* Brainstorming with people who may or may not be involved in the conflict is likely to generate a greater variety of creative and fair solutions.

7. *Identify and integrate the best plans for a win-win solution.* In evaluating the best plans or alternatives, consider what changes are necessary for a mutually beneficial solution.

EMBRACING CULTURAL DILEMMAS

People respond to interpersonal conflict in a multicultural environment in various ways. We may avoid the conflict or get angry and blame the other person. Or we may try to integrate and reconcile different points of view. This is the crux of what Trompenaars and Hampden-Turner refer to as dilemma theory. They discuss this theory at length in their book, *Building Cross-Cultural Competence: How to Create Wealth from Conflicting Values*. The book is based on data they collected from more than 50,000 surveys of businesspeople throughout the world.

According to this theory, cultural differences create seemingly contradictory differences or dilemmas. Rather than ignoring or smoothing over these differences, Trompenaars and Hampden-Turner argue we should embrace those positions and values that make us feel most uncomfortable. We do this by *not* locking into the idea that one position is right or good and the other is wrong or evil. Rather, we need to approach these differences with the idea that both parties in a conflict can learn something valuable from each other.

---

⑦ Where Am I Now?

Place an X on the dotted line to indicate how you feel about the following statements.

1. When making decisions at work, I feel it is better to be emotionally detached and objective.

   Agree .... Disagree

2. When discussing issues with a coworker, it is perfectly acceptable to express emotion.

   Agree .... Disagree

3. Becoming too emotional makes it difficult to think clearly.

   Agree .... Disagree

4. If I felt upset about something at work, I would not hesitate to express my true emotions.

   Agree .... Disagree

One of the cultural dilemmas cited by the Trompenaars and Hampden-Turner is called "neutral versus emotional." Neutral cultures (agreeing with statements 1 and 3 in the preceding "Where Am I Now") keep their emotions under control in business relations while emotional cultures (agreeing with statements 2 and 4) express their feelings openly. When Trompenaars and Hampden-Turner posed the question, "How would you behave if you felt upset about something at work?" participants in their workshops gave a variety of answers. For instance, participants from Japan, Ethiopia, and Poland were much more apt to adopt a more neutral orientation. In contrast, participants from Egypt, Cuba and Spain were much more likely to express their emotions openly (see Figure 7.2).

Regardless of our cultural background, we must strive to see beyond our limited view of others. Whereas one employee might separate emotion from objectivity, another employee might not. Understanding the value in both of

Figure 7.2 • Feeling Upset at Work

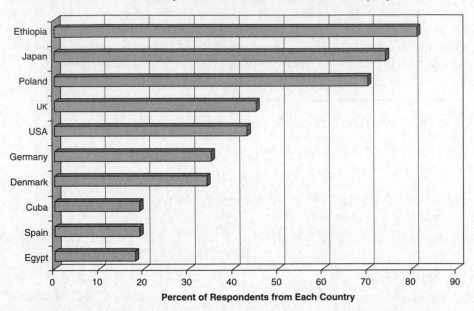

% of respondents who would NOT show emotions openly

Percent of Respondents from Each Country

SOURCE: Adapted from Fons Trompenears and Charles Hampden-Turner, *Riding the Waves of Culture* (London: Nicholas Brealey, 1997), p. 70.

these points of view is critical. Becoming emotional *may* make it harder to think straight. Similarly, trying to separate reasons from feelings *may* lead to a lack of trust and, at times, emotional leakage.

RESPONDING EFFECTIVELY TO MICRO-AGGRESSIONS

YOUR TURN   • • • • • •

According to the Council on American–Islamic Relations (CAIR), it is not uncommon for Muslims to hear comments by coworkers that lead to conflict and complaints. One common remark is, "Oh, he's such a peaceful person."

Why do you think this comment might trigger conflict?

_____

_____

_____

_____

Dr. Alvin Poussaint, psychiatrist, educator, and author of numerous studies on the health of African Americans, uses the word *micro-aggressions* to describe those everyday slights that often lead to conflict. It is helpful to remember that these slights are not necessarily mean-spirited and intentional. Often, they are the result of cultural misunderstandings.

Because of their diverse backgrounds, people may interpret the same action or comment very differently. Consider the following examples of micro-aggressions:

- A White supervisor comments, "Oh, he's so articulate," after hearing a Black employee speak "proper" English.
- A Latino questions why a White coworker should be leading a work initiative to promote cultural awareness.
- A woman tells her male coworker that he has no idea what it is like to raise a child while working full-time.
- Over lunch, a Korean is constantly being asked how Asians feel about various issues.
- In the restroom, an employee is upset because she overhears a coworker describe their new boss as a "slave driver."
- A visually impaired individual is complimented for her ability to look "so color coordinated" and fashionable.

Even though these comments might have been said with no intended malice, they sometimes come across as demeaning, insensitive, and biased. Understanding why may require us to put ourselves in somebody else's shoes. For instance, how might someone's cultural identity influence how they feel about the use of the term *slave driver*? How might diverse life experiences influence people's feelings toward being described as articulate?

YOUR TURN   • • • • •

Give an example of a micro-aggression that you find particularly offensive. What about your background might explain your views and feelings toward this micro-aggression?

_____

_____

_____

_____

When encountering a micro-aggression, our first impulse might be to lash out at the perpetrator or to ignore it altogether. Before responding, it helps to fine-tune your anger. If you suspect bias in a person's words or actions, you might want to probe further. What is the evidence? Are there alternative explanations? Perhaps you can solicit feedback from others as to how they might interpret what took place. While one option is to discuss what you read into a person's actions and ask for clarification, another option is to ignore the micro-aggression. In weighing your options, consider some of the situational factors we discussed previously, including the people involved in the conflict, the setting, the possible repercussions, and your state of mind.

When you are seen as the perpetrator, respect the other person's feelings and try not to get too defensive. Obviously, no one likes being accused of being insensitive or biased. Regardless of what someone is assuming about your behavior, it is helpful to

- Acquire information from the person who was offended. Specifically, what was offensive and why?
- Ask the person how he or she expects you to act and why.
- Thank the person for the feedback.
- Reflect on what you learned from this interaction.

If it is a misunderstanding, try to clarify what you meant. Also, communicating a heartfelt apology for what took place can be an effective way of dealing with the emotions that accompany micro-aggressions. Regardless of the conflict, saying "I'm sorry" may help achieve closure.

OTHER THINGS TO KEEP IN MIND

While no single approach to cross-cultural conflict works in all situations, it is important to remember the following:

- *Check assumptions.* As we take in information, we tend to make assumptions. If we do not unravel them, they can foster negative feelings and make conflict management more difficult. For example, we might notice that a person avoids eye contact. Rather than assuming, make sure you consider the possibilities regarding what this nonverbal communication might mean. Does it mean someone is inattentive, hostile, showing respect, or something else? For instance, direct eye contact is a sign of disrespect in many Hispanic and Asian cultures.
- *Listen actively.* Conflict can make it extremely difficult to engage in active listening. When we confront something that conflicts with our beliefs and

turns us off, we may become more emotional and self-centered. This makes it difficult to absorb and understand other ways of looking at the conflict. Restating what we think the other person is saying and asking for clarification can defuse emotions.

- *Build trust.* Without trust, people may be reluctant to share information out of fear that it might be used against them. How we define trust varies. To many of us, trust means that people can rely on what we say. However, suppose you find yourself doing business in a country such as China. In Chinese culture, trust means that we will protect other people's feelings and will not do anything that might cause them embarrassment.

- *Respect all parties involved.* In some cultures, people are hesitant to talk about emotions and the reasons for conflict. Therefore, they might feel uneasy about answering certain questions. Questions like, What is the conflict about? What part did you play in the conflict? and How do you feel about it? might seem intrusive. This is important to bear in mind before you assume you have an accurate reading on the views and feelings of those involved. However difficult it may be, respect people's decision to not open up or communicate about the conflict.

- *Deal with people's behaviors.* Criticizing an individual's beliefs as irrational or just plain wrong serves to erect a wall between you and that person. As an alternative, explain what behavior is preferable and why. For example, a worker in the United States might come from another country where workers enjoy flirting with each other. A good example of such a country is France, where exchanging glances and brushing up against each other is often tolerated. If this occurs in the U.S. workplace, behavior rather than beliefs should be the issue. By being aware of certain policies and their impact on the bottom line, you and your coworkers can avoid misunderstandings such as these.

- *Assess success.* One way of assessing the success of conflict management is to look at resulting relationships. Are you and other parties better able to communicate and deal with conflict, now and in the future?

> **DID YOU KNOW?**
> A recent National Urban League survey of U.S. workers addressed a variety of issues related to cultural diversity in the workplace. Fifty-seven percent of the respondents responded, "I trust my coworkers." Among African American workers, the level of trust was considerably less (44%). [6]

SELF-ASSESSING

Throughout this chapter, we have discussed a variety of conflict management skills. We can learn, practice, and improve these skills. In order to do this, we need to assess ourselves. The following self-assessment tool can be used when you encounter cross-cultural conflict (see Table 7.4).

Table 7.4 • Post Conflict Self-Assessment

Self-Assessment Form

Describe the conflict. _____

Place a checkmark next to the skills you believe you exhibited during the conflict.

I maintained my awareness of cultural differences regarding	I used the following communication skills	I applied conflict management skills by
____ Norms and values	____ Suspending judgment	____ Asking questions to gain cultural insight (see Table 7.2)
____ Possible stereotypical assumptions	____ Identifying values, goals, and feelings of others	____ Identifying cultural differences and influences
____ Communication styles	____ Using active listening skills	____ Exploring all positions and options
____ Power dynamics	____ Building trust	____ Avoiding ritual conversations
	____ Showing understanding	____ Seeking common ground
Comments:	Comments:	Comments:

RECOGNIZING THE COSTS OF CONFLICT MISMANAGEMENT

Mismanaged conflict is time-consuming and expensive. When we do a poor job of dealing with cross-cultural conflict, it can escalate and become more of a problem. Conflict mismanagement can negatively impact people's ability to work together and communicate well. It makes it more difficult for us to focus our efforts on producing a quality product. Customer service suffers. Additionally, there are the emotional costs. When conflict is handled poorly, feelings such as anger, fear, and alienation inhibit synergy and lessen productivity.

On an organizational level, the mismanagement of cross-cultural conflict can alienate people to the point that groups become polarized, morale suffers, and people consider changing jobs. Employee and customer complaints can lead to litigation and negative publicity costing companies millions of dollars. Other negative consequences include wasted time, lower morale, inability to focus on work, and feelings of mistrust, all of which impact the bottom line.

THE BOTTOM LINE

In the rapidly changing global workplace of today, managing cross-cultural conflict is a key business skill for all employees. This megaskill allows us to transform the inevitable conflicts we encounter into opportunities for growth, both personally and professionally. With the pressure to be ever more adaptive, efficient, and productive, effective conflict management allows us to focus on achieving individual and collective goals.

Furthermore, this key component of CQ allows us to shift our thinking and change our behaviors. Rather than viewing cross-cultural conflict as a negative, we view it as an opportunity to learn more about ourselves and others. Moving away from an overly competitive, win-lose approach allows us to embrace multiple realities and options, and, in turn, seek the best possible outcome for ourselves and others. In the end, this becomes a win-win proposition for us, our organizations, and consumers.

TO LEARN MORE

As sports teams in the United States become more culturally diverse, the likelihood of cross-cultural conflict increases. In many instances, the success of a team hinges on the ability of coaches and players to deal with conflict of this nature.

The movie *Remember the Titans* is based on a true-life story of a high-school football team that became racially integrated almost 40 years ago. The movie describes how Coach Herman Boone dealt with the conflict that was tearing his team apart. Watch this movie and take an in-depth look at the nature of the conflict, how Boone dealt with it, and the reasons for his success.

A Look Back: I Have Learned

✓ _____ What is meant by the terms *conflict* and *conflict management*.

✓ _____ How cultural differences may bring about conflict.

✓ _____ Why managing cross-cultural conflict starts with knowing ourselves.

✓ _____ The value of recognizing clashing cultural realities.

✓ _____ To ask certain questions to gain cultural insight.

✓ _____ How to avoid ritual conversations.

✓ _____ To see conflict as an opportunity.

✓ _____ How to reach a win-win solution.

✓ _____ What embracing cultural dilemmas entails.

✓ _____ How to respond effectively to micro-aggressions.

✓ _____ How to assess my own conflict management skills.

✓ _____ The bottom-line implications of managing cross-cultural conflict effectively.

Individual Action Plan

Think about one specific thing you can do to improve your skills in the area of managing cross-cultural conflict. Then complete the following plan during the next _____ (state time period).

Specific skill I want to improve first (refer to list of Performance Skills at the beginning of the chapter):

_____

My strategy:

_____

_____

_____

_____

In order to develop this skill, I will:

_____

_____

_____

_____

Possible obstacles include:

_____

_____

_____

_____

Resources I need:

_____

_____

_____

_____

I will measure my progress by:

_____

_____

_____

_____

Notes

1. Eric Hinton, "When a Diversity Crisis Occurs, How Should Your Company React?" Online October 31, 2005. Available: **http://www.diversityinc.com/members/3752.cfm**.

2. Gordon Allport, *The Nature of Prejudice* (Reading, MA: Addison Wesley, 1954).

3. Geert Hofstede, *Culture's Consequences: International Differences in Work-Related Values* (Beverly Hills, CA: Sage Publications, 1980).

4. Karen Young Kreeger, "Scientific Community Finds Value in Diversity Training." Online 8/9/2003. Available: **http://www.the-scientist.com/yr1997/feb/prof_970217.html**.

5. N. Allen and T. D. Hecht, "Team-Organization Alignment and Team Behavior: Implications for Human Resource Management," *Human Resource Management Research Quarterly*, 2000.

6. National Urban League, *Diversity Practices That Work: The American Worker Speaks*, June 2004, p. 11.

CHAPTER 8

CQ MEGASKILL: MULTICULTURAL TEAMING

Performance Skills

- *Promoting teamwork in virtual settings*
- *Using cultural differences and similarities as assets*
- *Recognizing and responding to fault lines*
- *Understanding how a team develops*

- *Anticipating cultural differences*
- *Decentering and recentering*
- *Building a multicultural team*
- *Holding ourselves accountable*
- *Promoting inclusion*

 **REFLECT BEFORE READING**

SCENARIO 1 Imagine you and other coworkers are sent to a team-building retreat. You are sitting in a briefing room, wearing a battle dress uniform. The facilitator of the exercise gives you a summary of what you can expect on the battlefield. You are given a game plan and a time of departure. You are told what you might encounter from the enemy by way of movement, deception, or opposition. Then, safety measures and contingency plans are discussed. Your task is to drive a military tank through a formation maneuver. Given very little direction and no prior experience, your team must learn how to handle this complex machine. As a member of a three-person team, you will alternate positions as a navigator, commander, and driver as the day unfolds. According to the leader, every part of this exercise relates to business and teaming. Specifically, you must achieve a particular task by following the hierarchy of command. Additionally, you must maintain focus and morale. Excellent communication and problem-solving skills are essential. Given this scenario, conducting tank maneuvers is a formidable challenge. However, you are all from the same organization, speak the same language, and know each other pretty well.

Consider how different this exercise would be if you found yourself in a similar situation but with a culturally diverse group of people you hardly know.

SCENARIO 2 As with first scenario, all of you are from the same organization and presented with the same task. But your relationships are much different. You have only limited knowledge of the other two members of your team. One member does not speak English fluently. All three of you have different communication styles. For example, you believe that showing strong emotions and speaking at the same time as someone else are inappropriate behaviors. Other members of your team do not feel that way. Unlike your teammates, you constantly smile to put them at ease. Lastly, you are of the opinion that conflict should be avoided at all costs. You are not sure how they feel about this.

Because of the communication differences, you are not certain everyone on your team fully understands the mission. To make matters worse, you are not sure you can trust them. After all, you do not know them all that well. And you have a difficult time taking orders from one of your team members, considering she is constantly deferring to you and seems afraid to take control. The fact that she is half your age makes it difficult to view her as someone with authority over you.

What I have described in this last scenario is typical of the challenges and potential clashes found on multicultural teams. These challenges can interfere with the team's ability to fulfill its mission. If you were part of this last scenario, how would you address these challenges? What personal experiences and training have prepared you for this scenario? What skills are you lacking?

· · · · · · · ▬▬▬▬▬▬▬▬▬▬▬▬▬▬▬▬▬▬▬▬▬

INTRODUCTION

The term **multicultural team** refers to a group of people from various cultural backgrounds who are involved in a cooperative effort. Multicultural team members differ in numerous ways, including gender, race, ethnicity, religion, sexual orientation, age, organizational background, communication style, fluency in one or more languages, values and beliefs, and disability.

Culture has become a key consideration in terms of understanding how teams in today's workplace can function more effectively. As an example, in recent years much has been written about the challenges posed by workers who adhere to a variety of religious beliefs and practices. A team comprised of people with different faiths, such as Muslims, Christians, Jews, and Buddhists, must have cultural intelligence to deal with a variety of issues at work. These include when to schedule meetings, what food to serve, how to regulate leave time for religious reasons, what to wear, and under what circumstances it is appropriate to discuss religion. Like other components of culture, religious differences have vast implications for building trust, managing conflict, promoting inclusion, and other behaviors necessary for building a high performance team. When we are able to anticipate, understand, and adjust to cultural diversity, whether it is expressed through religion or some other way, we become much more effective team players.

To be a great team player in the 21st century, we need to boost our CQ. Cultural differences have the potential to enhance or inhibit the effectiveness of teams. Too often, we simply focus on the people themselves and their differences. Cultural intelligence shifts that focus to whether we see the possibilities embodied in those differences, and whether we have the skills to leverage those differences. By enabling us to excel on multicultural teams, CQ provides us with the necessary tools to use cultural diversity to enhance team performance.

TEAMING—RELATIONSHIPS AND TASKS

A **team** refers to a relatively small number of people who are committed to achieving certain results for which they hold themselves accountable. We know from experience that a team's productivity and success hinges to a large degree on fostering relationships both within and outside of an organization. These relationships are crucial to establishing a common mission, building trust and rapport, and providing helpful feedback. At work, teams may include coworkers, managers, suppliers, consumers and clients, and community members. Teams have a wide range of responsibilities, including project management, problem solving, product development, employee discipline, and quality assurance.

---

⑦ Where Am I Now?

DIRECTIONS: For each statement, write the number corresponding to your answer: Always (5), Frequently (4), Sometimes (3), Rarely (2), Never (1).

As a team member,

1. _____ I actively strive to consider the impact of all decisions on everyone concerned.
2. _____ I focus primarily on the task at hand.
3. _____ I can safely assume that everyone will work well together if we have the will and skill to relate to each other effectively.
4. _____ I can safely assume that everyone will work well together if we focus on the task at hand.

Task behaviors, those behaviors oriented toward accomplishing certain objectives, range from defining objectives to gathering and evaluating information to problem solving and networking. Your responses to the preceding statements in "Where Am I Now?" give you some idea of how task-oriented and relationship-oriented you are. For instance, higher scores on the first and third statements point to relationships being a priority, while higher scores on statements 2 and 4 show a greater concern with accomplishing tasks.

Task behaviors interconnect with **relationship-building behaviors**, behaviors aimed at understanding, motivating, and communicating with others. Relationship-building behaviors might include the following:

- Showing appreciation.
- Setting ground rules and facilitating discussions in such a way that everyone feels included.
- Examining each other's assumptions.
- Collaborating and compromising when necessary to resolve conflicts.
- Being able to gauge strengths and weaknesses as a team.

As multicultural team members, we need to strive to achieve some kind of balance between task and relationship behaviors. In many organizations in the United States, teams tend to be very task-oriented. In such teams, the quality of relationships among team members is often an afterthought, or something that happens after a team begins its work. This is owing, in large part, to the bureaucratic, hierarchal structure of organizations. But being so focused on getting the job done is apt to be seen negatively by certain team members. To them, developing relationships come first. It is not that they are less committed to the task; rather, they go at it differently.

YOUR TURN

Some research suggests that gender affects the way we view teamwork. For example, work by Deborah Tannen shows that women focus more on team relationships and the process of problem solving, while men are more task- or solution-oriented. When working on teams, has this been your experience? Explain.

THE CULTURAL CONTEXT OF TEAMS

Imagine arranging a meeting to meet a government official in Riyadh, Saudi Arabia. You and a fellow team member are scheduled for an appointment, but you are not sure what to expect. Instead of being given a time to meet, you are told to drop by mid-afternoon. When you arrive at 3:00 P.M., you notice a number of people waiting in front of you. Presumably, all of these people were told to come "around mid-afternoon." What's more, the official disregards the order in which people arrived; rather, he arbitrarily chooses in what order the people waiting will be seen. Whether you take this as an affront will depend on your understanding of cultural context.

Cultural context refers to the ideas, values, beliefs, and other environmental influences that characterize the setting in which interaction takes place. Consider one environmental influence, **chronemics**, or the use of time. How many of us stop to think about whether business meetings should begin on time and follow an agenda? We may not think about this because of our **cultural baggage**, or those beliefs, values, and practices that we carry around with us. While many of us believe that using agendas is the way productive meetings are run, others might think differently. They might see this as too bureaucratic and impersonal; meaning there is no time or "open space" for other issues not on the agenda. In other cultural settings, team meetings might regularly start 15–30 minutes late, and deviating from the agenda is encouraged.

Teams do not exist in a vacuum. Tasks and relationships within a team cannot be analyzed apart from the cultural context outside of the team. These include the organizational culture as well as cultures in the larger society and beyond (see Figure 8.1).

Organizational culture refers to the structures, processes, rules, behaviors, and underlying assumptions that characterize an organization. For example, organizations differ in the amount of autonomy, responsibility, and accountability they give to teams. They also differ markedly in the degree to which they understand, embrace, and integrate diversity into their core values and day-to-day operations. For example, organizations differ greatly in their inclusiveness of employees who are gay, lesbian, bisexual, or transsexual. Depending on the organization, these differences may be tolerated, embraced, or viewed as "a problem."

Team members need to be aware of cultural context as it unfolds in the course of their interaction with each other, the organization, and the larger society. Consider a team within an organization whose members view the relative importance of individuals and groups differently. Some team members come from **individualist cultures**, cultures that emphasize the achievements and goals of individuals. These members are apt to think in terms of personal goals and assign less importance to group conformity. Other members come from **collectivistic cultures**, cultures that focus primarily on the welfare of the group as a whole. For them, cooperation and doing what is best for the team

Figure 8.1 • Teams Operate in a Cultural Context

are likely to take priority. To further complicate matters, this cultural difference is only one of many that may influence a team member's behavior.

According to research, countries with generally individualist cultures include the United States, Australia, the United Kingdom, and the Netherlands. Examples of countries with generally collectivist cultures are Vietnam, Singapore, China, and Pakistan. According to Hofstede's research on international differences in the perceptions and behaviors of more than 100,000 employees, a range or continuum of differences exists. In other words, societies may be highly individualistic, highly collectivistic, or somewhere in-between.[1]

Where Am I Now?

In Figure 8.2, you will find various approaches to teaming that tend to differentiate people with a group orientation (collectivistic cultures) or an individual orientation (individualistic cultures). Mark an X to indicate where you see yourself with regard to each approach.

Bear in mind that you can belong to a highly individualistic culture and still have a group orientation. Even though individuals may share the same general cultural background, they nevertheless respond to it differently.

Figure 8.2 • Approaches to Teaming

DIRECTIONS: Place an X on the dotted line to reflect where you think you are on the continuum.

Group Orientation		Individual Orientation
Avoid conflict	....	Confront conflict
Focus on preserving relationships	....	Focus on accomplishing tasks
Emphasize context (how it is said)	....	Emphasize content (what is said)

TO LEARN MORE

Go to **www.geert-hofstede.com/hofstede_dimensions.php.** Use the interactive chart to compare individualism and other dimensions of culture for over 80 countries.

 Applied • • • • • •

Rick Pitino, a highly successful professional and college basketball coach, remembers asking Bill Russell to speak to his team before a big game. Russell, formerly a member of the Boston Celtics and one of the greatest basketball players of all time, began by saying he was the most egotistical person in the room. But, he added, his ego was not about individual goals and accomplishments. It was a team ego, meaning it was all about the team.

Pitino recounts how his team took Russell's message to heart and played inspired, unselfish basketball that night. However, the effect of that talk was short-lived. Pitino's team soon reverted back to thinking more about individual statistics than sacrificing themselves for the sake of the team.

In retrospect, it was naive of Pitino to think he could instill a team ego by exposing his players to one locker room speech by one of the greats. He was not just dealing with a "me first" attitude on his team, he was trying to undo years of cultural conditioning. Indeed, one of the core values of U.S. culture is individualism.

THE IMPORTANCE OF TRUST

Trust refers to the feeling within a group that team members can depend on one another and assume their intentions are good. In the earliest stages of team development, trust is apt to be minimal. Consequently, people will tend to be guarded and hesitant to express differences. Only later, after learning from experience, can team members feel safe to open up about themselves and their culture.

According to Patrick Lencioni, author of the best-selling book *The Five Dysfunctions of a Team*, "Trust lies at the heart of a functioning, cohesive team.

Without it, teamwork is all but impossible."[2] Lencioni identifies "absence of trust" as one of the five team dysfunctions because it wastes time and energy, damages morale, makes asking for help difficult, hides people's weaknesses, and makes us jump to conclusions.

It is usually easier to trust people if they share our beliefs, values, and cultural backgrounds. Hence, building trust on multicultural teams will test us. CQ helps us meet this challenge.

Building trust motivates us and puts us at ease. With trust in other team members, we feel more comfortable being ourselves and bringing all of our diversity to the workplace. Trust allows us to believe in others, build a common purpose, and support team goals. If I trust my teammates, I am much more likely to be honest, do my job well, and share any knowledge I might have for the benefit of the team.

PROMOTING TEAMWORK IN VIRTUAL SETTINGS

The use of **virtual teams**, whose members use communication technologies to interact across distance, time, and organizational boundaries in pursuit of a common goal, has increased dramatically in recent years. Such teams tend to be more culturally complex than traditional teams since their members represent a wide variety of nations and cultures. Virtual teams, which may include employees only or employees and outsiders, are a staple of large global companies. However, small organizations operating from a single location can also benefit from virtual teams. This is particularly true if workers, suppliers, and other decision-makers are found at a variety of geographic sites.

Virtual teams are more apt to achieve their objectives when they consciously focus on their relationships as well as their tasks. Constantly using electronic means of communication such as e-mail, conference calls, videoconferences, and groupware, can make CQ even more important than in face-to-face teams.

As members of virtual teams, we are more likely to misunderstand, make incorrect assumptions, and hide problems. For instance, people may "misread" the substance of e-mail messages due to cultural differences. Because of their individualistic orientation, messages from team members in Western cultures may be more impersonal and to the point. E-mail from cultures with a more collective orientation may be longer and more focused on people's needs and interpersonal relationships.

Because members are apt to exhibit a wide range of opinions, values, and beliefs, it is not uncommon for them to experience considerable conflict. Although communicating virtually may facilitate our ability to brainstorm, making decisions and negotiating can prove more difficult. One of the major reasons for this is a lack of trust. Without frequent face-to-face interactions, people may find it more difficult to earn trust. And while so-called "swift trust" can develop solely through online interaction, this type of trust tends to be more fragile because it involves little relationship building.

The dispersed nature of virtual teams compounds the challenge of linguistic diversity. Almost all of us can relate to this if we recollect those experiences in which we were on the phone trying to understand someone who did not speak our language very well. No matter how hard we tried, we struggled to make sense of what was being shared.

Now consider how virtual team members might also encounter difficulties trying to communicate with those who speak the same language but with different degrees of fluency. Or imagine the misunderstandings that might arise when people who speak different languages use a translator. A recent example involves a nonprofit organization whose work promotes digital technology. An individual who speaks Russian received an e-mail from a fellow team member saying the Website design she just created was awesome. The Russian-speaking team member fired back an e-mail with a flaming message, pointing out that she felt disrespected and misunderstood. She conveyed to the entire team that this e-mail revealed the poor quality of their assessment. After more nasty e-mails and hurt feelings all around, another team member who also spoke Russian diagnosed the problem. The computerized translator they were using translated "awesome" to a word that meant "awful."

TO LEARN MORE

Go to **Google.com.** Type "EN-15038" (European Quality Standard for Translation Services). What is EN-15038? How does it promote the quality of translation provided to businesses and customers?

Frequent effective communication builds trust, which, in turn, leads to more open and meaningful communication. When communicating as a member of a virtual team, you can expand your CQ in a number of ways. As team members become more familiar with each other, they actively seek information about cultural differences. Openly discuss the challenges of building trust cross-culturally. When interpersonal issues arise, address them on the phone or through face-to-face meetings rather than via e-mail.

If possible, agree that when anyone on the team receives a message that appears culturally offensive or inappropriate, that person will withhold judgment until he or she can contact the message sender. When dealing with cultural diversity in virtual settings, it is important to give people the benefit of the doubt until more information can be gathered in a timely manner.

DID YOU KNOW?

Intel Corporation conducted research on a number of their high-performing virtual teams and studied what made these teams so successful. Their research points to specific CQ skills; namely,

- Respect among team members
- Understanding mutual expectations
- Trust
- Cooperation
- Listening

USING CULTURAL DIFFERENCES AND SIMILARITIES AS ASSETS

Years of research shows that culturally diverse teams have the potential to out-perform homogenous teams. Over time, diverse team members can generate more different ideas, be better problem solvers, and be more creative than members of homogenous teams. Specifically, diverse teams are better able to

- Consider a greater variety of perspectives and alternatives.
- Rely on a greater variety of contacts and information.
- Think "outside of the box."
- Think through issues by offering arguments and counterarguments.
- Adapt to changing circumstances.
- Question prevailing assumptions.

Developing our CQ allows us to realize these benefits. Only then are we able to focus on differences as an asset to be utilized, rather than as a challenge to be dealt with or overcome. All CQ megaskills, especially intercultural communication, conflict management, and the ability to shift perspectives, come into play when we ask ourselves how we can make cultural diversity a plus on teams.

While diversity can be an asset to teams, it can also be a liability, particularly if individuals lack CQ. There is the potential for more divisiveness, as is sometimes the case when new people join a team and bring new languages, agendas, and perspectives with them. According to research studies, cultural diversity on teams may result in greater difficulty learning to work together, poorer communication, lack of trust, and more absenteeism and turnover.

Diversity is only an asset when team members feel included, understood, and respected. When these conditions are present, there is a much greater likelihood of cooperation and **synergy**, meaning the output of the team as a whole is greater than what the individual members are capable of, acting alone.

Just as we may be unaware of cultural differences within a team, we also may be unaware of our similarities. By building a common purpose and focusing on similar backgrounds, values, and beliefs, we build trust and strengthen teamwork. For instance, sharing similar feelings about the importance of a common commitment can build unity amidst diversity. On a multicultural team, members may agree that there is more than one right way to communicate, lead, or resolve conflict.

DID YOU KNOW?

According to a recent survey conducted by the National Urban League, more than 5,500 U.S. workers shared what they think about differences in race and ethnicity, gender, job type, and age. Eighty percent responded, "I am comfortable working in diverse teams." Nearly as many (77%) responded, "I am expected to positively interact with people who are different from me." [3]

YOUR TURN   · · · · · · ――――――――――

Think back to a time when you were part of a team and felt supported by a teammate from another culture. Describe what this person did to make you feel this way.

_____

_____

_____

_____

RECOGNIZING AND RESPONDING TO FAULT LINES

A team may subdivide into smaller groups or factions. The reason for doing this could be any number of criteria, including nationality, religion, race, language, or any other type of cultural difference no matter how insignificant it might seem. When this occurs, **fault lines,** or divisions among team members, can erupt and interfere with the team's ability to come together and achieve its goals. These fault lines may create **in-groups,** those people with whom we identify, and **out-groups,** those people with whom we do not identify. Each member of a team may feel he or she shares more in common with some people than others.

As an example, we might find ourselves on a team made up of male and female coworkers. Within this group, fault lines may develop on the basis of gender. In this event, a team member's gender may determine whether you really listen to or feel some connection to that person. The welfare of the team can take a back seat to concerns about in-groups and out-groups.

Generally, we are more likely to show bias toward out-groups. If men on a team perceive each other as an in-group, they are more likely to characterize an aggressive woman as pushy or hostile but view a man with those same traits in a positive way. Or an in-group of women might view a man whose clothes are very coordinated, whose hair is always in place, and who regularly gets manicures and pedicures, in a negative light, even though these same traits in a female team member are seen as acceptable and even desirable.

We tend to see people in out-groups as less differentiated and less complex than people in in-groups. When members of our in-groups "screw up," we tend to blame the _individual_ team member. We might say the person is incompetent, made a mistake, or perhaps had a bad day. If the same thing happens with a member of an out-group, we are more prone to stereotype every member of that _group_ on the basis of one person's behavior.

What can we do? First, we can be aware of the possibility of fault lines undermining the team's ability to do its work. If some team members segregate themselves on the basis of language or some other similarity, make an effort to reach out to all members regardless of differences. Be aware of your own tendency to stereotype and constantly gravitate to people with whom you identify. By focusing on the superordinate goal of the larger team, we reset group boundaries and reconnect to the team.

Says John Dovidio, a psychologist who has studied teamwork in depth, "If you can establish a sense of groupness, of being on the same team even artificially and temporarily, that begins to create a foundation on which people can have more personal, deeper discussions and understanding."[4]

UNDERSTANDING HOW A TEAM DEVELOPS

Developing a team takes time and effort. This is particularly true of high-performance multicultural teams. In such teams, building trust and commitment across cultures requires a certain level of comfort and familiarity. These things do not happen by chance. There are stages of development and, at each stage, cultural diversity must be taken into account.

Throughout the process, team members continually learn to trust each other, adapt, reflect, and assess. As they do, stereotypical notions and first impressions become less and less important. Instead, ability, commitment, passion, and reaching a common goal become the center of attention.

As Table 8.1 shows, different processes, questions, and strategies are relevant during each stage of team development. All stages interrelate and reflect a building process. Too often, we bypass or pay scant attention to what goes on during the early stages of forming, storming, and norming. When we do, developing into a high-performing team is that much more difficult.

YOUR TURN · · · · · ──────

As teams move through the five stages of development (Table 8.1), summarize what you think distinguishes a great team from a good team.

_____

_____

_____

_____

_____

_____

Table 8.1 • Five Stages of Team Development

STAGE 1—FORMING—MEMBERS GET TO KNOW EACH OTHER AND "FIND THEIR PLACE"

Team Tasks/Activities	Questions Team Members Ask Themselves	Strategies for Overcoming Cultural Barriers
• Get-acquainted period • Focus on developing a sense of belonging and team's reason for coming together • Minimal work accomplished	• Why are we here? • What do we know about each other? • What talents and resources do we bring to the team? • What are our similarities and differences?	• Listen actively • Get to know individual behind the label • Make sure general expectations understood by everyone • Begin the process of building trust through effective communication

STAGE 2—STORMING—MEMBERS WRESTLE WITH ADDRESSING THE ISSUES

Team Tasks/Activities	Questions Team Members Ask Themselves	Strategies for Overcoming Cultural Barriers
• Individuals jockey for position and influence within team • Discuss resources and constraints • Minimal work accomplished	• Who does what, and why? • What cultural differences exist and why might they be important? • What differences might reduce team cohesion by dividing the team into subgroups?	• Move out of your cultural comfort zone • Acknowledge and respect culturally different ways of communicating and making decisions

STAGE 3—NORMING—MEMBERS ESTABLISH RULES AND RESPONSIBILITIES

Team Tasks/Activities	Questions Team Members Ask Themselves	Strategies for Overcoming Cultural Barriers
• Share skills and knowledge • Manage conflicts • Focus on clarifying goals and developing cohesion • Moderate work accomplished • Build trust	• What decisions should be made together or individually? • How can diversity generate better team decisions? • What similarities can further increase trust?	• Seek everybody's input in order to agree on ground rules • Value diverse opinions and avoid **groupthink**, the tendency to think like everyone else

STAGE 4—PERFORMING—MEMBERS WORK TOGETHER TOWARD A COMMON GOAL

Team Tasks/Activities	Questions Team Members Ask Themselves	Strategies for Overcoming Cultural Barriers
• Implement "vision" of the team • Solve problems • Become more close-knit, synergistic	• Are language differences interfering with teamwork? • Do members with different perspectives feel safe to speak up?	• Cultivate authentic and effective communication • Put yourself in other people's shoes

STAGE 5—EVOLVING—MEMBERS LOOK BACK AND LOOK AHEAD

Team Tasks/Activities	Questions Team Members Ask Themselves	Strategies for Overcoming Cultural Barriers
• Look back and reflect • Adapt as tasks, team members change • Assess where team is and where it wants to be • Team dissolves if it fulfills task and is no longer needed	• What kind of balance has been struck in terms of focus on cultural differences and similarities? • Have team members tapped the creative power of their differences? • What could we do better to facilitate teamwork?	• Identify individual and collective strengths and weaknesses • Assess ability to use conflict to better decision making and team performance • Identify training needs

Source: Adapted from Allan Drexler, David Sibbet, and H. Forester, *The Team Performance Model*, NTL Institute for Applied Behavioral Science (1988), and Bruce Tuckman, "Developmental Sequence in Small Groups," *Psychological Bulletin 63* (1965), pp. 384-399.

ANTICIPATING CULTURAL DIFFERENCES

Rather than assuming others will think and act like us, we need to anticipate the possibility of differences. Team members who assume they are similar are often shocked to uncover differences in their values, outlooks, and life experiences. As we learn to anticipate cultural differences, we learn to treat each individual as an individual.

YOUR TURN   · · · · · ·

Examine the following list of personal characteristics. Circle five terms that describe coworkers you would *least* prefer having on your team.

Shy	Arrogant	Unselfish	Friendly
Self-centered	Animated	Sympathetic	Critical of others' ideas
Soft-spoken	Very nurturing	Passive	Seeks praise from others
Sensitive	Obedient	Rebellious	Punctual
Independent	Avoids conflict	Competitive	Humble

Analysis: Ask yourself why you chose these five terms. How do your choices relate to your cultural background? Explain.

_____

_____

_____

_____

_____

Even though many of us resist or avoid teaming with certain types of people, we may have no choice. As a member of a work team, we may find ourselves teaming with people who "turn us off" because they are very sensitive, or animated, or self-centered. One helpful technique in a situation such as this is to view these traits as dimensions of diversity rather than as annoying behaviors. As such, they are like any other difference that might impact the bottom line. By anticipating differences, we are less apt to be overwhelmed by them and more apt to react to them positively.

Anticipating cultural differences means being sensitive to the value of doing things in a variety of ways, and adapting when necessary. Differences can manifest themselves in a great variety of ways, including the following:

Approaches to Decision-Making. Teaming across cultures can bring out a variety of expectations surrounding the task of making a decision. In

Western cultures, there tends to be more of an emphasis on answering the question. This is at odds with the tendency in some Asian cultures to view decision making in terms of defining the question. Because the emphasis in these cultures is on the question rather than the answer, team members pay more attention to what issues are being raised and whether there is a need for a decision. By not focusing solely on the answer, consensus is more likely. The answer to the question follows from how we construct the question.

Communication Style. As discussed in Chapter 6, the ways people communicate, or their communication styles, vary considerably. Consider, for instance, how animated we are when we communicate. Raising one's voice and wildly gesturing with one's hands might be interpreted by some team members as an indication of displeasure or outright conflict. While this might be true some of the time, this type of communication style may simply indicate excitement and intensity.

Attitudes Toward Past, Present, and Future. Team members may not place the same emphasis on traditions and the importance of history. Further, future considerations (long-term goals) and present concerns (organizational policies and procedures) may factor into decision making for some much more than others.

Attitudes Toward Conflict. Some team members may view conflict as positive; that is, as a way to promote divergent thinking, creativity, and well-thought-out solutions. Therefore, it might be embraced or even encouraged. In contrast, in many Eastern countries people avoid conflict on teams as much as possible. If it does occur, it is seen as potentially embarrassing and therefore, people try to quietly work out their differences of opinion. For further discussion, see Chapter 7.

YOUR TURN · · · · · ·

Would you rather be the best player on a losing team or an average player on a winning team? What does your answer reveal about you, your cultural upbringing, and whether you are a "team player"?

_____

_____

_____

_____

_____

_____

These briefly discussed differences address only a few of the innumerable possibilities we might encounter on multicultural teams. Clearly, we do not have the luxury of assuming that team members will think, act, and respond as we do. By anticipating cultural differences, we are able to communicate and work together much more effectively. By increasing our knowledge of what differences might emerge and how they might show themselves, we can be better prepared for this eventuality.

DECENTERING AND RECENTERING

Once we have an idea of the cultural differences on the team, we then employ the skill of **decentering**, moving away from our own "center" or perspective and adopting the other person's point of view. For instance, if we are interacting with someone with a different communication style than ours, we attempt to adapt our own way of communicating by adopting the other person's style.

Decentering combats the tendency to assume that our way is the right way, and therefore their way must be wrong. Making this assumption is a common trap we fall into, especially when cultural differences prove to be subtle. By asking questions, paraphrasing, and testing our assumptions, we can keep the focus on others. Suspending judgment is critical.

Recentering means building a bridge between your perspective and that of another person to form a new, more effective way of interacting. Recentering builds on decentering. Once you acknowledge differences and then explore those differences through decentering, you then recenter by finding specific similarities. By recentering, you and others find common ground and use that knowledge to come back to the center. For example, the entire team might discover their views overlap. As with any skill, decentering and recentering can be learned and improved with practice.

BUILDING A MULTICULTURAL TEAM

Building a multicultural team is a results-driven, collaborative process. **Team building** is the process of enabling a group of people to achieve their goal. Team building is more than an event that happens to a team. Rather, it is a process undertaken by all team members, and it can vary depending on the size and nature of the team.

As stated earlier, the development of a multicultural team goes through stages. As it does, one of the biggest mistakes a team makes is not spending enough time to get to know one other. When this occurs, fault lines may develop at the first sign of conflict threatening team unity. Without common commitment, a team is just a collection of individuals who are going through the motions of working together.

YOUR TURN · · · · · · ────────────

What factors impact your willingness to join and remain committed to a team? Does your cultural background have something to do with why these factors are important to you?

_____

_____

_____

_____

_____

Team-oriented activities that involve everybody are an integral part of the team-building process. Through role playing, simulations, journals, and appropriate games, members of a multicultural team develop greater awareness and appreciation for what they share in common, such as

- Goals and experiences
- Core values and beliefs
- A passion to achieve a goal
- Trust in each other and their abilities
- The need for developing awareness, knowledge, and skills

A team-building exercise, for example, may put you in an uncomfortable and unfamiliar cultural zone. Once you respond, you receive formal and informal feedback from others, including other team members, customers, and clients. But then, you need to take what you learned with you.

CQ **Applied** · · · · · · ────────────

WIBttP ("What I bring to the party") has been shown to be an effective multicultural team-building strategy. It is a low-risk process that team members can use to begin or further the process of developing multicultural relationships. WIBttP involves asking team members to take a few minutes to consider what they might feel comfortable sharing about themselves. Specifically, they might share a work or life experience that might be relevant to the team's goal or some other aspect of their diversity. As they do this, other members of the team are asked to listen carefully, noting any special skills and experiences they might want to explore at a later date.

This team-building exercise allows team members to share a considerable amount of information about themselves in a short period of time. Also, it eases people into the process of learning about each other in a way that is not usually threatening. That said, some members may still be hesitant to participate because they do not want to bring attention to themselves, for individual or cultural reasons.

> **TO LEARN MORE**
>
> Go to http://wilderdom.com/InitiativeGames.html to see a variety of thoroughly described team-building activities.

HOLDING OURSELVES ACCOUNTABLE

Accountability is one of the building blocks of effective multicultural teaming. Each and every team member needs to hold themselves and each other accountable, meaning we need to accept responsibility for our individual and collective actions. For example, members need to

- Follow through on shared goals and objectives.
- Respect and leverage diversity.
- Interact in agreed ways, especially with regard to communicating, managing conflict and change, and solving problems.
- Periodically assess themselves and the team.

Accountability is not simply the job of the team leader, organization, or individuals higher up in the chain of command. Anybody who fails to follow through on his or her commitment needs to be held accountable by the team.

Personal assessment promotes personal accountability by targeting the ability to progress and achieve certain results. Assessment tools, such as the following "Where Am I Now?" section provide insight into specific, critical areas of multicultural teaming.

By repeatedly evaluating ourselves, we gain insight into our ability to improve in critical areas of multicultural teaming. Assessment data provides us with a baseline against which we can chart our progress over time. We cannot know how far we have come unless we know where we started.

Where Am I Now?

Self-Assessment: 5 Critical Areas of Multicultural Teaming

DIRECTIONS: For each statement, write the number corresponding to your answer: Always (5), Frequently (4), Sometimes (3), Rarely (2), or Never (1). As a team member:

Self-awareness

_____ I evaluate and reevaluate my ability to team with people who are culturally different from me.

_____ I suspend my reservations about other cultural values in an attempt to learn more about those values.

_____ I am aware of my values.

_____ I modify my values when necessary.

_____ I am aware of my own cultural diversity when I interact with other members of my team.

Communication

_____ I can effectively relate to team members who do not respond to directives from management the same way I do.

_____ I think about how my ways of communicating are perceived by people from other cultures.

_____ I facilitate group interaction.

_____ I scrutinize my own language and behavior for possible meanings that may be offensive to others.

_____ I become even more attentive when I sense someone's communication style is different from mine.

Building trust

_____ I take time to learn about others' backgrounds and values.

_____ I actively strive to consider the impact of all decisions on everyone concerned.

_____ I reinforce others in behavior that supports respect for cultural diversity.

_____ I take responsibility for helping all team members feel welcomed and comfortable.

_____ I pay attention to feelings as well as the words exchanged among us.

Managing conflict

_____ I react positively when there are differences of opinion.

_____ I see conflict as an opportunity for more effective teaming.

_____ I suspend judgment before reacting to conflict.

Bottom line

_____ I am aware of the goals and objectives of my team.

_____ I am aware of the value of diversity to my team.

_____ I am aware of how my personal development in the area of diversity impacts the team's bottom line.

_____ I use my diversity and the team's diversity as resources to achieve our bottom line.

[____] Point Total

Analysis: Our goal should be to improve our point total each time we assess ourselves. Also, check each critical area over time. Are there areas for which you consistently score low? If so, what might you consider doing differently to improve your scores?

Accountability is ongoing. Once we assess ourselves, we need to change our behavior and work on our weaknesses. This might mean communicating with customers differently, attending training, and reaching out to team members who may feel like cultural outsiders.

PROMOTING INCLUSION

A Tale of O is advertised as the world's best-selling video on diversity. In this video, the implications of a person's status as an insider (X) or an outsider (O) are explored in the context of the workplace. *A Tale of O* describes insiders as individuals who are fully accepted in a job setting for any number of reasons while outsiders refer to those who are excluded. The video is based on the work of its narrator, Rosabeth Moss Kanter, author of thirteen books and a consultant to major corporations around the world.

A Tale of O examines how language, race, religion, job position, or even hair style and length can make people feel like an insider or an outsider on teams. Even though Xs and Os may work in the same setting and find themselves on the same team, their feelings of inclusion tend to be very different (see Table 8.2). This makes it difficult for a team to do its best work.

Gender is one of many differences that can make a team member feel excluded. In a team that does work for a large financial services corporation, one female works with eight men. She has relatively little power and feels isolated because she is the only woman in her office. Because there is no clear-cut organizational code of conduct, team members are left on their own. She describes the work environment

Table 8.2 • Experiencing Teamwork as an X and an O

Cultural **X**	**Blend in;** cultural identity is a non-issue	Feeling of **acceptance,** sense of community	Can **be yourself** and act naturally	**More power and opportunity** to learn from others, mentors, networks	**Evaluated on** the basis of your **performance** (what you do)
Cultural **O**	**Stand out;** feel "under the spotlight," cultural identity is an issue	Feeling of being **left out** in certain situations, sense of isolation	**Pressure** to side with Xs or be **more like them**	**Less power and opportunity** to learn from others	**Performance may be overshadowed** by who you are

YOUR TURN

As team members, we tend to be more aware of being excluded than included. When participating on teams, has this been your experience? Explain.

_____

_____

_____

_____

as male dominated. The men on her team make a habit of looking at porn on the Internet, talking about trips to sex clubs, and commenting on females' body parts. Even though the female employee in this situation reported it to the ethics hotline and confronted specific managers about this behavior, it has not stopped. She was seen as the one who had a problem, not the men.

Teams work best when there is **inclusion,** meaning *all* members feel a sense of belonging and respect. High-performance multicultural teams draw on the talents and best ideas of all of their members. They do this in a variety of ways, including broadening participation, building on each other's ideas, and valuing everyone's contributions. Promoting inclusion can take more time, and it certainly takes more effort.

Multicultural teams in the U.S. armed forces have been successful largely because of their inclusiveness. A U.S. marine provides insight into how his unit developed this quality:

My unit was made up of Whites, Hispanics, Italians, Indians, and one guy who did not say what he was nor did anyone care. There were people from the South, the Midwest, the Northeast, and all points in between. The first thing the drill instructors told us was that we were no longer White or Black. Once you become a Marine, you are neither light nor dark, you are only a Marine. Through all of our differences, we had to learn to function as a well-oiled machine.

Because of their interconnected roles and statuses, this team of marines depended on each other for survival. Research illustrates that intragroup collaboration of this nature may be far more effective in promoting inclusion than preaching and teaching about the importance of working together. By committing to **superordinate goals**, shared goals that require all members of a group to unite and work together, team members begin to see each other differently.

YOUR TURN   · · · · · ——

Picture yourself on a culturally diverse team of coworkers. What is one thing you can do to promote a sense of oneness on the team and reach out to those who may feel left out?

_____

_____

_____

By becoming more aware of those situations in which people may feel like cultural insiders and outsiders, we put ourselves in a position to promote inclusion. With this knowledge, we are able and motivated to become better communicators, broadening the scope of interaction and socialization. Additionally, we find ourselves reaching out to people who may feel they cannot be themselves. This benefits everyone on the team, in that it increases our collective ability to make use of everybody's assets and generate better ideas.

THE BOTTOM LINE

Multicultural teaming can provide a tremendous competitive edge. Potentially, it can increase flexibility, creativity, and productivity, and it can lead to better problem definitions and solutions. But cultural diversity, when ignored or devalued, can have a dramatic, negative impact on the bottom line as well. This is the reason why many multicultural teams are less efficient and less productive.

While "getting along" and creating synergy are important, they are only a means to a goal. The *ultimate* purpose of a team is to achieve certain results. This can only occur if members of multicultural teams develop their CQ.

A Look Back: I Have Learned

✓ _____ What is meant by a team.

✓ _____ To differentiate between task behaviors and relationship-building behaviors.

✓ _____ That teams exist in a cultural context.

✓ _____ Why virtual teaming poses unique challenges.

✓ _____ How CQ allows us to use cultural differences and similarities as assets.

✓ _____ How fault lines develop on teams.

✓ _____ To identify five stages of team development.

✓ _____ Why it is important to anticipate cultural differences.

✓ _____ How to decenter and recenter.

✓ _____ Why bulding trust is critically important.

✓ _____ Why it is important to promote inclusion.

✓ _____ How and why multicultural teaming impacts the bottom line.

Individual Action Plan

Think about one specific thing you can do to improve your skills in the area of multicultural teaming. Then complete the following plan during the next _____ (state time period).

Specific skill I want to improve first (refer to list of Performance Skills at the beginning of the chapter).

_____

My strategy:

_____
_____
_____
_____

In order to develop this skill, I will:

_____
_____

_____

_____

Possible obstacles include:

_____

_____

_____

_____

Resources I need:

_____

_____

_____

_____

I will measure my progress by:

_____

_____

_____

_____

Notes

1. Geert Hofstede, *Culture's Consequences: International Differences in Work Related Values* (Beverly Hills, CA: Sage Publications, 1980).

2. Patrick Lencioni, *The Five Dysfunctions of a Team* (San Francisco, CA: Jossey-Bass, 2002), p. 195.

3. National Urban League, *Diversity Practices That Work: The American Worker Speaks* (New York: Author, June 2004), p. 7.

4. Ellis Cose, *ColorBlind: Seeing Beyond Race in a Race-Obsessed World* (New York: HarperPerennial, 1997), p. 241.

CHAPTER 9

CQ MEGASKILL:
DEALING WITH BIAS

Performance Skills

- *Understanding the nature of prejudice and stereotypes*
- *Distinguishing between stereotypes and generalizations*
- *Becoming aware of personal biases*
- *Understanding the dynamics of bias*
- *Recognizing the many faces of discrimination*
- *Responding to bias effectively*
- *Unlearning personal bias*

 REFLECT BEFORE READING

When he was CEO of General Electric (G.E.), Jack Welch issued a challenge to his company. The challenge was to make G.E. "boundaryless." **Boundaryless behavior** is interaction that is free of the walls and layers that people build between themselves and others. To be successful, Welch believed that G.E. had to remove barriers that inhibit creativity, waste time, limit vision, and impede change.

· · · · · · · ·

INTRODUCTION

Dealing with bias is a critical component of cultural intelligence (CQ) because it allows us to read people more accurately. When we show **bias**, we interpret and judge other people and their way of life in terms particular to our culture. How we see and relate to others is filtered through our own cultural expectations. Because we are so immersed in our culture, we are often unaware of our biases and how they predispose us to look at people a certain way.

While the amount of bias varies from person to person, some bias is found in everyone. Due to the pervasiveness of bias, we can describe it as a cultural universal. Beverly Tatum, author of the critically acclaimed book *Why Are All the Black Kids Sitting Together in the Cafeteria? And Other Conversations About Race*, suggests that we think of bias the same way we would think of smog. Each day people breathe it in without even thinking about it. Sometimes it is so thick we can see it, but at other times it is less visible. But while we may be oblivious to the effects of smog and bias, their cumulative effect over time is significant.[1]

Even though encounters with bias are a daily occurence, it is all too easy to locate bias in everyone except oneself. Unfortunately, lack of awareness of personal biases makes it difficult to manage, unlearn, and accept responsibility for acting the way we do. When our perceptions are biased, we are likely to assume certain things about people that are not true. This hampers our ability to communicate, team, lead, and manage conflict effectively. Moreover, workers who show bias are bad for business. Bias wastes time, saps energy, and makes everyone's job more difficult. As we learn to deal with bias, we become more aware of it in ourselves, we become more sensitive to it in others, and we learn to respond to it appropriately when it surfaces.

YOUR TURN   · · · · ·

Can you think of a situation at school or at work in which you were judged on something other than merit? If so, what was the situation and how did you feel?

_____

_____

_____

_____

Biases permeate the workplace. For example, we may expect women to record minutes at a meeting. When we see two male colleagues standing next to each other—one White and one Black—we may assume that the White male occupies the higher position. We might give a person with a disability assistance, without even asking if he or she needs or wants it. These views are not genetic or inborn. Rather, they have been shaped and reinforced by our cultural upbringing.

What would it tell you about the person pictured in Figure 9.1 if you knew his sexual orientation was different from yours? What if you knew he was over 70 years of age? HIV positive? Formerly on welfare?

Figure 9.1 • Are You Biased Towards This Person?

How would knowing this information affect your ability to

- Communicate with him?
- Value his ideas?
- Work closely with him on a project?

EXAMPLES OF BIAS

Biases assume many different forms. These include biases based on race, gender, ethnicity, geographic region, job classification and position, education, social class, political affiliation, disability, and so forth. Given the cumulative effect of culture on our thinking and behavior, bias may reveal itself at any moment.

Consider how reporters' social class backgrounds might filter their view of the world. If reporters come from privileged social backgrounds, might they be apt to cover stories or describe the world differently than those who have had to constantly struggle for social acceptance and economic stability? Like other manifestations of culture, our social class filters our understanding of many different issues.

Table 9.1 • Does Gender Make a Difference?	
Background Information on Assistant Vice President	**Evaluators' Rating**
Both man and woman highly competent	Man and woman viewed as equally competent, but woman is less likable
Competency of both man and woman unknown	Man viewed as more competent than woman; both are equally likable

Source: Madeline Heilman, *Journal of Applied Psychology,* Vol. 89, No. 3, 2004.

Gender Bias

According to research, we learn gender bias from our culture. In one experiment, evaluators were provided with information about individual male and female assistant vice presidents working for an aircraft company. Evaluators rated these assistant VPs in terms of likability and competency.

Each evaluator was provided with background information, including the assistant VP's gender and competency. Competency was either "unknown" because no performance review had been completed, or "highly competent." Findings from this experiment appear in Table 9.1.

According to Heilman's data, it appears we give men but not women the benefit of the doubt when questions arise regarding competency. When a highly competent man occupies a position of leadership, we see him as likable. Why don't we see women the same way? If you were an evaluator in this experiment, how would you respond? Do you make certain assumptions about female leaders, particularly in male-dominated fields?

Perhaps the answers to these questions can be found in the cultural "gender schemas" we have been exposed to in the United States. **Gender schemas**, those images of what it means to be male or female, are part of our cultural upbringing. In the United States, we *learn* to see males as independent, intelligent, and rational, and women as nurturing, irrational, and dependent.

Unfortunately, laws can protect the rights of men and women but they cannot mandate changes in our thinking. In spite of facts and figures and examples that show both men *and* women can be excellent leaders, bias continues to infiltrate and distort our thinking.

Word Usage

The late Ossie Davis, well-known writer, actor, and social commentator, offered some insight into how culture, and specifically the English language, impacts our bias toward

DID YOU KNOW?

According to a recent study conducted by Catalyst, a women's research organization, men consider women to be less adept at problem solving. This same study found that both men and women view women as being more skillful when it comes to supporting and rewarding. And both sexes say men are more apt to excel at delegating responsibility and influencing superiors. What is interesting is how these responses tend to fall along the lines of stereotypical thinking. Men are better at taking charge, while women are more accomplished nurturers. If we believe this, are we apt to view men as running things, and women as supporting them?

whiteness and blackness. Davis found synonyms of whiteness had far more positive implications than synonyms for blackness. Language, as many studies have shown, can affect our beliefs about ourselves and each other.[2]

Melissa, a student of mine, brought this to my attention in a vivid way by describing what she did as part of a presentation in her African American literature class. She opened up *Webster's Dictionary*. Without telling the students what she was doing, she gave them all definitions of the word *black*, such as impure, not good, sullen, and evil. She then read the definitions for *white*, pure driven snow, innocent, harmless, and without malice. When she asked the students to pick the characteristics they prefer, everybody picked those associated with the color *white*. Melissa added, "The class was 90% Black."

Words are powerful, in that they create images in our minds. Moreover, they influence our thoughts and actions. For example, consider how you would feel if someone refers to people with whom you identify as "problem people" versus "people who have problems" just like anybody else. Simply changing the order of these words evokes very different feelings. If poorly chosen, words can negatively impact people. It is also true that well-chosen ones can offer hope, motivate, and strengthen relationships.

UNDERSTANDING THE NATURE OF PREJUDICE AND STEREOTYPES

Bias is the foundation of prejudice and stereotypes. **Prejudice** is an irrational, inflexible prejudgment. When we exhibit prejudice, we form conclusions about people before we get to know them. Most people are very reluctant to acknowledge their prejudices. Yet, making irrational prejudgments is something we do on a regular basis.

Numerous theories attempt to explain why prejudice is found in everyone. According to the culture theory, prejudice is embedded in our culture. Consequently, we cannot escape prejudice since it is learned through everyday interaction with the media, family, friends, coworkers, and strangers.

We frequently learn prejudice by observing and modeling those individuals with whom we have personal and long-lasting relationships. The prejudgments we learn from these relationships can begin to mold our thinking very early in life. For example, we may not have the frame of reference to critically evaluate what we hear from a parent, relative, or close friend. What lessons do we learn if we hear derogatory jokes and stereotypical comments in the presence of others, and observe that no one intervenes?

Ask yourself, "Which of the following individuals would make a good American citizen—John, Ahmad, Jamal, Carlos, Yoshi?" When a group of youngsters, 6–11 years old, were asked this question as part of a survey by Sesame Workshop, creator of TV's *Sesame Street*, almost half said all these individuals would make a good citizen.[3] But what about the other half? Where and how did they learn to prejudge people on the basis of their names? And how likely is it that these prejudices will continue to shape their thinking as adults?

YOUR TURN   · · · · · ·

When did you last encounter prejudice? And when did you last sense that you were showing prejudice toward others?

_____

_____

_____

_____

Of the two prior questions, which one is easier for you to answer? Why?

_____

_____

_____

_____

Often, we make prejudgments on the basis of **stereotypes**, unreliable over-generalizations about people that do not take individual differences into account. When we stereotype a group of individuals, we assume they are all the same even though they are not.

While stereotypes are typically negative, they do not have to be. For example, we might stereotype Asian Americans by portraying them as strong in research and technical areas. Even though we are focusing on a positive attribute, the effect is a lack of understanding. This particular stereotype may limit our ability to see Asian Americans as individuals. In addition, this stereotypical image may limit people's opportunities. For instance, we may assume that Asian Americans are not the best candidates to be managers because we associate this population with technical proficiency rather than interpersonal skills.

Look at Figure 9.2. Which of these people look like an "American"? Research by Project Implicit (**http://implicit.harvard.edu**), found that respondents are much more likely to see European faces, as opposed to Asian faces, as American.

Figure 9.2 • Who Looks American?

DISTINGUISHING BETWEEN STEREOTYPES AND GENERALIZATIONS

We hear stories and comments about groups of people all the time. Many of these are not factual; rather, they are stereotypical. Unlike stereotypes, generalizations represent tendencies or patterns. Generalizations are flexible; stereotypes are rigid. When we generalize, we make assumptions about a group; however, we seek further information before we decide if the assumption fits particular individuals within the group.

Being able to distinguish between fact and fiction, between generalizations and stereotypes, is a skill. This skill enables us to treat people as individuals but, at the same time, realize that a group of individuals *may* tend to act a certain way because of their cultural background.

YOUR TURN • • • • •

Which of the following are stereotypes and which are generalizations? Mark S for stereotype and G for generalization.

_____ People in wheelchairs appreciate offers of assistance.

_____ Asian American women tend to prefer not to drink ice water after childbirth.

_____ Because someone is a Latina, she will be respectful of elders and family oriented.

_____ European Americans are acquisitive and competitive.

_____ In the United States, decisions are often made by majority rule.

(*Note:* Answers and analysis found at end of chapter.)

Understanding the difference between generalizations and stereotypes makes it possible for us to be aware of cultural differences and similarities, and at the same time, be ever mindful of individual differences. In short, we need to recognize the uniqueness of each individual we meet.

In an effort to combat bias in the workplace, some diversity trainers actually reinforce stereotypes. Some trainers teach that Whites are materialistic, competitive, and individualistic; Asians are passive, religious, and future-oriented; Latinos are family-oriented and affectionate; and Native Americans are spiritual and live in harmony with the earth. While their intent is to point out cultural differences, trainers who do this promote stereotypical assumptions by ignoring the diversity within each of these groups.

BECOMING AWARE OF PERSONAL BIAS

 ### Where Am I Now?

DIRECTIONS: For each statement, mark M (most of the time), O (often), S (sometimes), R (rarely), or N (never).

1. _____ I educate myself through workshops, classes, reading, and other activities to learn more about bias and what forms it takes.

2. _____ I am aware of those times when my bias "leaks out."

3. _____ I understand how my bias might influence my behavior.

4. _____ I am aware of those instances when my bias influences my judgments of others.

5. _____ I seek feedback from a variety of people in order to become more aware of my biases.

As we build our CQ, we seek opportunities to promote awareness and understanding of our own biases.

Bias is problematic because it is the outgrowth of assumptions that may be invisible to us. As biases are reinforced, they become rigid and inflexible. Consequently, we tend to cling to our biases even in the face of evidence that proves us wrong.

Why is it important for us to be aware of our biases? If we are aware of them *and* if we are concerned about them, research shows that we have the power to control our biases. Conversely, lack of awareness or concern will make it more certain that our biases will control us.

A good example is Alice, a mixed-race elementary-school teacher. As she sees it, White males do not care about diversity, nor do they have any interest in learning about different cultures. Recently, she has become friends with a few White male teachers in her department who do not fit this stereotype. After becoming aware of her bias toward White males, Alice now is more apt to monitor her thinking when she communicates with others. The less she assumes, especially with regard to White males, the more she is apt to treat people as individuals. Slowly, she is developing the realization that race or gender is not a reliable indicator of someone's thoughts about diversity.

YOUR TURN   · · · · · · ━━━━━━━━━

Two of my biases are

1. _____

_____

2. _____

_____

Unconscious Bias

For many of us, acknowledging our own biases is a formidable challenge. If we refer back to the definition of bias, it becomes clear that we all have biases. Nevertheless, acknowledging our biases can be extremely difficult.

Our bias may be unconscious, meaning we are not aware of it. It is as if our brain has been programmed to take biased, mental shortcuts. Recently, scientific research has shown that we can be fully committed to fairness and equality, yet still possess negative prejudices and hold on to stereotypes. Consequently, unconscious bias may influence our perceptions even though we claim otherwise.

Might unconscious bias explain why women are more likely than men to see their doctor, but less likely to receive proper care? Research suggests that the gender bias of doctors might have something to do with this. Doctors are more likely to dismiss what women say, seeing their complaints as more psychological than physiological. Even when women express concerns about chest pains and other symptoms of heart disease, doctors may be less likely to take complaints seriously. Women report being told by their doctors, "There's nothing to worry about," or "You're overreacting." Doctors are no different from other highly educated and trained professionals when it comes to being unable or unwilling to see their own biases.

In spite of our best efforts to control bias, it can emerge at the most inopportune times. Feeling stress or simply relaxing can allow unconscious bias to emerge. Also, situational factors can play a role, such as the setting, the diversity of the audience, and our familiarity with the people who happen to be present.

Figure 9.3 • Which Words Describe Which Person?

lazy	honest
honest	lazy
sneaky	educated
educated	sneaky
uneducated	hard-working
hard-working	uneducated
threatening	law-abiding
law-abiding	threatening

The Implicit Association Test

The Implicit Association Test (IAT) is designed to measure hidden bias, or what people really feel regardless of whether they are aware of it. In other words, the IAT seeks to avoid socially acceptable or politically correct responses that often skew the results of other tests. For example, how many of us claim we are color-blind even though we are not? This is particularly true in a country like the United States, which prides itself on fairness and treating people the same.

The IAT gauges which words and images trigger positive and negative reactions in the test takers. Responses represent quick, nonreasoned assumptions about people of different races as well as gays, women, and people from other countries.

Time is a factor for a reason. The IAT is based on the idea that our initial, spontaneous response is a better indicator of how we really feel. More time gives us more opportunity to cover up our true feelings. Therefore, timed responses measure implicit or more hidden attitudes. According to numerous studies, implicit assumptions are a better predictor of behavior than explicit or more fully expressed opinions.

Figure 9.3 contains the kind of descriptors found on the IAT. When taking the IAT under time pressure, people of all races in the United States are more likely to pair White faces with positive terms and Black faces with negative terms. According to Mahzarin Banaji, one of three researchers who designed the IAT, the test "measures the thumbprint of the culture of our minds."[4]

Major findings of the IAT, based on the responses of more than 2 million people, can tell us something about our own hidden biases. According to IAT data,

1. We are all biased, regardless of what we say.
2. Among the biases, large majorities show implicit biases against gays and lesbians, Arab Muslims, and the poor.
3. Some of us show bias toward our own group. For example, minorities generally internalize the same biases as majorities.

TO LEARN MORE

Test yourself for hidden bias. Go to **https://implicit.harvard.edu** and take the Implicit Association Test. To better understand the test and your results, go to **https://implicit.harvard.edu/implicit/demo/faqs.html.**

UNDERSTANDING THE DYNAMICS OF BIAS

Being Blind to Cultural Differences: A Wise Choice?

Is it possible or even desirable to be blind to differences in race, ethnicity, or some other dimension of culture? Being blind to cultural differences may be particularly problematic in certain professions. Salespeople, for example, may lose or jeopardize a sale because they fail to consider the relevance of cultural differences. Imagine you are a real estate agent. To your way of thinking, the most important considerations when selling homes are their location, size, condition, and amenities. Unknown to you, however, your prospective buyer is also concerned with the relationship among physical space, human feelings, and emotions.

Buyers with ties to eastern Asian societies may believe that a life force or *qi* flows through structures like homes and office buildings. Whether the design helps or hinders the flow may be crucial to the sale, for a "good building" in harmony with nature will increase the luck and fortune of the people inside.

Or maybe your client, who comes from the Middle East or East Asia, is looking for a home with a room for prayer. Many Muslims pray five times a day, facing the east, toward Mecca. While it is important to be knowledgeable about these cultural preferences, we should not assume someone of a certain cultural background will necessarily feel this way. Rather, as clients become more diverse, both real estate agents and builders should be open to these possibilities and be prepared to adjust.

In other fields such as medicine, culture may be viewed as a nonissue. Some psychiatrists, for example, consider their field of study to be scientific, rational, and devoid of cultural bias. However, this may not apply to diagnoses of mental illness. Unlike other illnesses that may be diagnosed with a brain scan or a blood test, diagnoses of mental illnesses leave more room for error. There is no lab test for mental illness. Rather, its identification depends on verbal and nonverbal cues which may vary from culture to culture. For instance, a secular psychiatrist may interact with a deeply religious patient who mentions hearing the voice of God and believing in spirits. Is this patient mentally ill?

Like the rest of us, psychiatrists who lack cultural intelligence run the danger of using themselves and their own cultural standards as the measure for judging normality. If this occurs, being blind to the cultural differences of patients may actually contribute to a misdiagnosis. The difficulty lies in recognizing cultural cues, interpreting them accurately, and integrating this information into diagnoses and treatments.

Linking Bias to Behavior

YOUR TURN   · · · · · ·

If we are aware of our biases, we can monitor and try to manage them before they are shown through behavior. But it is also true that changing our behavior may decrease or eliminate a personal bias. What is one behavior you can change that might have this effect?

_____

_____

_____

What is the relationship between the bias that is hidden inside of us and the behavior we show to others? Most diversity training focuses on increasing awareness of personal biases and their impact on human relations. This approach is based on the premise that once we become aware of our biases, many of which might be unconscious, we will then be able to behave and express ourselves appropriately.

Social psychologists have found that changing one's attitude does not necessarily lead to a change in behavior. For instance, A.W. Wicker's review of research found that just the opposite can occur; that is, our behavior drives our attitudes.[5] This is the thinking behind the approach taken by the U.S. military. While military leaders admit they cannot eradicate bias and force troops to like one another, they do insist on certain behaviors. Through behavior modification, they seek to promote cooperation and trust. By continually emphasizing and reinforcing the importance of teamwork, the objective is to bring attitudes in line with these expectations, no matter who is involved. The bottom line drives this approach, in that one's life and the success of one's mission might be jeopardized by intolerance and discrimination.

People in the workplace are judged on the basis of their behavior, not their hidden biases. But while bias does not dictate our behavior, it can influence it in a pretty consistent way. In one classic experiment, White interviewers exhibited different behaviors with Black and White applicants. With Blacks, White interviewers generally sat further away, made more speech errors during the course of the interview, and ended it sooner.[6]

YOUR TURN   · · · · · · ━━━━━━━━

Describe a a situation in which you felt biased but your behavior did not show it.

_____

_____

_____

Describe a situation in which you did not feel bias but your behavior showed bias.

_____

_____

_____

All of us, at some point, project an image contrary to how we really feel. We may be sitting at a meeting and trying to look interested even though we are bored to death. This same dynamic may occur with bias. For example, we may try to act in a way that hides our bias in order to fit in or conform to a certain code of conduct in the workplace. Therefore, it is difficult to be sure of someone's motive by observing their behavior.

As a result, what we read into interpersonal interactions can be deceiving. A recent study by a team of psychologists found that Whites with more negative views of racial minorities sometimes go out of their way to act friendly and are more careful about what they say. According to the researchers, this leads some African Americans and other minorities to prefer interacting with highly-prejudiced Whites who are adept at masking their real feelings, as opposed to certain low-prejudiced Whites who might act more openly and honestly.[7]

Whether we feel bias and act on it will depend on the situation. Consider those times when a person's feelings may or may not match his or her behavior. A good example would be a web designer who creates a beautiful site that is all Flash—soft, attractive animation full of beautiful images—but offers no text options. For someone with a visual impairment, this type of content is very difficult if not impossible to access, yet the designer probably does not realize it.

WHEN BIAS LEAKS OUT

Even though we may try to cover up our bias, it can leak out. We may be completely unaware of this, while the person on the receiving end may be overwhelmingly aware. Just because we think we are behaving in an unbiased manner, it does not mean we are.

Certain cues *may* point to bias in ourselves and others. While bias leakage can be overt and easy to pinpoint, it can also show up in less obvious ways. For instance, body language can point to bias: expressions, stance, eye contact, or even how far away we stand while talking.

YOUR TURN   · · · · ·

Think of someone who maintains he or she is not biased, but you think otherwise. What cues point to bias in that individual?

_____

_____

_____

_____

Even when bias in others seems obvious, do not assume. Rather, seek more information. For example, what would you read into a supervisor questioning the appropriateness of a Black female's beaded corn rows? In a situation such as this, it is usually a good idea to ask for clarification and maybe share how you feel. You might ask, why is the hair style inappropriate? If the supervisor offers an explanation, is the reason job-related? For instance, what is company policy? Are there specific rules regarding dress and appearance, and why? Reflect on other possible explanations for the comment. If appropriate, share how you feel about the comment.

It helps to have some knowledge of the person who shows what you perceive as bias. Is the behavior in question out of the ordinary or is it part of a pattern? Before jumping to conclusions, think through your response. Serious, repeated behaviors should be reported to someone in authority whom you can trust. This might be an individual, a committee, or even a "hotline" set up for this purpose.

WHAT IS DISCRIMINATION?

While all cultures classify people, how we treat people on the basis of these classifications varies from culture to culture. A good example is the way we treat older workers. In many cultures, older workers are highly valued and treated with reverence and respect. In the United States, older workers are often devalued and not viewed as cost-effective. A common stereotypical belief is that technological expertise, innovation, and flexibility are the domain of youth.

Age is constantly an issue, according to human resource managers. Often, older candidates for jobs are not even given the opportunity of an interview. If they do get an interview, they may hear comments such as, "We're looking for someone with young ideas," or "Don't you think you're overqualified?"

Discrimination, the unequal treatment of a group or individual, may be difficult to see because it can be so subtle. For example, one recent study of racial discrimination in the workplace shows that it is not typically the "in-your-face" variety. Rather, discrimination is often hidden and **institutionalized;** that is, unequal treatment is built into the policies, procedures, and practices of an organization. Consequently, people may not even be aware they are targets or perpetrators of this kind of discrimination.

For example, a person of color might be turned down for a mortgage request. This decision might be based on factors that have nothing to do with the individual. Studies show that lenders are far more likely to turn down such a request from a minority applicant than from an equally qualified White applicant. Furthermore, lenders provide minority applicants with less assistance in completing the necessary paperwork.[8]

If we just look for discrimination *between* different groups of people, we would be unaware of much discrimination. For example, a common form of discrimination *within* a group is **colorism**, unequal treatment based on the lightness, darkness, or other color characteristics of an individual. Colorism is found among Asian Americans, African Americans, Latinos, and other groups. Recently, a major restaurant chain was found in violation of Title VII of the Civil Rights Act of 1964. Title VII protects against discrimination on the basis of skin color as well as race, sex, national origin, or religion. According to the African American server who worked at one of the chain's restaurants in Atlanta, he was called "porch monkey," "jig-a-boo," "blackie," and other derogatory names by his manager. His manager was a light-skinned African American.

RECOGNIZING THE MANY FACES OF DISCRIMINATION

We can be victimized by discrimination for any number of reasons. Imagine a company looking to hire new employees. The company, looking to fill a number of positions, advertises in a number of large urban areas and receives hundreds of responses. Which of the following factors do you think would determine whether job applicants got calls for interviews?

1. Experience
2. Academic background

3. Résumé and cover letter
4. Specific job skills
5. Name

For most of us, answers 1 through 4 are relevant and worthy of consideration and 5 is totally irrelevant. A real-life study, however, shows otherwise. Recently, economists at the University of Chicago and the Massachusetts Institute of Technology sent 5,000 résumés to 1,250 employers who ran help-wanted ads in Chicago and Boston.[10] Some job applicants were given names we associate with Blacks, such as Tyrone, while others were given White-sounding names, like Greg. Each employer received four résumés: an average Black applicant, an average White applicant, a highly skilled Black applicant, and a highly skilled White applicant.

Prior to sending out the résumés, the researchers had been told that the employers looking for help were seeking to diversify their workforce and hire qualified minorities. Nevertheless, those résumés with "White-sounding names" elicited 50% more callbacks than those with "Black-sounding names." In addition, highly qualified Black applicants got fewer calls than lower-skilled White applicants. Even so-called equal opportunity employers discriminated.

YOUR TURN

Place a check beside the following real-life scenarios that involve discrimination.

_____ **SCENARIO 1.** As a female bartender for a casino in Las Vegas, you are required to conform to certain appearance standards. In addition to being required to wear makeup, you are weighed periodically, with the understanding that you are allowed to gain only a certain amount of weight. If your appearance does not conform to the guidelines, you will be suspended without pay and may be fired.

_____ **SCENARIO 2.** You are a hostess or host at a restaurant. Your job is to greet customers as they arrive and seat them at their table. A few customers have complained about your appearance; specifically, the tattoos covering your arms and much of your legs as well as your body jewelry. The manager moves you to another position where the public will not see you.

_____ **SCENARIO 3.** As a worker at a fast-food chain, your job is to take orders from people in their cars who are using the drive-through lane. You are not yet fluent in English but you manage to understand your customers, even though you sometimes have difficulty. The other day, a customer drove through and became annoyed by your inability to understand what he was saying. The customer, who happens to be a well-known politician, complained to your manager, who in turn fired you.

All three scenarios describe different forms of discrimination. However, all forms of discrimination are not covered by law. While the legal implications of these scenarios are beyond the scope of this book, it is interesting to note that in the first real-life scenario involving a casino company in Reno, Nevada, the court affirmed the right of employers to adopt "reasonable" dress and grooming standards. The other two scenarios are hypothetical. In general, the legality of decisions based on language or appearance tend to revolve around whether they relate to a person's ability to do his or her job and whether these requirements are uniformly applied to all employees.

In each scenario, employees were treated differently for so-called business reasons. Appearance and English-speaking skills can and do impact the bottom line. However, in these examples, are we catering to other people's biases in order to be more profitable? What do you think?

_____

_____

_____

_____

_____

_____

PERCEPTIONS OF DISCRIMINATION

In a study by the John J. Heldrich Center for Work Development at Rutgers University, U.S. workers were asked about discrimination on the job. Data from this survey show starkly different perceptions of the pervasiveness of discrimination.

Looking at the data in Figure 9.4, it is almost as if workers interact in very different workplaces. In comparison to White workers, African American workers perceive considerably more unfair treatment on the job.

Findings from another study conducted by the Pew Hispanic Center examined the perceptions of Hispanics in particular. According to this survey, the vast majority of Hispanics think discrimination is a problem. Interestingly, an overwhelming majority see Hispanics discriminating against other Hispanics as part of this problem.[11] Discrimination of this nature can be due to a variety of factors, including differences in education and income. In other instances, discrimination among Hispanics may occur because of differences in cultural backgrounds and countries of origin.

EXPERIENCING DISCRIMINATION

Is discrimination widespread? According to the latest research, that depends on who you ask. According to one poll of six ethnic groups, African Americans are most likely to say they experience discrimination because of ethnic heritage,

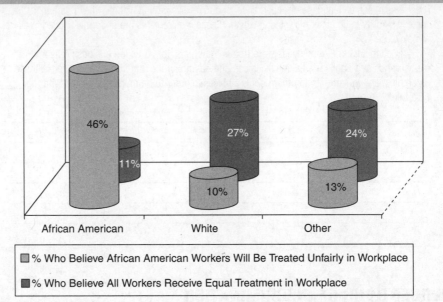

Figure 9.4 • Perceptions of Workplace Discrimination

■ % Who Believe African American Workers Will Be Treated Unfairly in Workplace

■ % Who Believe All Workers Receive Equal Treatment in Workplace

SOURCE: "A Workplace Divided: How Americans View Discrimination and Race on the Job," John J. Heldrich Center for Work Development, Rutgers University.

followed by Jews and Hispanics. Results from the poll, conducted prior to the terrorist attacks of September 11, 2001, appear in Figure 9.5.

If this same poll was conducted today, responses might be markedly different, especially for Arab Americans. Equal Employment Opportunity Commission (EEOC) data show that in the aftermath of 9/11, Arabs or even people who look Arab are much more likely to be singled out as possible terrorists and treated unequally.

People experience discrimination for a variety of reasons. A study conducted by researchers at Rice University examined cultural bias toward people whom we perceive as obese. This relatively small-scale study examined the experiences of overweight shoppers in a large city. Findings illustrate how sales clerks are affected by our weight-conscious culture. Clerks in this study discriminated against overweight shoppers, especially when these shoppers dressed casually. Much of the discrimination was subtle, including sales clerks who acted rude and unfriendly. While some question whether these sales clerks might be rude to everyone, the findings are in line with numerous other studies that lend credence to discrimination of this nature. Interestingly, the clerks in this study were less apt to discriminate if they thought the customer was trying to lose weight.[12]

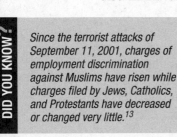

DID YOU KNOW?

Since the terrorist attacks of September 11, 2001, charges of employment discrimination against Muslims have risen while charges filed by Jews, Catholics, and Protestants have decreased or changed very little.[13]

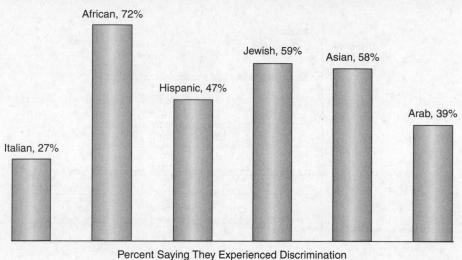

Figure 9.5 • Experienced Discrimination?

African, 72%

Jewish, 59%

Asian, 58%

Hispanic, 47%

Arab, 39%

Italian, 27%

Percent Saying They Experienced Discrimination

SOURCE: James Zogby, *What Ethnic Americans Really Think*. (Zogby International, 2001).

RESPONDING TO BIAS EFFECTIVELY

(?) Where Am I Now?

DIRECTIONS: For each statement, mark M (most of the time), O (often), S (sometimes), R (rarely), or N (never).

1. _____ I speak up when others feel belittled or harassed because of their race, gender, or sexual orientation.

2. _____ I challenge organizational policies and procedures that lead to the unfair treatment of certain people.

3. _____ When the opportunity presents itself, I discuss the issue of bias with others.

4. _____ I intervene in some way when I observe others showing bias.

5. _____ I seek feedback to clarify anything I perceive as bias.

6. _____ I see my response to bias as a way to promote learning and growth for everyone involved.

The preceding "Where Am I Now?" points to a number of constructive responses to bias. Statements to which you responded S, R, or N indicate those areas you might want to focus on and practice.

Figure 9.6 • Forms of Disrespect in the Workplace

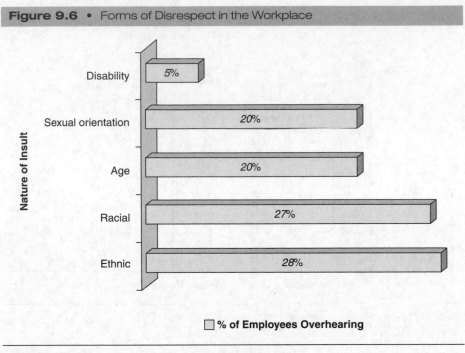

SOURCE: Survey conducted by International Communications Research (Media, PA, 2004).

As stated earlier, bias can reveal itself in the form of prejudice, stereotypes, and discrimination. Consider how you would respond if you heard a coworker make a sexually inappropriate comment, use a racial or ethnic slur, or ridicule someone because of his or her age, sexual orientation, or disability?

According to a recent national survey of U.S. workers, the most frequent form of disrespect was the use of sexually inappropriate language, reported by 28% of women and 35% of men. The frequency of other common forms of disrespect is shown in Figure 9.6.

Think back to the *last* time you and others with you overheard an inappropriate comment directed at someone's language, race, sexual orientation, age, disability, or some other dimension of diversity.

• What was your reaction?

_____

_____

_____

• How did it affect you and why?

_____

_____

_____

- What might you have done differently? Why?

  _____

  _____

  _____

It is easy to misinterpret comments. If possible, strive to maintain a dialogue rather than a monologue. As you learn more, you might discover that you misread a facial expression or off-handed remark. Perhaps what you construed as intentional, mean-spirited bias is actually an innocent cultural misunderstanding.

When we encounter bias, numerous options exist. Today, people targeted by bias are less likely to ignore it and walk away. This is especially true in the workplace. Speaking up, approaching management, and filing lawsuits are all viable options. Or you may decide to try to put the bias behind you and move on.

CQ Applied · · · · · · ·

Katie, a financial consultant, deals with bias constantly because of her appearance. In many situations people assume that Katie, a White blonde female, is unintelligent and relies on her striking looks to get ahead. Instead of confronting these people and their biases, Katie simply focuses on her work and strives for excellence. If she is overly concerned about what others think, she finds she cannot do her job well. Simply put, she lets her actions speak for her.

Acknowledging the existence of bias and understanding its nature helps us move beyond guilt and finger-pointing to promoting understanding. It is usually a good idea to explain how you feel as a result of what you perceive as bias. Artist Adrian Piper, who teaches at Wellesley College in Massachusetts, has created business cards to make us think about how we might react to bias. When she encounters **racism**, the belief that some racial groups are naturally superior or inferior to others, Piper distributes the business card pictured in Figure 9.7.

Figure 9.7 • One Person's Reaction to Racism

Dear Friend,
I am Black.
I am sure you did not realize this when you made/laughed at/agreed with that racist remark. In the past, I have attempted to alert White people to my racial identity in advance. Unfortunately, this invariably causes them to react to me as pushy, manipulative, or socially inappropriate. Therefore, my policy is to assume that White people do not make these remarks, even when they believe there are no Black people present, and to distribute this card when they do.
I regret any discomfort my presence is causing you, just as I am sure you regret the discomfort your racism is causing me.

YOUR TURN • • • • • • ━━━━━━━━

Create your own business card, one that might raise the consciousness of someone who shows bias.
What would you print on the card? _____

_____

_____

_____

_____

_____

UNLEARNING PERSONAL BIAS

 REFLECT BEFORE READING

You take a test for bias. It shows that you have biases toward Native Americans. Which of the following strategies is most effective in changing the way you view Native Americans?

1. Decorating your office with artwork by Native American artists.

2. Joining a team in which you have to work closely with Native Americans.

3. Reading books about the contributions of Native Americans.

4. Participating in a diversity training workshop that deals with strategies for combating racial bias.

Why do you think the strategy you chose is most effective? _____

_____

_____

_____

_____

While all of these strategies can change the way you view Native Americans, probably the most effective is joining the team, especially if your participation on the team is personal, intensive, and long-lasting. No one strategy, however, is sufficient.

Research shows that we can unlearn biases. However, it is not easy. Since bias is reinforced over time, it becomes ingrained. Consequently, it may be more realistic to begin with reducing or managing bias as opposed to eliminating it.

Unlearning bias requires conscious and continuous efforts on the part of the individual. The first step is to acknowledge our biases. This is not as easy as it sounds. Many of our biases are hidden or unconscious, as discussed previously. Because we internalize biases from our everyday environment, seeing them takes work.

It helps to acknowledge any discomfort or fear that might "kick in" around certain groups of people. Does your nonverbal communication reflect this discomfort? Do you tend to prejudge certain individuals because of their appearance, dress, or mannerisms? If so, ask yourself why? Awareness, reflection, and critical thinking are critical.

Bias can be reduced significantly when members of racially and culturally mixed groups work together to accomplish common goals. Consider research that has been done in the area of cooperative contact. Many social scientists have studied how group identification impacts our biases.

In one classic study by Dr. Muzafer Sherif, boys at a summer camp were divided into two competing groups.[14] Their competitive relationship fed intergroup hostility. Then, Sherif created situations in which boys in both groups had to work together for a greater goal. In one case, for example, this meant pulling a truck that was stuck. Experiences such as these significantly reduced their bias and hostility toward each other.

YOUR TURN   · · · · · ────────────────

What recent cooperative experience served to reduce or eliminate a bias of yours?

_____

_____

_____

How can we apply Sherif's findings to human relations skills? When individuals from diverse groups and backgrounds come together to achieve shared goals, bias can be significantly reduced. This is particularly true when everyone feels accepted, interacts frequently, and gets to know one another personally. Interaction of this nature has been found to change our thinking about others more than studying cultural differences or just talking about intolerance.

Contrary to popular belief, it is not enough to simply live in a diverse community or work with diverse coworkers. To unlearn bias, we need to engage people we might otherwise avoid. Furthermore, we need to get "up close and personal." Some organizations have programs that encourage employees to do this very thing, such as cross-cultural mentoring and volunteering with diverse community groups. Experiences such as these increase the likelihood that we will develop meaningful relationships with people who make us question our biases.

THE BOTTOM LINE

When we address the bottom-line effects of bias, we tend to concern ourselves with those who are directly victimized. **Co-victimization** means that you can feel the effects of bias even if you do not experience it directly. For example, sexual harassment can poison the climate of an entire workplace, make everyone feel uncomfortable and guarded, and lead to mistrust.

Bias can become a **self-fulfilling prophecy**, meaning bias can create expectations that cause people to act in ways consistent with how they are expected to act. For example, people will live down to expectations that reflect bias. If we assume young people or old people cannot do something simply because of their age, our expectations may place limits on what *they think* they can do. Self-fulfilling prophecies lower expectations and reduce performance.

Bias hurts everyone, including the person who knowingly or unknowingly displays it. If we show bias, it cuts us off from new ideas from individuals and groups. By putting up a wall between us and others, bias limits our opportunities to grow and learn from others and build our cultural intelligence.

By dealing with bias and thereby doing the personal growth work necessary to lessen, control, and eliminate bias, we become more adept at reading people accurately. Without the distraction and distortion of bias of all kinds, we can think more clearly, relate more effectively, adapt more quickly, and be more productive. Furthermore, we will become more comfortable with cultural diversity, and more confident in our ability to capitalize on it.

A Look Back: I Have Learned

✓ _____ What is meant by bias.

✓ _____ How bias and culture interrelate.

✓ _____ How bias takes different forms.

✓ _____ How to differentiate between stereotypes and generalizations.

✓ _____ Why our personal biases are often invisible to us.

✓ _____ How bias may impact behavior.

✓ _____ What is meant by discrimination.

✓ _____ How to unlearn bias.

✓ _____ Why and how bias impacts the bottom line.

Individual Action Plan

Think about one specific thing you can do to improve your skills in the area of dealing with bias. Then complete the following plan during the next _____. (state time period).

Specific skill I want to improve first (refer to list of Performance Skills at the beginning of the chapter).

_____

My strategy:

_____

_____

_____

_____

In order to develop this skill, I will:

_____

_____

_____

_____

Possible obstacles include:

_____

_____

_____

_____

Resources I need:

_____

_____

_____

_____

I will measure my progress by:

_____

_____

_____

_____

Answers

Your Turn (see p. 207)

  S   People in wheelchairs appreciate offers of assistance.

  G   Asian American women tend to prefer not to drink ice water after childbirth.

  S   Because someone is a Latina, she will be respectful of elders and family oriented.

  S   European Americans are acquisitive and competitive.

  G   In the United States, decisions by groups of people are often made by majority rule.

Each of the stereotypical statements (marked S) portrays everyone within a group as alike. Qualifiers, such as *many*, *often*, or *commonly* are missing. It is important to use precise language. Saying "some people of this culture," or referring to a "custom practiced by many" allows us to be more accurate.

Notes

1. Beverly Tatum, *Why Are All the Black Kids Sitting Together in the Cafeteria? And Other Conversations About Race* (New York: Harper Collins, 1997).

2. O. Davis, "The English Language Is My Enemy." In C. D. Eckhardt, J. F. Holahan, and D. H. Stewart (eds.), *The Wiley Reader* (New York: John Wiley and Sons, 1976), pp. 312–313.

3. Ellen Edwards, "For Kids, There's No Place Like Home," *The Washington Post*, 2/26/03, p. C4.

4. Shankar Vedantam, "See No Bias," *The Washington Post Magazine*, January 23, 2005, pp. 12+.

5. A. W. Wicker, "Attitudes versus Actions: The Relationship of Verbal and Overt Behavioral Responses to Attitude Objects," *Journal of Social Issues*, 25, 1969, pp. 41–78.

6. Paul L. Wachtel, "Racism, Vicious Circles, and the Psychoanalytic Vision." *The Psychoanalytic Review*, 88, Oct. 2001, pp. 653–672.

7. Richard Morin, "Words That Matter," *The Washington Post*, July 31, 2005, p. B5.

8. John Yinger, *Closed Doors, Opportunities Lost: The Continuing Costs of Housing Discrimination* (New York: Russell Sage Foundation, 1995).

9. Gallup Poll, 2005.

10. The University of Chicago Graduate School of Business, "Racial Bias in Hiring." Online Spring 2003. Available: **http://www.chicagogsb.edu/capideas/spring03/racialbias.html**.

11. Associated Press, "Hispanic Hope Persists Despite Discrimination," *Baltimore Sun*, 12/18/02, p. 19A.

12. "Obese Shoppers Say Clerks Not Helpful," **abc7.com**. Online 5/14/2005. Available: **http://abclocal.go.com/kabc/health/041105_hs_obese_shoppers.html**.

13. U.S. Equal Employment Opportunity Commission.

14. Muzafer Sherif, *In Common Predicament: Social Psychology of Intergroup Conflict and Cooperation* (Boston: Houghton Mifflin, 1966).

CHAPTER 10

- - - - - - - -

CQ MEGASKILL: UNDERSTANDING THE DYNAMICS OF POWER

Performance Skills

- *Understanding the nature of power*
- *Tuning in to our power*
- *Recognizing privileges*
- *Identifying our minority and majority statuses*
- *Understanding the repercussions of power*
- *Treating people with respect*

 REFLECT BEFORE READING

Imagine you are participating in a diversity workshop. Next on the agenda is something called "the privilege walk." According to the leader of the workshop, the idea behind this exercise is to give participants the experience of feeling what it is like to be excluded on the basis of power.

Scenario: The leader instructs you and other participants to form a line in the center of the room, standing shoulder to shoulder. She then reads a list of social and economic privileges, such as attending a private school or growing up in a well-to-do neighborhood. If the privilege applies to you, you are instructed to step forward.

Then, the leader describes a number of social and economic disadvantages. These disadvantages include, "I can turn on the television or read the newspaper and see many negative images of people like me." This time, if the statement applies to you, you are told to step back. As the exercise unfolds, the space separating those who are privileged and those who are disadvantaged slowly becomes more noticeable.

After the exercise, participants discuss what they felt when they stepped forward and backward. Some coworkers were found more toward the front of the line. They share how they felt both lucky and guilty. Comments from those with fewer privileges, found near the back, reveal their frustration and resentment.

The exercise reminded them of how difficult it is to "catch up" to others no matter how hard they try.

The leader invites you and other participants to share your feelings about the privilege walk. She explains that the best way to learn about power and privilege is by examining our own lives. Some resent being singled out as more privileged. Others see it differently, explaining the discrimination they encounter almost daily due to their lack of privilege. They counter, "It's good for others to know how it feels."

However, one woman of mixed race shared that the entire activity was a nightmare in her eyes. "As if I needed one more reminder in my life of the discrimination I must endure and the lack of status I must deal with on a daily basis. It was so publicly degrading that I left the room in tears and have had trouble communicating with some people in that room ever since."

- - - - - - -

YOUR TURN

If you were part of this exercise, would you find yourself closer to the "more privileged" or "less privileged" group? Why?

_____

_____

_____

If you were part of this exercise, where would you *want* to be standing—closer to those with a great deal of power, closer to those with little power, or somewhere in the middle? Why?

_____

_____

_____

_____

INTRODUCTION

Like other megaskills, understanding the dynamics of power has vast implications for success in our chosen profession. This aspect of cultural intelligence helps us understand how people view and define power, how power operates, and how it is distributed. Equally important, we develop a clearer picture of how the dynamics of power impact each of us. Do we and should we act differently toward others based on our power and theirs? Do we recognize how we and others use power? How does power affect our assumptions about others?

In order to make sense of the dynamics of power, we need to make the connections between our lives and the cultural context in which we find ourselves. These connections are relevant both at home and abroad. While power is distributed unequally throughout the world, the degree of inequality and the nature of that inequality vary depending on numerous situational factors. Similarly, how people view and use power varies within and between cultures.

Understanding the dynamics of power is probably one of the most difficult megaskills to examine. In the United States, discussing it with others or analyzing it can be an uncomfortable experience, especially when we examine power on a personal level. While power is seen as a natural occurrence in human relationships in many other countries, power in the United States is more apt to be seen as unnatural and something to abuse.

In an effort to put some distance between ourselves and power, we may push it to one side or it may lie hidden from our view. This is all the more reason to take a closer look at the nature of power and its ramifications for the way we think, feel, and interact.

UNDERSTANDING THE NATURE OF POWER

Power refers to the ability to bring about change. When defined this way, it is clear that we all have power. Regardless of our title, job, status in life, or family background, all of us can make a difference. When we participate in decision making, serve as a mentor, and team with others, we exercise power.

At work and in other settings, some of us have more power than others for a variety of reasons. Certain people have power because of their personal characteristics, such as a magnetic or charismatic personality. Other sources of power include money, personal connections, good interpersonal skills, and support from others. In the case of directors, managers, and supervisors in organizations, their positions provide them with the authority to make things happen by enabling them to influence and even control others.

YOUR TURN . . . . .

Getting results is very different for the powerful and the powerless. Think back to the last time someone with power over you asked you to do something. What was your response? Now imagine how you would react if the person making the request had little or no power. Would your response have been any different? Why?

_____

_____

_____

_____

Power affects the way people view us and relate to us. Often, people are nicer to those with power, even if that person happens to be obnoxious or is very self-centered. When we communicate with someone with more power than us, we may be less spontaneous and more aware of our language, both verbal and nonverbal.

Consider the way we view and react to **sexual harassment**, unwelcome sexual attention that creates a hostile work environment or affects people's work performance. In recent years, sexual harassment has come to be seen as an act that says more about power than sex. For instance, it is more likely that someone in power will harass someone with less power than vice versa. People sometimes wonder why people who are harassed do not complain or bring charges against the perpetrator. Perhaps they feel no one will listen to them or believe them because they lack power.

⑦ Where Am I Now?

DIRECTION: For each statement, write the number corresponding to your answer: Always (5), Frequently (4), Sometimes (3), Rarely (2), or Never (1).

1. _____ I am aware of those situations in which I do have power.

2. _____ I am aware of those situations in which I do not have power.

3. _____ I understand how power influences the way people relate to me.

4. _____ I understand how a person's power influences the way I relate to him or her.

5. _____ I am aware of my earned and unearned privileges.

6. _____ I give everybody the same amount of respect, regardless of their power.

7. _____ I am aware of those situations in which I exclude others because of their power.

8. _____ I use my knowledge of the dynamics of power to reach out to those who may feel excluded due to their lack of power.

☐ Point Total

Strive to improve your point total over time. As your understanding of the dynamics of power increases, you will exhibit these skills more often.

PERCEPTIONS OF POWER

Because the U.S. culture is highly individualistic and very competitive, power is very often viewed in terms of economic, political, and social domination. In this context, power is viewed as a scarce resource that is possessed by the "higher-ups." But if we define power as bringing about change, power is not limited to individuals who have achieved a certain ranking. For example, secretaries and receptionists wield power by virtue of how they interact with customers. Also, they are in a position to influence who has access to those in power.

I am reminded of Rayheen, a recent immigrant to this country who spoke very little English. She shared with me how a receptionist who spoke "easy

English" made it possible for her to gain the information she needed to find a job. In this context, the receptionist wielded considerable power. While she might not have known it at the time, her ability to communicate effectively in this particular situation opened up a life-changing opportunity for Rayheen.

Power can be a difficult concept to grasp and discuss, especially to those of us who are not aware of our power and privilege. Also, many of us have preconceived, biased notions about who is most likely to have power. When students come into Tom's class for the first time, they are likely to talk to his assistant, Linda, as if she is the teacher. Or they will ask each other, "Is he the teacher?" Because of a diving accident that paralyzed him from the neck down, Tom uses a wheelchair. To many of his students, he does not fit the image of a teacher. Even his coworkers will sometimes try to talk to Tom through Linda, or they will act as if he is not present.

CULTURE OF POWER

As previously stated, we can trace power to an individual attribute. However, power is also part of the larger system or culture in which we find ourselves. For this reason, we might hear people use the phrase, **culture of power**. In *Uprooting Racism*, Paul Kivel defines the culture of power as an environment created by those in power "that places its members at the cultural center and other groups at the margins." This term underscores the fact that power is more than an individual phenomenon. We can only make sense of how power is defined, expressed, and distributed by examining our environment.

If there is a culture of power, what does it look like? Visualize a specific, familiar setting. Then ask yourself the following six questions:

- Who is in charge?
- Who is respected?
- Who is listened to?
- Who has the most resources?
- Who makes the important decisions?
- Whose experiences are valued the most?

If the culture of power benefits us, we may have a difficult time seeing it, feeling it, or understanding its impact. In certain groups, power may be based on a variety of things, including gender, religion, nationality, physical appearance, language, sexual orientation, social class, and age.

As an example, someone might experience a male culture of power in certain workplaces. In a male culture of power, what men say and do carries more weight. Men are at the center of things, so to speak, while women may feel insecure and invisible as they try to fit into this culture as much as possible.

As I become more aware of cultural diversity, I have gradually grown more aware of those times when others feel excluded by the relationships within an organization as well as its physical environment. As an example, I belong to a health club. Upon joining, I became aware of a culture of power that was anything but diverse in terms of age. In the more than 100 images in the club, from advertisements to photographs, there is not one senior citizen. The entire staff of more than 20 people represents an age group of young and middle-aged adults. The music that is piped in through the sound system appeals to younger rather than older people. To try to be more inclusive in terms of their music, the club asks people to indicate their preference for music by accessing their Website. But will people of all ages be equally inclined to do this? Even though the club serves many seniors, its culture of power is not inclusive in terms of age.

Although we may notice our own exclusion, it is important for us to tune in to the exclusion of others as well. To do this, we need to work at recognizing and carefully listening to those who are denied access to the culture of power. Shifting perspectives can also make us aware of how we may unknowingly exclude certain people. In other words, ask yourself, "If I were of a different age, race, gender, or ethnicity, how would I feel at this moment or in this circumstance?" Or ask, "Who might feel left out, disrespected, or even unsafe at this point in time?" We might do this when working on a team, getting to know a client, or selling a product to a customer.

CQ Applied

Becoming familiar with the culture of power at work will help you deal with a variety of diversity issues, including religion. An Orthodox Jew comments on how lucky she was to be one of many observant Jews at her firm.

> *It was already accepted that there would be an early departure for the Sabbath on Fridays in the winter. My non-Jewish/religious managers would watch the clock for me on Fridays and practically kick me out the door if they thought I was going to be late for the Sabbath. All firm outings and parties had kosher caterers brought in. If there was a kosher member on an audit team, even client lunches were held in kosher restaurants to the extent possible. There was great effort made to hold all activities on nights other than Fridays and Jewish holidays.*

Often, an organization's track record in one area of diversity says something about their commitment in other areas. In order to become more familiar with the culture of power in a specific workplace and whether they fit in, prospective employees might ask the following questions. Does the organization

- Address discrimination and harassment through policies and procedures?
- Provide some type of ongoing diversity training for its employees?
- Provide mentoring and support systems to all employees?
- Consider cultural intelligence in performance reviews?
- Systematically address the need for respecting cultural differences in all relationships involving customers, clients, and coworkers?

Table 10.1 • Cultural Expectations and Power Distance

Behaviors	Expectations	
	Small-Power Distance Cultures	**Large-Power Distance Cultures**
Demonstration of power by those in authority	Do not openly demonstrate power or pull rank	Openly show power
Direction from those in authority	Delegate power and give subordinates important assignments	Hold on to power and provide clear direction to subordinates
Relationship between supervisor and subordinate	Socialize together and develop personal relationship to some degree	Generally, relationships should be impersonal and formal

POWER DISTANCE

Power distance refers to how much equality or inequality people within a particular society accept or expect. The power distance of relationships ranges from relatively equal to very unequal. Power distance, which varies from culture to culture, might reveal itself in the expectations and behaviors that govern relationships between supervisors and subordinates (see Table 10.1).

Geert Hofstede, an international management scholar, studied power distance in his research of IBM employees working in 40 countries. In some countries, such as India and Colombia, workers both expected and accepted large differences in power. In these "large-power distance" countries, workers gave people with power a tremendous amount of respect and deference. In other "small-power distance" countries, such as Germany and the United States, relationships were more equal. People valued equality for everyone. Consequently, workers were more likely to question those in power at times, speak their minds, and provide frequent feedback.[1]

TO LEARN MORE

Go to **www.geert-hofstede.com/hofstede_dimensions.php.** Use the interactive chart to compare power distance differences for over 80 countries.

TUNING IN TO OUR POWER

One of the best ways to learn about power is by examining ourselves in different situations. For instance, we might examine our power at home, among friends, and possibly at work.

YOUR TURN

Follow directions in Table 10.2.

Table 10.2 • When Do I Have Power?

I Am Powerful

Think of a real-life situation in which the following occurs:

- I am taken seriously. In other words, when I talk, people listen.
- I am in a position to influence others, even when they do not agree.
- I am given a great deal of respect.
- I have extensive resources at my disposal.

Describe this situation:

_____

_____

_____

_____

_____

_____

_____

_____

I Am Powerless

Think of a real-life situation in which the following occurs:

- I am not taken seriously and ignored often.
- I am often bypassed or dismissed when decisions are made.
- I am frequently disrespected, usually without consequences.
- I have limited resources at my disposal.

Describe this situation:

_____

_____

_____

_____

_____

_____

_____

_____

One of the most effective ways of tuning in to our power is to be conscious of those situations in which we do and do not have power. How do we act and react differently to others when we are powerful and powerless? And how does our degree of power affect how we feel about ourselves and others?

In some instances, gender differences provide us with answers to these questions. In particular, research shows male and female differences in demeanor, use of space, and body language:

Demeanor   Powerful people tend to interrupt others while speaking more than less-powerful people. Since women are more apt to occupy positions of lesser power, they are more apt to be interrupted by men, defer to men, and remain quiet while men are talking.

Use of Space   Those with more power tend to take up more **personal space,** the area surrounding a person over which he or she makes some claim to privacy. Personal space varies from culture to culture. But almost everywhere, a pattern emerges when men and women are talking. Men are allowed much more freedom when it comes to intruding into a women's personal space than vice versa.

Body Language   Outside of personal relationships, touching and smiling can tell us something about power. While men are more likely to touch women, women are more apt to smile at men. Interestingly, touching can convey power and dominance while smiling sometimes symbolizes submission or appeasement.

PRIVILEGES: EARNED AND UNEARNED

Privileges are rights or benefits enjoyed by a particular person or a select group. Those in power are apt to enjoy a wide range of privileges. Some are economic, but they can be social and psychological as well. Privileges rooted in power might include participating in decision making, accessing resources and information, being heard, and not having to think about "passing" or assimilating.

In certain situations, some individuals may cover up their differences or try to pass as members of more powerful or mainstream cultural groups. As an example, gay and lesbian professionals may pass as heterosexuals in order to enhance their prospects for upward mobility. A lawyer who typically wears a yarmulke outside of court may have to think long and hard about whether it is in the best interests of his client to do this inside of court.

What we view as a privilege reflects our cultural background. For example, how many of us consider paying bills, maintaining a car, and working 9 to 5 as incredible privileges? Many people do, both in this country and around the world. One such person is a middle-aged woman who in her words was "locked in a psychiatric ward" after being diagnosed with bipolar disorder, a disability marked by extreme mood swings. To her, these jobs or responsibilities are privileges or freedoms to be savored and enjoyed.

YOUR TURN · · · · · ·

Imagine that you *had* to change your race, gender, *or* sexual orientation. Which of these would you change and why?

_____

_____

_____

_____

What privileges would you gain from this change?

_____

_____

_____

_____

What privileges would you lose?

_____

_____

_____

_____

Earned privileges, those advantages that reflect effort and achievement, are what motivate many workers. **Unearned privileges** refer to those advantages that we have due to who we are or circumstances beyond our control. In theory, unearned privileges have no place in U.S. organizations. Yet reality tells us otherwise.

What dictates your ability to move up the bureaucracy or chain of command may have more to do with who you know rather than what you know. What we do or are capable of doing may take a back seat to who we are. For example, being male or female, Black or White, married or single, and Christian or non-Christian may provide us with unearned privileges. Unearned privileges can factor into hiring, promotion, decision making, networking, and evaluations.

In her classic study, *Men and Women of the Corporation*, Rosabeth Moss Kanter discusses the significance of numbers, particularly as it relates to privileges. She concludes that those individuals who are few in number often encounter significant interpersonal problems and are treated as outsiders.[2] To be specific, they may be stereotyped and made to feel as if they are under a spotlight because of all the attention they receive. The few may feel stuck by virtue of the **glass ceiling**, those barriers that keep certain people out of the highest positions.

In the workplace, those treated as outsiders may include the following:

- A male moving into a predominantly female position or occupation, such as nursing.
- A female moving into a traditionally male position or role, such as engineering or construction work.
- A visually impaired person working in an office in which everyone else is not.
- A person who is an English language learner joining a team of people who speak English exceptionally well.

RECOGNIZING PRIVILEGES

Recognizing privileges can be difficult. If we live in a society that emphasizes individual achievement and fairness, such as the United States, we are taught to believe that privileges are earned through hard work. Indeed, many would argue that the playing field in the United States is level. According to this argument, the only thing holding an individual back is a lack of initiative or drive.

This is the concept of **meritocracy**, the idea that people deserve what they get. During childhood, many of us have been taught this lesson in a variety of ways. The lesson was an attempt to make sense of life's inequities and motivate us to apply ourselves. After all, if you work hard, you will get more than someone who does not.

Only later do some of us discover that life is not fair, and not all privileges are earned. Coming to grips with the concept of unearned power and privilege is unsettling, because it causes us to question whether there really is a meritocracy.

THE INVISIBILITY OF PRIVILEGE

> **YOUR TURN** · · · · · ━━━━━━
>
> Are you more aware of those situations in which you have privileges or those in which you lack privileges? What might account for this?
>
> _____
>
> _____
>
> _____
>
> _____

Table 10.3 • Thinking About Power		
Person One	**Person Two**	**Person Three**
Tall	Very short	Average height
White	White	Black
Male	Female	Female
Average weight	Average weight	Overweight
Age in 40's	Age in 70's	Age in 30's

In a workshop given by Jane Elliott, a noted diversity trainer, she invites three participants to the front of the room. Elliott points out some of the differences among the individuals, including the characteristics shown in Table 10.3.

Elliott then proceeds to ask each of these three people,

"How often do you think about your *height?*"

"How often do you think about your *race?*"

"How often do you think about your *gender?*"

"How often do you think about your *weight?*"

"How often do you think about your *age?*"

YOUR TURN   · · · · · ·

Take some time to think about the possible responses of the three individuals:

1. Which person do you think thought about *height* most often?

2. Which person do you think thought about *race* most often?

3. Which person do you think thought about *gender* most often?

4. Which person do you think thought about *weight* most often?

5. Which person do you think thought about *age* most often?

(*Note:* See answers at the end of the chapter.)

Examine your answers to each of these five questions. Why do you think you answered the way you did?

_____

_____

_____

_____

_____

_____

Invariably, people think about their minority statuses more than their majority statuses. In the previous Your Turn, some minority statuses in the United States are brought to our attention, including being short in stature, Black, female, overweight, and over 70.

People who possess a **minority status**, meaning a position that lacks power and privilege in society, may find themselves thinking about this status in situations where they feel left out, devalued, or excluded in some manner. As an example, employees with cancer may be relieved of important duties or even laid off by managers who assume their illness will make it impossible for them to do their job. Consequently, cancer patients who are undergoing chemotherapy may be hesitant to disclose their condition or treatment for fear of the consequences. Like many employees with other disabilities, people with cancer may excel at work. However, because of their minority status and the threat of bias, they may constantly find themselves thinking about people's perceptions and reactions.

Conversely, those with power are less apt to think about it. For example, White men rarely if ever think about the power they have because of their race and gender. White men, along with other majorities, tend to be blind to their privileges.

Consider the following sequence of events. A White male is not going to think twice about the fact that he can hail a cab on his way to work even though he just came from the gym and is wearing sweats and a skull cap. He takes that for granted, rather than saying to himself, "If I had been a person of color, the taxi driver might have avoided me." Or when a White male walks into a hotel to attend a conference, he is not going to be aware of the fact that nobody mistook him for the porter, valet, or some other hotel employee. At the end of the day, he is not going to reflect on how he benefited from his majority status.

IDENTIFYING OUR MINORITY AND MAJORITY STATUSES

YOUR TURN   · · · · · ·

I consider myself

   a. A minority.

   b. A majority.

   c. Both; it depends on the situation.

   d. Neither.

Explain why:

_____

_____

_____

_____

Rather than examine people as members of a majority *or* minority, it is more instructive and inclusive to think of ourselves as members of both. A **minority group** refers to a category of people who are singled out, marginalized, and denied equal opportunity and equal access to power. On the other hand, a **majority group** is generally more accepted and included, afforded more opportunities, and has greater access to power.

The difference between these two types of groups is not a matter of numbers or percentages. Even though a group is a numerical majority, its members might still lack opportunity and power. People of color in South Africa and women in the United States are good examples.

The differences between minority and majority may apply to groups as a whole, but not to all individuals within a group. For instance, some minority individuals have considerable power due to their wealth. Likewise, some majority individuals may have minimal power because of their appearance, family background, or job.

All of us are both minorities and majorities. The society and situation we find ourselves in may impact our access to power and opportunity. For instance, being fluent in a particular language may work in our favor only some of the time. Whether we are a minority or majority depends on the status or statuses under consideration.

How would the privileges of a White male with a learning disability who also happens to be gay compare with a Hispanic female who is heterosexual, well-off financially, and a recent immigrant to the United States? What we

Table 10.4 • My Majority and Minority Statuses

Status	What Am I?	Majority Status	Minority Status
Religion			
Ethnicity			
Sexual orientation			
Age			
Language			
Skin color			
Weight			
Wealth			
Gender			

have here is a mix of majority and minority statuses. Because of the importance we attach to race and gender in the United States, we tend to overlook other statuses. For instance, we may view a lower-class White male as belonging to a majority while an upper-class African American male is seen as a minority group member.

Identifying our majority and minority statuses allows us to understand more fully the role power and privilege play in our relationships. In Table 10.4 are a variety of statuses that distinguish one individual from another. Examine how each type of status relates to you. First, describe your specific status. For example, next to religion you might describe your status as a Muslim, Christian, Buddhist, Jew, Mormon or possibly some other faith. Then, place an X in the column of Table 10.4 to indicate whether this status of yours is considered a majority or minority status in the United States.

UNDERSTANDING THE REPERCUSSIONS OF POWER

Power, or lack of it, has numerous repercussions for the individual and the way others relate to him or her. It may influence people's ability to perform. Consider the effectiveness of women in leadership positions. Do they have enough support? Do they get credit for their accomplishments? Do they have the resources and information they need? Is their effectiveness hampered by stereotypical images of women leaders, such as the "bossy woman," or the stereotype of women being too emotional, too petty, or too detail-conscious?

While the distribution of power can influence one's performance, how we as individuals use and react to power are critical. How would you feel if your boss is a fitness fanatic and you are not? Because of the value she attaches to fitness, your boss encourages employees to attend workouts at a nearby fitness center before work. You consider this an infringement on your free time. Your boss, who works out every morning, constantly praises those employees who join her on a regular basis. Making matters worse, you feel like you are "out of the loop" on some business issues that happen to be discussed before and after these workouts. This seems unfair to you.

To the boss, a level playing field exists. After all, everybody has an equal opportunity to participate. Or do they? Because of their demands at home, a nagging injury or medical condition, or some other factor beyond their control, some might opt not to participate. Others might simply prefer doing something else, like sleeping later. To their way of thinking, people are being treated differently and unfairly because of their lack of power and privilege. The inability of the boss to acknowledge this is in itself a privilege and may be a source of tension.

TREATING PEOPLE WITH RESPECT

YOUR TURN   • • • • •

Imagine you are eating at an upscale French restaurant. Your waiter, while leaning over and serving drinks to you and your guests, loses his balance. The glass of red wine he is serving tumbles onto your expensive white shirt. What is your immediate reaction? What do you do?

_____

_____

_____

_____

According to many CEOs, you can tell a lot about a person by the way she or he treats a waiter in a restaurant. This is called the "waiter rule". The rule also applies to the way we treat bellhops, hotel maids, security personnel, janitorial staff, and mailroom clerks. According to CEO Bill Swanson, the way people treat others who have less power tells us a lot. Swanson writes, "Watch out for people who have a situational value system, who can turn the charm on and off depending on the status of the person they are interacting with." He continues, "Be especially wary of those who are rude to people perceived to be in subordinate roles."[3]

Other CEOs share similar observations about the waiter rule:

> "People with situational values have situational ethics, and those are people to be avoided."
> "They're saying, 'I'm better. I'm smarter.' Those people tend not to be collaborative."
> "To some people, speaking in a condescending manner makes them feel important, which to me is a total turnoff."
> "Sitting in the chair of CEO makes me no better of a person than the forklift operator in our plant. If you treat the waiter, or a subordinate, like garbage, guess what? Are they going to give it their all? I don't think so."[4]

Regardless of our position and power, we should respect subordinates just as much as we do peers and superiors.

TO LEARN MORE

Treating everyone with respect serves to level the playing field. In her article, "Checking Bias at the Door: 10 Ways to Level the Playing Field," found at **www.michaelwmorris.com/Papers%20in%20pdf/mediamenWallace.htm.pdf,** author Linda Wallace examines specific things a manager can do to avoid cultural misunderstandings and level the playing field when communicating with employees.

STEREOTYPES AND FEELINGS OF GUILT

YOUR TURN   · · · · · ——————

How does your status as a minority or majority affect the way you feel about yourself?

_____

_____

_____

_____

Rarely are power and privilege addressed in the workplace. When they are, stereotypes are common. For example, we might label a group such as straight White males as oppressors. Rather than focusing on the diversity within this group, we might simply blame them for all of the ills of society. When this group is the focus, we might find ourselves using descriptors such as selfish, arrogant, clueless, insensitive, narrow-minded, and conservative. When this occurs, White males may feel like they have to constantly apologize. Discussions about cultural diversity and power cease to be seen as a vehicle for learning about one another. Rather, discussions of this nature turn to assigning and avoiding blame.

When the subject of power is broached in the workplace, the forum in which these discussions typically take place is diversity training. Unfortunately, stereotypical feelings of guilt often make these discussions unproductive. The following quotes from participants in diversity training are not uncommon.

> "It seems to me that diversity training is based on the belief that if some people are made to feel guilty, they will be more sensitive. If that's the case, it doesn't work. It only makes me, and others like me, more resentful. We're being treated like children. I'm tired of being taught by minorities who feel oppressed and make me feel guilty. One 63-year-old trainer went on and on about how her grandmother was called a 'nigger' and how that memory still stays with her. Give me a break. I had nothing to do with that. It is an affront to me. I hate racism, and resent those people who use this kind of language."

> "Diversity training is all about how the White male has oppressed minorities over the years. We have gone from the racist 1960s to blaming Whites for everything and anything in the twenty-first century. If Black and women employees—mostly lesbians—keep up their whining, businesses will just pick up and move to other countries where they don't have to deal with this minority crap."

Paul Kivel, an educator and author, recalls a workshop he conducted on racism. In order to promote more in-depth discussion, he attempted to divide the participants into a caucus of Whites and a caucus of people of color. This prompted a number of Whites to say, "But I'm not White." Kivel was surprised by their reaction. Although these people looked White, they were not comfortable with being labeled White. A White woman stood up and remarked, "I'm not really White because I'm not part of the White male power structure that perpetuates racism." Then a White gay man stood up, and pointed out, "You have to be straight to have the privileges of being White." A White, straight, working-class man said, "I've got it just as hard as any person of color." Finally, a middle-class White man proclaimed, "I'm not White, I'm Italian."[5]

Whites are disinclined to see themselves as part of a group, as others do. They may disavow their whiteness or claim some other identity to avoid feelings of guilt. They do not want to be seen as racist, nor do they want to be stereotyped. When society does racialize Whites, it tends to paint whiteness with a broad brush. By defining themselves as victims, certain Whites may be showing their discomfort with a racial status that makes them out to be oppressors and hides their individual circumstances.

> **TO LEARN MORE**
>
> Go to **www.loden.com/video.html.** Familiarize yourself with a 30-minute video program, "Dialogue on Diversity: Straight White Men Speak Out." The Website discusses reasons for this program, its content and target audiences, and how to order.

THE BOTTOM LINE

Understanding the dynamics of power makes power more visible and manageable. We cannot leverage power if we do not understand culture and its relationship to power. Neither culture nor power can be examined apart from each other.

This CQ megaskill allows us to improve our interpersonal skills and, in turn, increase our productivity. By developing our understanding of the dynamics of power, we become more adept at tuning in to our own power, the power of others, and the ways in which power manifests itself in a variety of cultural situations. Additionally, we are in a better position to anticipate misunderstandings, build trust and relationships, and deal with conflict effectively.

● ● ● ● ● ● ● ●

A Look Back: I Have Learned

✓ _____ Why understanding the dynamics of power is a megaskill.

✓ _____ What is meant by power.

✓ _____ How people from diverse cultural backgrounds perceive power.

✓ _____ What is meant by the culture of power.

✓ _____ How to tune in to my own power and lack of power.

✓ _____ To distinguish between earned and unearned privileges.

✓ _____ To identify minority and majority statuses.

✓ _____ To understand the repercussions of power.

✓ _____ How power, stereotypes, and feelings of guilt interrelate.

✓ _____ How power impacts the bottom line.

Individual Action Plan

Think about one specific thing you can do to improve your skills in the area of understanding the dynamics of power. Then complete the following plan during the next _____ (state time period).

Specific skill I want to improve first (refer to list of Performance Skills at the beginning of the chapter).

_____

My strategy:

_____
_____
_____
_____

In order to develop this skill, I will:

_____
_____
_____
_____

Possible obstacles include:

_____
_____
_____
_____

Resources I need:

_____
_____
_____
_____

I will measure my progress by:

_____
_____
_____
_____

Answers

Your Turn *(see p. 240)*

1. Very short (height)
2. Black (race)
3. Females (gender)
4. Heavy (weight)
5. 70s (age)

Notes

1. Geert Hofstede, *Culture's Consequences: International Differences in Work Related Values* (Beverly Hills, CA: Sage Publications, 1980).

2. Rosabeth Moss Kanter, *Men and Women of the Corporation* (New York: Basic Books, 1977).

3. Del Jones, "CEOs Vouch for Waiter Rule: Watch How People Treat Staff," *USA Today*, April 14, 2006, pp. B1+.

4. Ibid.

5. Paul Kivel, *Uprooting Racism* (Gabriola Island, BC, Canada: New Society Publishers, 2002), p. 8.

BIBLIOGRAPHY

ABC News. (2000). *Hopkins 24/7* [Television series].

Allen, N. J., & Hecht, T. D. (2000). Aligning teams within organizations: Implications for human resource management. *Human Resources Management Research Quarterly, 4,* 1–4.

Allport, G. (1954). *The nature of prejudice.* Reading, MA: Addison Wesley.

Alvord, L. A., & Van Pelt, E. C. (1999). *The scalpel and the silver bear.* New York: Bantam Books.

Anton, M. (2003, May 25). Aspiring doctors see more through art. *Baltimore Sun,* p. A10.

Anzaldúa, G. (1999). *Borderlands.* San Francisco: Aunt Luke Books.

Ashe, A. (1993). *Days of grace.* New York: Ballantine Books.

Axtell, R. (1991). *Gestures: The do's and taboos of body language around the world.* New York: Wiley.

Barbian, J. (2003, February 1). Diversity training. *Training Magazine.* Available at **www.trainingmag.com/msg/search/article_display.jsp?vnu_content_id=1809715**

Bateson, M. C. (1968). Insight in a bicultural context. *Philippine Studies, 16,* 605–621.

Bertrand, M. (2003, Spring). Racial bias in hiring. *Capital Ideas, 4*(4). Research from the University of Chicago Graduate School of Business. Available at **www.chicagogsb.edu/capideas/spring03/racialbias.html**

Birdwhistell, R. (1970). *Kinesics and context: Essays on body motion communication.* Philadelphia: University of Pennsylvania Press.

Bogardus, E. (1925, July/August). Social distance and its origins. *Sociology and Social Research, 9,* 216–225.

Boiney, L. (2001, Fall). Gender impacts virtual work teams. *The Graziadio Business Report.* Available at **http://gbr.pepperdine.edu/014/teams.html**

Burgoon, J., & Hale, J. (1988). Nonverbal expectancy violations: Model elaboration and application to immediacy behavior. *Communication Monographs, 55,* 58–79.

CIA. (2005). *The World Factbook.* Available at **https://cia.gov/cia/publications/factbook/geos/xx.html**

Cose, E. (1993). *The rage of a privileged class.* New York: HarperCollins.

Cose, E. (1997). *Colorblind: Seeing beyond race in a race-obsessed world.* New York: HarperPerennial.

Covey, S. (1989). *The seven habits of highly effective people.* New York: Simon & Schuster.

Crozier-Hogle, L., & Wilson, D. B. (1997). *Surviving in two worlds.* Austin: University of Texas Press.

Davis, O. (1976). The English language is my enemy. In C. D. Eckhardt, J. F. Holahan, & D. H. Stewart (Eds.), *The Wiley Reader* (pp. 312–313). New York: Wiley.

DeAngelis, T. (2001, April). Thwarting modern prejudice. *Monitor on Psychology, 32*(4). Available at **www.apa.org/monitor/apr01/prejudice.html**

Dixon, K. A., Storen, D., & VanHorn, C. E. (2002, January). *A workplace divided: How Americans view discrimination and race on the job.* New Brunswick, NJ, and Storrs, CT: Rutgers University John J. Heldrich Center for Workforce Development, with University of Connecticut Center for Survey Research and Analysis.

Doane, A., Jr. (1997). Dominant group ethnic identity in the United States: The role of "hidden" ethnicity in intergroup relations. *Sociological Quarterly, 38*(3), 375–397.

Drexler, A. B., Sibbet, D., & Forrester, R. H. (1988). The team performance model. In W. B. Reddy & K. Jamison (Eds.), *Team building: Blueprints for productivity and satisfaction.* Alexandria, VA: NTL Institute for Applied Behavioral Science.

Du Bois, W. E. B. (1903). *The souls of black folk: Essays and sketches.* Chicago: McClurg.

Edwards, E. (2003, February 26). For kids, there's no place like home. *The Washington Post,* p. C4.

Ekman, P. (1980). *Face of man: Universal expression in a New Guinea village.* New York: Garland.

Furuiye, A. (1991). I am plural, and I am singular. First written for *Who Cares?!* (Newsletter for members of ©Kosmopolitan Association International). Available at **www.digitrends.com/crossingcultures/fury.htm**

GMAC Global Relocation Services. (2006). *2005 Global Relocation Trends Survey Report.* Woodridge, IL: Author. Report produced in association with National Foreign Trade Council (NFTC) and the SHRM Global Forum.

Goldstein, A., & Suro, R. (2000, January 16). A journey in stages. *The Washington Post,* p. A24.

Goleman, D. (1998). *Working with emotional intelligence.* New York: Bantam Books.

Golson, B. (1999, September 23). Creating and deconstructing cultural identity. *Yale Daily News,* n.p.

Graves, E. (1998). *How to succeed in business without being white.* New York: HarperCollins.

Hall, E. (1966). *The hidden dimension.* Garden City, NY: Doubleday.

Hall, E. (1976). *Beyond culture.* Garden City, NY: Anchor.

Heilman, M. E., Wallen, A. S., Fuchs, D., & Tamkins, M. M. (2004, June). Penalties for success: Reactions to women who succeed at male gender-typed tasks. *Journal of Applied Psychology, 89*(3), 416–427.

Hinton, E. (2002, October 31). When a diversity crisis occurs, how should your company react? *DiversityInc Magazine.* Available at **www.diversityinc.com/public/department86.cfm**

Hispanic hope persists despite discrimination. (2002, December 18). *Baltimore Sun,* p. A19.

Hofstede, G. (1980). *Culture's consequences: International differences in work-related values.* Beverly Hills: Sage.

Humphreys, J. (2003). *The multicultural economy 2003.* Athens: University of Georgia, Selig Center for Economic Growth.

Interpersonal failure. (2005, September 28). *Inside Training Newsletter,* p. 1.

Jackson, P., & Delehanty, H. (1995). *Sacred hoops.* New York: Hyperion.

Jones, D. (2006, April 14). CEOs vouch for waiter rule: Watch how people treat staff. *USA Today*, pp. B1+.

Kanter, R. M. (1977). *Men and women of the corporation*. New York: Basic Books.

Kao, G. (2000, September). Group images and possible selves among adolescents: Linking stereotypes to expectations by race and ethnicity. *Sociological Forum, 15*(3), 407–430.

Kim, H., & Markus, H. R. (1999). Deviance of uniqueness, harmony, or conformity? A cultural analysis. *Journal of Personality and Social Psychology, 77*, 785–800.

Kipnis, K. (1998, Spring). Quality care and the wounds of diversity. APA *Newsletters, 97*(2). Available at **www.apa.udel.edu/apa/archive/newsletters/v97n2/medicine/quality.asp**

Kivel, P. (2002). *Uprooting racism*. Gabriola Island, BC, Canada: New Society.

Kohls, L. R. (1984). *The values Americans live by*. Washington, DC: Meridian House International.

Kreeger, K. Y. (1997, February 17). Scientific community finds value in diversity training. *The Scientist, 11*(4), 17.

Lederer, W. J., & Burdick, E. (1958). *The ugly American*. New York: Norton.

Lencioni, P. (2002). *The five dysfunctions of a team*. San Francisco: Jossey-Bass.

Linton, R. (1936). *The study of man*. New York: Appleton-Century-Crofts.

Lutz, C. (1988). *Unnatural emotions: Everyday sentiments on a Micronesia atoll and their challenge to Western theory*. Chicago: University of Chicago Press.

Madrid, A. (1988, May/June). Missing people and others: Joining together to expand the circle. *Change, 20*, 55–59.

Morin, R. (2005, July 31). Words that matter. *The Washington Post*, p. B5.

M2W. The Marketing-to-Women Conference. Information available at **www.m2w.biz/fastfacts.html**

National Urban League. (2004, June). *Diversity practices that work: The American worker speaks*. New York: Author.

Nissel, A. (2006, May 10). What are you? Life as a bi-racial. NPR's *Morning Edition* [Radio broadcast]. Retrieved from **www.npr.org/templates/story/story.php?storyId=5395390**

Obese shoppers say clerks not helpful. (2005, April 10). MSNBC Business News. Available at **www.msnbc.msn.com/id/7454822/**

O'Brien, D. (2005, October 21). Americans, Canadians really are like two peas in a pod. *Baltimore Sun*, pp. D1+.

Oetting, E. R., & Beauvais, F. (1991). Cultural identification theory: The cultural identification of minority adolescents. *International Journal of Addiction, 25*, 655–685.

Pearce, W. B., & Pearce, K. (2000). Extending the theory of the coordinated management of meaning (CMM) through a community dialogue process. *Communication Theory, 10*(4), 405–424.

Pew Hispanic Center/Kaiser Family Foundation. (2002). *2002 National Survey of Latinos*. Available at **www.hispaniconline.com/pol&opi/02_nat_survey_latinos.html**

Pitino, R., & Reynolds, B. (2000). *Learn to succeed: 10 traits of great leadership in business and life*. New York: Broadway Books.

Pitts, J. (2005, September 25). Beauty that is more than skin deep. *Baltimore Sun*, p. E1.

PRWeb Press Release Newswire. (2005, April 12). Memo to global executives: Learn Spanish.

Senge, P. (1999). *The fifth discipline*. London: Nicholas Brealey.

Seymour, M. (2002, July 29). Call me crazy, but I have to be myself. *Newsweek*, 16.

Shapiro, S. (2005, March 11). Medicine and modesty. *Baltimore Sun*, pp. E1+.

Sherif, M. (1966). *In common predicament: Social psychology of intergroup conflict and cooperation*. Boston: Houghton Mifflin.

Smith, D. (2002). *If the world were a village: A book about the world's people*. Toronto: Kids Can.

Sue, D. W. (2001). Multicultural facets of cultural competence. *Counseling Psychologist, 29*, 790–821.

Tannen, D. (1994). *Talking from 9 to 5: How women's and men's conversational styles affect who gets heard, who gets credit, and what gets done at work*. New York: Morrow.

Tatum, B. (1997). *Why are all the black kids sitting together in the cafeteria? And other conversations about race*. New York: HarperCollins.

Topics: Civic communication. (1994, July). Civic Practices Network. Available at **www.cpn. org/topics/communication/neworleans.html**

Trompenaars, F., & Hampden-Turner, C. (1997). *Riding the waves of culture: Understanding cultural diversity in business*. London: Nicholas Brealey.

Trompenaars, F., & Hampden-Turner, C. (2000). *Building cross-cultural competence: How to create wealth from conflicting values*. New Haven: Yale University Press.

Tuckman, B. (1995). Developmental sequence in small groups. *Psychological Bulletin, 63*, 384–399.

Vedantam, S. (2005, January 23). See no bias. *The Washington Post Magazine*, pp. 12+.

Vedantam, S. (2005, December 10). Psychiatry ponders whether extreme bias can be an illness. *The Washington Post*, pp. A1+.

Vega, A. (2006). Americanizing? Attitudes and perceptions of U.S. Latinos. *Harvard Journal of Hispanic Policy, 18*. Available at **www.ksg.harvard.edu/hjhp/vol/2006/ vega/pdf**

Wallace, L. (2001, July 30). Checking bias at the door: 10 ways to level the playing field. *DiversityInc Magazine*. Available at **www.diversityinc.com/public/ department86.cfm**

Wentling, R. M., & Palma-Rivas, N. (1997, December). *Diversity in the workforce series, report #3. Barriers to diversity initiatives*. Berkeley: University of California, National Center for Research in Vocational Education. Available at **http://ncrve.berkeley.edu/ Abstracts/MDS-936/MDS-936-Barriers.html.**

Wicker, A. W. (1969). Attitudes versus actions: The relationship of verbal and overt behavioral responses to attitude objects. *Journal of Social Issues, 25*, 41–78.

Williams, G. (1996). *Life on the color line: The true story of a white boy who discovered he was black*. New York: NAL/Dutton.

Wood, J. (2003). *Communication in our lives*. Belmont, CA: Wadsworth.

Wu, F. (2003). *Yellow: Race in America beyond black and white*. New York: Basic Books.

Yinger, J. (1995). *Closed doors, opportunities lost: The continuing costs of housing discrimination*. New York: Russell Sage Foundation.

Yunker, J. (2005). *The Web globalization report card 2005*. San Diego: Byte Level Research.

Zogby, J. (2001). *What ethnic Americans really think*. Utica, NY: Zogby International.

INDEX